MODERN AMERICAN HISTORY ★ A Garland Series

Edited by
ROBERT E. BURKE
and
FRANK FREIDEL

James Middleton Cox
Age 74

JAMES M. COX ★ Journalist and Politician

James E. Cebula

Garland Publishing, Inc.
New York & London ★ 1985

Copyright © 1985 James E. Cebula

All rights reserved

Library of Congress Cataloging-in-Publication Data

Cebula, James E., 1942–
  James M. Cox : journalist and politician.

  (Modern American history)
  Bibliography: p.
  Includes index.
  1. Cox, James M. (James Middleton), 1870–1957.
  2. Presidential candidates—United States—Biography.
  3. Ohio—Governors—Biography. 4. Journalists—Ohio—
  Biography. 5. Presidents—United States—Election—
  1920. 6. Ohio—Politics and government—1865–1950.
  7. United States—Politics and government—1901–1953.
  I. Title. II. Series.
  E748.C88C43 1985   973.91'3   85-16259
  ISBN 0-8240-5666-3

All volumes in this series are printed on acid-free,
250-year-life paper.

Printed in the United States of America

For

Anne and Judy

CONTENTS

ACKNOWLEDGMENTS 9
EARLY LIFE 11
THE NEW CITY AND THE NEW JOURNALISM 19
A BUSINESSMAN TURNS TO POLITICS 29
A CAMPAIGN FOR THE COMMON GOOD 39
ECONOMY, SYSTEM AND EFFICIENCY: PLURALISM IN OHIO 45
COMBATING "RIOT AND REVOLUTION:" STRUCTURAL REFORM 53
DEFEAT AND VINDICATION 63
WAR GOVERNOR 73
EMERGENCE OF A PROGRESSIVE PRESIDENTIAL CANDIDATE 88
WINNING THE NOMINATION 101
COX AND THE ELECTION OF 1920 109
COX AND THE NEW DEMOCRATIC PARTY 119
PUBLISHER AND ELDER STATESMAN 127
EPILOGUE 138
TABLES 141
NOTES 147
ESSAY ON SOURCES 171
INDEX

Acknowledgments

Many people helped with this manuscript and I will always be grateful to them for their generosity. The staffs of libraries where I did research, with few exceptions, went out of their way to make the task easier and more rewarding. David Larson, then of the Ohio Historical Society, stayed late as I plowed through the Cox Executive Papers. The research personnel at the Library of Congress Manuscripts Division and at the University of Kentucky library led me to several collections that I did not know existed. Librarians at the University of Cincinnati, especially Sally Moffitt and Harriette Wolfe, tracked down sources not available in the University library system. James M. Cox, Jr., opened his father's personal papers to me and the employees at the *Dayton Daily News* made the work of organizing the Cox Papers much less arduous then it otherwise would have been. Si Burick and James Reston graciously provided me with insights into a man who helped them get started in journalism.

A number of scholars offered valuable criticism of the work at various stages of its development and they have my sincere thanks. Daniel Beaver, who directed the project as a doctoral dissertation, George Engberg, Zane Miller, and William Baughin all offered helpful suggestions for change during early drafts of the manuscript. Austin Kerr read and criticized chapter two. Al Sumberg and Kurt Wimer, who introduced me to the subject, read an early version of chapter twelve. Martin Fausold critiqued an early revision of the entire manuscript. The general editors of the series Robert Burke and Frank Freidel have my gratitude for taking the time to read the manuscript and for agreeing to include it in the series. Special thanks go to David Burner and Tony Deye for generously giving of their time and editorial skills and for suggesting both conceptual and language changes.

The University of Cincinnati and my colleagues at Raymond Walters College, especially Ted Cook, have my appreciation for the support given me while preparing this manuscript for publication. Thanks also to Rosemary Weaver, who with good humor and dedication to detail prepared the manuscript for publication and to Elaine Plummer who helped with the proofreading. As always, my friends and family have my gratitude for their encouragement and genuine interest in the project. While all of these people made this a better book, I alone bear the responsibility for any of its shortcomings.

Cincinnati, Ohio   James E. Cebula

I
EARLY LIFE

During the last third of the nineteenth century and early in the twentieth century, as the United States changed from a predominantly rural-commercial society to an urban-industrial one, community leaders at all levels sought appropriate responses to the changed conditions. Among the political leaders who emerged were numerous businessmen and professionals who had achieved financial success and positions of power in the increasingly complex industrial economy. With values, in many cases, closely linked to their rural and small town backgrounds, these new era politicians plunged vigorously into the urban environment. Consisting of representative figures like Thomas L. Johnson and Samuel "Golden Rule" Jones in the cities, and Robert La Follette and Hiram Johnson on the state level, they tried to deal systematically with the changed political, social, and technological structure of urban America. Their prime concerns were to create an acceptable order and to adjust the values of middle-class democracy to the pace and rhythm of urban-industrial life.

A mixture of self-interest and a desire for consensus provided much of the motivation for these reformers. The preservation of the liberal ethic of economic individualism, which they saw as the core of the American democracy, was an essential part of the programs that emerged. The system they helped set in motion stood, however, tinged with ironies and contradictions.[1]

James Middleton Cox of Ohio typifies this new leadership. His career in journalism and politics, stretching from the late nineteenth through the mid-twentieth century, provides a vehicle for looking at numerous aspects of the approach of his generation to the urban milieu—an approach characterized by one scholar as America's "initial experiment in bureaucratic order."[2] Throughout his public life, Cox worked to reconcile the conflicting values of efficiency and freedom. Tom Taggart, former mayor of Indianapolis, a power in Indiana politics, and a political associate of Cox in national politics, underscored this conflict in values when he observed that "people will never know the real James Cox, he gives the impression of being a practical politician and a hard headed executive but he is really the most ideal[istic] man I ever knew in politics."[3] Cox's careers as a journalist-businessman, two-term congressman, three-time governor of Ohio, and 1920 presidential candidate was shaped by the ambivalent pull of the ideal and the practical. Moving from an impoverished rural and small town background to the city, he rapidly gained wealth, influence, and prestige. By the time he reached the pinnacle of his political power, Cox had come to equate efficiency in government with democracy, and came to believe that government officials, through the positive use of power could serve the people by mediating among community groups to establish a balance between ideals and self interest.

Cox grew up on a farm in Butler County, which lay in southwestern Ohio, approximately thirty miles north of Cincinnati. Described as "prosperous and wealthy" in 1837, Butler County developed into a rich farming district. In 1847 Henry Howe, an Ohio gazetteer, noted that the county out-stripped every other Ohio county in corn, wheat, oats, and pork production. The farmers in the district turned to the "flourishing post towns" of Hamilton, Middletown, and Paddy's Run to market their products. From these service centers, the produce of the area made the journey down the Miami Canal to Cincinnati for processing.[4]

After the War of 1812, Gilbert Cox, James' grandfather, left New York for a brief visit with friends in the southwestern Ohio farm village of Franklin. He stayed and married Anne Craig, whose brother had founded the settlement of Jacksonburg, twelve miles to the southwest in Wayne Township. In the spring of 1817, Gilbert and his bride left Franklin and crossed the Miami River on rafts to Jacksonburg to establish a homestead. Three years later Gilbert Cox had completed a stone house that served the Cox family throughout the nineteenth century. The future journalist's grandparents farmed the land and raised eleven children, naming the youngest after the father. Young Gilbert gained title to the land after the death of his parents. He married Eliza Andrews, a girl from a log cabin farm one mile from the Cox residence. Seven children resulted from the marriage, and the youngest, James Middleton Cox, was born on March 31, 1870.[5]

Jacksonburg prospered in the beginning largely because it was on the road from fertile Darke County to Cincinnati. By 1830, it contained four stores, two hotels, and a pork processing plant. But it declined rapidly after a bridge connected the west bank of the Great Miami River with Middletown. Its fate was sealed when the Dayton, Hamilton, and Cincinnati Railroad by-passed the town in 1851. In 1890, the village population numbered only 77.[6]

Along with others in Jacksonburg, the Cox family fell upon hard times. Although they retained the land, family unity disintegrated. Young James' parents were divorced and Eliza Cox went to live with her married daughter, Anne, in Middletown. Gilbert Cox, who retained custody of the three male children, soon remarried and continued to operate the farm. His new wife brought three additional children to the crowded house. Cox had nothing to say about his father's second wife in his memoir, an omission which probably indicates his attitude toward her.[7]

As a boy, Cox lived a strenuous life on his father's farm. Confronting "a good deal of drudgery," he remarked with pride in *Journey Through My Years*"

> It was hard work in season and out. In Summertime we were in the fields at sunrise; we came in for dinner at eleven o'clock, had supper at four o'clock and then followed the plow or sickle till sundown.[8]

Proud as he might later become of his youth on the farm, he bitterly resented his father who looked upon his sons as nothing but hands with which to draw profit from the land.

Along with this antagonism toward his father, Cox maintained a sense of his own individuality, and a strong desire to succeed. A neighboring farmer sent seven sons to nearby Miami University, Cox recalled, while his father held his sons on the land. Denied access to a formal education, Cox later came to believe that this denial drove him to better himself. What structured education young Jim received, he acquired in the one room schoolhouse of Jacksonburg, which he attended irregularly until he was sixteen. He read the old McGuffey eclectic readers, and later attributed his continued interest in "good" reading to their influence. He absorbed their messages on rugged individualism, the dignity of labor, the desirability of thrift, and the need for honesty and charity. Early in life, when confronted by the crude domination of his father, Cox later reflected that the McGuffey books and similar reading provided him with an emotional outlet.[9]

Cox's makeshift education also embedded the roots of his conception of the United States. Recalling his early reading of American history, *Venable's History of the United States* stood out in his mind as a "thoroughly good work." Written in 1880 by William Henry Venable, the book emphasized the continuity of political and social institutions.

Venable portrayed the Hamiltonians as agents of the commercial and manufacturing interests and the Jeffersonians as representatives of the agrarian masses. In contrast to the the Whig historians, Venable suggested that the Civil War resulted from violations of states rights. America's international wars, as well as the political confrontations of the party system, indicated the progressive realization of American ideals for the midwestern historian. Venable's basic ideas, tempered by Cox's primitive pragmatism, helped provide the young farm boy with a rough commercial and political rationale that endured throughout his life.[10]

A prescript of Venable's contributed to Cox's choice of a profession. He implored his readers to keep up with the times and to observe the inevitable progress of civilization and the arts by reading "the most important current news of the day."[11] Young Cox displayed a fascination with contemporary events and the manner in which they reached the public. While still a student, he turned to Murat Halstead's *Cincinnati Commercial Gazette*, "the most widely read newspaper in the west." The voice of the nationally known mugwump Republican, the paper spread the economic influence of Cincinnati into its hinterlands. By the eighties, Halstead had become closely tied to the GOP machine in the Queen City. At the same time, however, he pressed for positive governmental responses to the problems of the growing city. The *Commercial Gazette* helped mold Cox's social and political outlook. It also represented a window to urban America, providing young Cox a view of the attractions, opportunities, and perils of city life.[12]

In part a product of his immediate environment, and what he read, Cox also reflected the social climate of the time. His character mirrored the attitudes that one historian described as a "vivid pattern of anxiety, frustration, [and] guilt."[13] The seemingly unending physical drudgery of rural life, the domination of his father over the family, the aspirations of youth—all challenged Cox to leave the land. He recalled years later:

> In the middle of the forenoon, while I was following the plow, I would often see one of the neighborhood school teachers starting to work, and about four in the afternoon while I still had long hours of toil ahead of me, I would see the teacher coming home. This spectacle might have given spur to my ambition to make a brief pedagogic career the stepping stone to something better.[14]

At sixteen, he set out for a larger town.

In 1886 Cox moved to Middletown, eight miles east of Jacksonburg, to live with his mother. Situated between Cincinnati and the emerging metropolitan center of Dayton, Middletown stood along the Miami Canal and was serviced by four railroads. A growing paper manufacturing and tobacco processing center, the town also served the mercantile interests of nearby farm communities. When Cox arrived, it had an estimated population of 4,500 but grew to 7,681 by 1890.[15]

Young Cox continued his education in this bustling environment. The relationship he developed with his brother-in-law, John Q. Baker, gave his aspirations definition. Baker taught at a one room high school in nearby Amanda, and shared this experience with Cox while tutoring him for the Ohio teachers examination. Ohio law in the 1880's required certified teachers to demonstrate skill in orthography, reading, writing, theory of teaching, English grammar, and the history of the United States. In addition, the applicants were to be of "good character." Traditionally, candidates demonstrated their ability to read and write before a politically appointed board of examiners. After a year of Baker's guidance, Cox decided to take the examination. Journeying to Hamilton, the county seat, Cox took the teachers examination and, he recalled later, "to my surprise received a two years' certificate to teach."[16]

At the age of seventeen Cox took his first teaching assignment at West Middletwon, and a year later, moved to the paper producing village of Rockdale, located south of Middletown. In his third year of teaching he "graduated from there to what was known as the best country school in the county, the Titus District School, two miles north of Middletown."[17]

While teaching, Cox became acquainted with Paul J. Sorg, the town's most influential man. A local booster observed that "scarcely any branch of manufacturing in Middletwon has gone on without his [Sorg's] particiaption—tobacco, pumps, farm machinery, bicycles, naval equipment, gas, paper, banking, railroads . . . ." In addition, he brought the Pennsylvania Railroad to Middletown. Sorg also sat on the Middletown school board and used his influence to put Cox in charge of the evening school. Modeled after a similar one in Cincinnati, the school operated during the winter months and catered to adults and children who worked during the day. Cox's introduction to Sorg probably came through his mentor, John Q. Baker, who also published the *Middletown Weekly Signal*, the town's Democratic newspaper. Sorg was the area's leading Democrat.[18]

Teaching, however, soon became an "incidental pastime" for Cox. Before long, Baker introduced his protege to journalism. The combination of journalism and teaching provided Cox with a distinctive theory of communication which he would come to rely upon throughout his life. As a teacher, Cox gained his first opportunity to communicate with others on a professional level. He believed that education could shape human nature and conceived of teaching as communicating information to solve the problems of life. When his interests turned to journalism, he naturally saw the press as a vehicle to educate people and he justified his change of profession by reasoning that he would reach a larger audience. Cox recalled, "printer's ink had moved into my blood."[19]

While still employed as a teacher, Cox delivered the entire edition of the *Middletown Weekly Signal* on Saturdays. Journalism gradually absorbed more of his time. During the week, he spent his evenings as a printer's devil and helped put the paper to bed. By 1891 as Middletown continued to grow, the need for a daily paper led Baker to turn his weekly into the *Middletown Daily Signal*. Cox left the classroom to devote his energies exclusively to journalism, becoming the paper's only reporter. In addition, as circumstances demanded, he worked as pressman, typesetter, or make-up man.[20]

At the time Cox transferred his energy from education to journalism, the rapid expansion of urban America fostered a parallel growth in newspaper publishing. Joseph Pulitzer bought the *New York World* in 1883, and turned it into the first American newspaper geared to the quickening tempo of urban life. Through extensive, but concise, news coverage, and aggressive support of labor unions and reform causes, Pulitzer's *World* won wide readership. Beyond this, the paper's features, cartoons, stories, and advertising made it attractive to city dwellers. Although Pulitzer's paper made use of sensationalism, it generally maintained a balanced perspective. Imitators, such as William Randolph Hearst, absorbed Pulitzer's techniques, but sacrificed balance, and the result was "yellow journalism." The new journalism spread throughout the urban centers and represented a triumph of business enterprise and technological innovation. The personal journalism of James Gordon Bennett, Horace Greely, and Murat Halstead could no longer function in the increasingly impersonal city. A large amount of capital was needed to acquire the necessary newspaper equipment, to hire the reporters and skilled workers, to provide a wide breadth of coverage, all of which was essential for a mass oriented newspaper. In addition, advertising in the emerging consumer economy took on an important role for publishers and middle-income wage earners caught up in the rapid pace of life in the sprawling cities. The rival claims of large-scale producers and retailers provided an avenue for impersonal comparative shopping. Without advertising, the metropolitan dailies could not thrive. It became the principal source of revenue for newspapers, and they became more and more dependent upon business and industry, rather than readers, as their major source of income. Consequently, more and more of the large papers reflected the opinions of entrenched economic interests who were the leading advertisers, while the day to day treatment of news became sensational to attract readers. Eventually, Cox absorbed these lessons.[21]

Association with the *Daily Signal* brought Cox into the mainstream of Middletown's business, political, and social life, but the *Signal* hardly reflected the new journalism. The paper consisted of four pages, three of which contained mainly imported pre-set newsprint. The city page, Cox's domain, reported the local news. His reporting was free of sensationalism, consisting of sober accounts of social news, local governmental transactions, real estate transfers, hotel arrivals, and the weather. A city notes column he wrote gave free advertising to local merchants and forthcoming events in Middletown society. Also, civic boosting and periodic ethnic and racial slurs appeared in these columns from time to time. Cox later referred to these early days with the *Signal* as a valuable experience that "enabled me to meet the leading men of the town." But, when an opportunity came to move to Cincinnati, the largest metropolitan center in the region, Cox took it. At last, he later said, he had earned the "chance to write my own story."[22]

As Cincinnati expanded in the 1870's and 1880's, the *Enquirer* and other large Queen City dailies extended their circulation into the suburbs, regional towns, and rural areas. To increase circulation, in such places, the papers ran columns of suburban news. But partisan political journalism still exerted a strong influence, and when the *Enquirer* sought news from Middletown, it turned to the Democratically-oriented *Daily Signal* for material. Cox, the only reporter on the paper, was hired as the *Enquirer* Middletown columnist. He forwarded notes to the Cincinnati paper about industrial accidents, marriages, and "the receipts of the post office for the last month."[23] According to a subsequent legend, the opportunity for Cox to join the *Enquirer* on a full time basis came when he outwitted reporters from other papers in reporting a large train wreck near Middletown. In one account, Cox kept competing reporters from using the telegraph line by having the telegrapher send that day's edition of the *Daily Signal* to the Cincinnati office while he rushed to the scene to report the event. He returned to the telegraph office and filed his story. Cox himself never mentioned this episode, but John T. McCarthy, the *Enquirer* editor, did offer the young reporter a full time job in Cincinnati.[24] Removed from the restrictive environment of a small town paper, he next learned the operations of a large metropolitan daily and gained experience in the company of professional journalists. Cox covered the railroads for the *Enquirer*, staying in Cincinnati for two years.[25]

By 1892, the Queen City had forfeited commercial supremacy in the Midwest to Chicago. Nevertheless, continued population growth and physical expansion created a "potentially explosive" situation.[26] In the previous decade, the city had experienced several labor riots. Spontaneous strikes frequently occurred during the two years Cox spent in the city, and the courts regularly employed the injunction to prevent violence. Simultaneously, the population was moving beyond the basin area surrounding the old commercial city, a shift which placed a severe strain on urban services. Politically, George B. Cox, the leader of the Republican Party in the city, initiated a new era by forming a coalition of mugwump reformers, political leaders who resided well beyond the basin area, gas and traction interests, and traditionally Republican blacks. To accommodate these various interests, city government extended and diversified existing municipal services and facilities such as police and fire protection, the water works, and the park system. In addition, city officials sought to regulate industrial smoke, gambling, prostitution, and public utilities. In the time James Cox spent in Cincinnati, the city was caught up in the urban search for order.[27] Years later, when Cox found himself in a position to meliorate urban problems, he remembered the Cincinnati he observed in 1892, and drew parallels from this early experience.

As the railroad reporter for the *Enquirer*, Cox covered a part of Cincinnati life essential to prosperity. During the 1850's, Queen City business leaders, preoccupied with preserving river trade and other traditional transportation links, failed to compete vigorously for railroads. While in smaller cities to the north, such as Dayton and Springfield, urban boosters successfully established connections with east-west rail lines and diminished the size of Cincinnati's hinterland, the Queen City continued to "protect existing investments."[28] Cincinnati did not have a direct connection with any northern railroad system of national proportion until 1872, when the Cincinnati and Springfield Railroad linked the city with the New York Central system. In the following year, the river-oriented city still continued to look southward for its commercial ties, and finally, in 1873, began construction of the city-owned Cincinnati Southern Railroad to connect it with Chattanooga, Tennessee. In spite of these sporadic advances in rail transportation, as late as 1890 Cincinnati had failed to attract a national trunk line. Cincinnatians had begun "to feel themselves in a backwater of commercial life in which there was a danger of an ultimate stagnation of industrial enterprise."[29]

While on the staff of the *Enquirer*, Cox witnessed the consolidation of Cincinnati railroad holdings and the struggle for power that the process represented. In reporting the creation of local railroad "empires", he made enemies among influential people.[30] Early in 1894, Cox wrote a story that cast an unfavorable light on the stock manipulations of Samuel Felton, president of the "Queen and Crescent" system. Felton had leased the Cincinnati Southern and his railroad consolidation linked Cincinnati to New Orleans. Cox soon discovered that he had entered forbidden territory when Felton used his influence with John R. McLean, owner of the *Enquirer*, to "let out" young Cox. John T. McCarthy, the editor of the paper who instructed him to write the story, offered Cox another job rather than fire him.[31]

Confronted by the "thoughtless injustice" of the business leaders in the city, Cox became disenchanted with Cincinnati journalism. Married to Mayme Simpson Harding of Cincinnati in April of the previous year, they now expected a child. With his position on the *Enquirer* suddenly jeopardized, he searched for new opportunities.[23]

A few days before Cox had been pressured by Felton, Paul J. Sorg, the multi-millionaire industrialist from Middletown, had won a special election to the third Ohio congressional seat. The success of a Democrat during a period of Republican ascendancy added significance to Sorg's victory. Immediately, he became a likely candidate for higher office, perhaps the governship. The new congressman needed a secretary. John Q. Baker, aware of Sorg's political potential, asked him to hire Cox. Two days after the election, Sorg journeyed to Cincinnati and dined with Judge John F. Neilen of Hamilton, Ohio, at the St.

Nicholas Hotel on Fourth Street. There, Neilen also interceded on behalf of Cox. As a result of support from these key party operatives, Sorg offered the young reporter the job. Cox and his family moved to Washington.³³

Late in the nineteenth century, Washington, much like Cincinnati, had experienced a great transformation in its physical development. The growth of government contributed to this expansion during the decades of the 1880's and 1890's. As the bureaucracy expanded, population increased, and the need for additional urban services multiplied. Community organizations appeared throughout the city to put pressure on Congress for a voice in the operation of the city. Gradually, in response to new needs, the District began developing additional sources of electric power, reservoirs, underground electric lines, extended streets and lighting, new rail transportation facilities, and a park system. The effort, however, did not proceed smoothly. One historian characterized the process as ridden with "frustration and impotence."³⁴

In retrospect, Cox looked upon his tenure in Washington as training for his chosen career in journalism and politics. He mused: "As I look back upon the fifty-third Congress, I feel that the interest which I took in live public questions and in the Senate and House debates upon them was the equivalent to a university course." The observation provides a useful insight into the character of the twenty-five-year-old Cox and the insecurity he felt as a result of his make-shift education. Despite his uncertainty and his wife's pregnancy, Cox was willing to leave Cincinnati for Washington and the instability of politics, demonstrating the emergence of a strong and independent will to find an active place in public life. For the time being, however, he had to be content with proximity to men making policy for the nation.³⁵

Years later, reflecting upon the men he had observed, Cox categorized them according to the ideals he accepted as best for America. He admired men of hard work, determination, honesty, rugged integrity, and progressive ideas. Those who did not meet these standards he castigated. Of Calvin Brice he noted, "His election to the Senate cast discredit upon the state of Ohio." Richard Olney, on the other hand, seemed "ruggedly honest according to his own lights, and of a blunt determination that seemed revealed in his bulldog face and figure," and Hoke Smith gave "the impression that he was always in command of himself." Lucius Quintus Cincinnatus Lamar "was the ablest man the south ever produced," and Orville H. Platt "was one of the Senate's hardest working and most conscientious members . . . he gave the chamber its leadership until the day of the insurgents dawned." Thomas B. Reed, on the other hand "was the first autocrat of the speaker's chair." Edward D. White of Louisiana he saw as a "special representative of sugar, but a man of integrity." Benjamin R. Tillman "was much derided by the conservative press; but I never felt any doubt as to his sincerity and honesty." In sharp contrast, Cox explained, "was Stephen B. Elkins of West Virginia, a man of wealth who represented great corporate interests." "It was the healthy revulsion from Senators like Elkins and the selfish greed behind them," Cox claimed, "which resulted in a long-overdue amendment for the direct election of Senators."³⁶

During his stay in Washington, Cox developed an awareness of the roles of specific interest groups in society. Knowing that Sorg would have to face reelection soon and believing the election would be close (Sorg had won by only 1,400 votes in the special election), Cox proposed that special care be taken with the interests of the residents of the National Home for Disabled Soldiers located in the district near Dayton. Since the home traditionally voted Republican, Cox reasoned that helping to transfer veterans to the district would gain their loyalty, and work to Sorg's advantage. Sorg liked the idea. Looking after patronage and keeping close touch with the pension system became Cox's primary duties. He personally examined individual cases at the pension bureau, and eased the transfer of veterans to Dayton. Cox attributed Sorg's narrow reelection to his efforts. The vote for Sorg in the Soldier's Home increased enough to help provide victory by 202 votes. In the election of 1894, only two Democrats won congressional seats in Ohio.[37]

Cox never outgrew his concern for the veterans; nor did he forget how the use of influence had promoted political objectives. He recalled, too, that in Washington he "learned how Congress works and [had] become acquainted with the practical side of politics—the logrolling and maneuvering on tariff, rivers and harbor improvement, and other questions." What he saw and learned made him sympathetic to the voices demanding change. Populism and the urban progressive movements especially attracted him. His rural background attuned him to agricultural discontent. His experiences in Middletown, Cincinnati, and Washington magnified in his mind the problems of the city and of government on all levels. In those years, he wrote, "a demand for correction of social and economic abuses was rising and great changes would have to be made." By the time Cox left Washington, he had become "aligned with progressive tendencies of the time."[38]

In 1896, when Paul Sorg decided not to seek reelection, Cox had to find a new position. He had served Sorg effectively, and the Middletown tobacco processor, paper manufacturer, and banker offered him a job with his "diversified interests." But journalism remained Cox's paramount concern and he told Sorg of his ambition to operate a newspaper free of outside control. After first looking around for newspaper property in Toledo, Cox decided to purchase the *Evening News* in nearby Dayton for $26,000. Sorg had enough faith in Cox to loan him $6,000. An experienced financier with an established reputation, Sorg also helped Cox float stock on the open market to finance the rest of the venture. Cox opposed this method of raising the necessary capital lest it hamper his journalistic freedom, but he reluctantly consented to the deal.[39]

II
THE NEW CITY AND THE NEW JOURNALISM

The *Dayton Daily News* had a long history of partisan journalism when James Cox took control. As Dayton's Democratic newspaper, it claimed an ancestry going back to the *Miami Herald* and *Dayton Republican Gazette* which had appeared in 1826 to espouse "Jacksonian principles." Never prosperous, Democratic papers succeeded in Dayton only for brief periods as political journals. By 1849 Clement Vallandingham took control of the Democratic party press employing the name *Daily Empire*, and used the paper to launch his political career. By 1876 the *Dayton Democrat*, begun in 1874, had passed into the hands of John Gates Doren. "A foe of bossism and a friend of the workingman," Doren earned little money with the paper, but did provide the Democrats with a political vehicle that helped them come to power in Dayton during the 1880's. In 1890 Doren sold the *Democrat* to Charles H. Simms and F. T. Huffman. They unsuccessfully expanded into the morning field with the new *Morning Times*, and the newly named *Evening News* also floundered. When Cox and the Dayton News Company bought them out in August 1898, Simms and Huffman had only 2,600 subscribers. Discontinuing the morning paper, Cox followed the trend to afternoon dailies by continuing the evening edition as the *Dayton Daily News*.[1]

Cox believed Dayton lacked a truly metropolitan newspaper. Local publishers had failed fully to develop the potential market for newspapers. While the circulation of Dayton papers languished, the *Cincinnati Times-Star's* suburban edition dominated circulation in the city and surrounding area. The local papers still existed primarily as political voices. Carrying brief summaries of telegraphic news and day-old, pre-set "boiler plate" shipped from Cincinnati, they printed advertising copy, Cox recalled, "without change from one season to another. I found watermelons advertised in the Christmas holidays and ice skates on the fourth of July." The twenty-eight year old Cox decided to take advantage of the opportunity Dayton provided for metropolitan journalism.[2]

Cox viewed the newspaper as constituting a basic component of the metropolitan order. Industry, commerce, transportation, and journalism, he believed, played interrelated roles in the development of the city. In an enthusiastic booster editorial, Cox early described Dayton as the hub of a "large geographic wheel" with the various interurban lines serving the city as "spokes". Noting a metropolitan competition between Dayton and Cincinnati, he optimistically observed that the communities between the two centers increasingly looked towards Dayton because of the city's "diversified industries, aggressive stores and intelligent businessmen." Urging Daytonians vigorously to assert their independence from the Queen City, Cox pledged that the *News* would do its part in the struggle for metropolitan identity.[3]

During the late 1890's, the *Cincinnati Post* and the *Cincinnati Times-Star* engaged in circulation battles to win control of the Dayton market. Cox entered the struggle and challenged their journalistic imperialism. In addition to consolidating his holdings, Cox began an aggressive advertising sales program and launched an intensive circulation drive. Offering special advertising rates to Dayton merchants and boosting the city to his readers, Cox and the *News* gradually won the circulation battle in Dayton. Within six months sales of the

Times-Star fell from "the thousands" to a "few hundred". While engaged in continued competition with the Cincinnati papers in the outlying areas south of Dayton, Cox helped to strengthen the Gem City's ties to other satellite towns by extending circulation into Xenia, Piqua, and Greenville early in 1899—towns then recently connected to the city by a series of interurban railroads.[4]

Three years later, the Cincinnati newspapers abandoned the Dayton market and the *News* claimed it dominated circulation in the city and outlying areas within a radius of twenty miles. In addition to aggressive sales techniques, several other factors contributed to this success. An improvised triple-deck gasoline-powered press enabled the *News* to go to bed two hours later than its competition and still reach the streetcorners earlier with up-to-date news. The Cox paper had a monopoly on the Associated Press wire service in Dayton until 1900. When the Associated Press began to sell its news to any buyer in 1901, Cox purchased a double AP wire service. This connection consistently gave him more news copy than his competition. At the same time, the efficient interurban lines out of Dayton permitted the *News* to reach the streets in outlying areas, such as Franklin twenty miles to the south, a quarter hour before the Cincinnati papers. Aware of the validity of Horace Greeley's advice to small town journalists "that the subject of deepest interest to an average human being is himself; next to that he is concerned about his neighbors," Cox made suburban columns regular features. They not only fostered loyalty to Dayton but won readers in outlying towns and allowed Cox and the *News* to enhance Dayton's regional dominance.[5]

The emergence of the *News* as a regional paper confirmed Dayton's transformation into a metropolitan center and industrial city. During the canal era the commerce and industry of Dayton centered around the processing of regional farm products, but the railroad gradually redirected the economy. Cheap and efficient transportation as well as mechanical innovations in agricultural processing promoted large scale operations in the major urban centers. Consequently, between 1850 and 1880, Dayton's small scale foundries, linseed oil processors, farm equipment manufacturers, coopers, distilleries, and flour mills either disappeared or diversified their activities.

During the railroad era, Dayton's growth centered around the production of transportation equipment. As early as 1849, the firm which eventually became the Barney and Smith Car Company began to build railroad cars in a plant located on the periphery of the geographically small city. Initially "The Barney" produced passenger and freight cars and later built sleeping cars for George Pullman before Pullman turned to manufacturing his own cars. As the national railroad network reached completion at the end of the nineteenth century, Barney and Smith diversified production to include street and traction cars. These products, directed to an urban market, soon became the firm's primary source of revenue. With the advent of the urban market, the company more than tripled its size employing in 1908 more than 4,000 people in what had become a sprawling downtown plant.[6]

By the 1890's, industrialists had clearly adapted their entrepreneurial skills to the demand for urban services and consumer goods. The rise of the National Cash Register Company demonstrated this new orientation. In 1878 the cash register firm of John Patterson employed only seventy-nine people and occupied the second and third floors of a small downtown building. During the next twenty years, Patterson moved to suburban South Park and built a giant corporation housed in fifteen buildings. In step with the quickening pace of commercial and urban life, he advertised that the "cash register is needed and can be sold wherever money is handled." Through saturation advertising, sales trainee programs, patent controls, an efficient assembly line process, and ruthless cut-throat competition, Patterson ultimately gained control of the world market in cash registers. In 1908 "the Cash," by then the largest firm in Dayton, employed more than 5,000 people.[7]

As Dayton underwent this industrial transformation, it experienced great physical change. A "new city" emerged. Until after the Civil War, Dayton had remained within its original boundaries. In 1868, however, the city carried out its first general annexation when it added from beyond the rivers the growing residential suburbs of North Dayton, Riverdale, and Dayton View. The annexation also included the large industrial tracts east of the Miami Canal. These additions were quickly tied to the "old city" by a series of street car lines. During the next forty years, as the rise of the new industries occurred and James M. Cox built the *Dayton Daily News*, the city added large areas of land in all directions. It also tripled its population from 38,678 in 1880, to 116,577 by 1910. As a result of this growth, the Gem City stood in 1910 as the metropolitan center of the upper Miami Valley.[8]

Simultaneously, city government responded to the increased demands for improved municipal services. In 1864, in a wooden city, a professional fire department replaced the volunteer fire companies. As the city developed new residential and industrial areas, additional fire houses were added. In 1869 Dayton voters approved a bond issue to construct a sanitary water works that went into operation in the following year. In 1870 the wooden Main Street bridge was rebuilt of iron to handle safely the increased traffic between Dayton View and the central business district of the expanding city. In 1873 city officials created a Board of Police Commissioners to govern the newly reorganized, armed, and uniformed police force of the crowded city.

The simultaneous additions of new services demonstrated the complexity of the growing city. A Board of Health was created in 1888 and two years later the city belatedly began to build a sewage system that it completed in 1908. Street paving began in 1888 and twenty years later the city had 58 miles of paved roads. Experimenting with new governmental forms to manage the transformed city, in 1900 a Board of City Affairs was created to serve as a bi-partisan executive body. Reconstituted in 1902, as the Board of Public Service, these changes presaged the Dayton City Manager Plan. In 1898 Dayton became one of five cities in Ohio to operate a state employment office to provide some order to the search for labor and jobs.[9] Through this growth and creativity a new and vastly different city had emerged.

When James M. Cox purchased the *Dayton Daily News* in 1898, he observed in Dayton characteristics of "a growing city," but one lacking a regional newspaper. By 1900 the Gem City had grown to a population of 85,333 and was the fifth largest manufacturing center in the state.[10] One historian of the city wrote that "Beginning with 1897 a tide of unprecedented prosperity set in which continued in full force for a period of ten years."[11] Cox considered Dayton the keystone of an area from Lima and Springfield to the north and Cincinnati to the south that was "alive with industry." In addition, the novelty of eight electric interurban lines were under construction or already completed into the city. With these feeders, location, and industrial productivity, he foresaw Dayton becoming an important trading center.[12]

In this milieu, Cox and the *News* transformed journalism in Dayton. The *Dayton Journal* noted Cox's entrance into the Gem City newspaper arena with condescension and doubt:

    The Evening News has been sold and will hereafter be a Democratic paper. Democratic papers have never paid in Dayton and never will. Four of them have failed.

The *Journal* proved a poor prophet. Before long, Cox and the *News* confronted the other Dayton publishers with advertising innovations, journalistic crusades, special features, expanded news, circulation building contests, and political independence.[13]

To increase the value of advertising and make it commercial communication, Cox adopted the rule that the *News* would accept no advertising unless it had the right to make changes in format. This technique not only assured readers of advertising credibility; it also promised advertisers an attractive presentation. To entice leading merchants to expand their advertising, Cox made private deals to the effect that "if no worthwhile results accrued" the advertiser need not pay. If business improved, the *News* won a steady customer. The plan worked well, and before long Cox stopped making special arrangements and "imported a good ad-writer" from Chicago.[14]

During these building years, Cox characterized the *News* as "the People's paper." Crusades appeared regularly. While they aroused the curiosity of readers, they also brought lawsuits. One of the more dramatic of these exposes involved the efforts of A. E. Appleyard and Company to acquire a new right of way for the Dayton, Lebanon, and Cincinnati interurban railroad through newly developed residential sections. The *News* campaigned vigorously against granting the right of way, charging political collusion. Appleyard countered with a criminal libel suit and the sheriff pad-locked the *Daily News* office. Doubting the ability of Cox to post bond, the other afternoon papers published extras announcing the closing of the *News*. Through a political connection, Cox raised bail and within a half hour after the lawsuit became news, issued an extra "emblazoned with the story of the closing that had not closed." The courts eventually dismissed the suit and the D.L.&C. failed to get the right of way. "This experience," Cox recalled, "did the paper a great deal of good. We installed a three-deck press . . . and red ink disappeared from our ledger."[15]

As the situation demanded and money permitted, Cox added special features. Almost immediately after taking control he added a woman's editor and a society section. Syndicated newsletters, stock market quotations, and book serializations soon became regular attractions. *McClure's Saturday Magazine* supplement won wide readership for the Saturday edition. The local news staff expanded as circulation grew. The double Associated Press wire service provided extensive sports coverage as well as national and international news. Trips to Washington, D. C. and New York were awarded the most diligent clippers of special coupons printed in the *News*. Charitable institutions also benefited through periodic $500 wagers with the paper's competition over the issue of circulation leadership. The purses went to local hospitals. Special editions and supplements highlighted industrial and suburban development while Cox periodically devoted an entire page to the prospects of the Gem City.[16]

Although the *News* remained loyal to the Democratic Party, it was not a house organ. When Cox purchased the paper, Joseph Dowling, the Montgomery County Democratic Party chairman, became a leading stockholder in the Dayton News Company. Cox and Dowling soon came into conflict. In 1902 Cox struck for independence and purchased all the outstanding stock with personal notes. Rather than be a "kept editor," he turned the *Dayton Daily News* into a profitable business and used its news columns and editorial page as a personal voice. Initially, he had taken the position that the editorial page bore no relationship to the news columns. The news should "be a reflection of what is happening in the world," he asserted in 1900. As he moved toward independence, the distinction blurred. Eighteen months later he wrote:

> When the press takes an independent course, when it opposes wrong and attempts no longer to disguise facts for political effect, then will better conditions prevail generally and the press will occupy its proper place as a public benefactor, a blessing to the world, a protection to the people.

As the *News* increasingly became a financial success, Cox became politically more independent. In 1904 Cox and Dowling battled through rival delegations at the Ohio Democratic convention for control of the Montgomery County Democratic Party. Cox supported Alton B. Parker in 1904, but in the following spring he asserted that the Democratic Party had entered a "new era." "The issues of the twentieth century eclipse the great theories of years gone by— different questions demand different considerations. The one great principle of Democracy is that the people rule." In spite of this receptiveness to a new politics, Cox believed the problems of the day lay in the people and not the system. The role of the independent *Dayton Daily News* was to educate. Cox editorialized:

> We do not hope to reform things in a day. The evil is too deep-seated to be cured by a newspaper article. But please God, just so long as we have the power to write we shall call attention to the hypocrisy as we find it: just so long as it is a newspaper, the *Dayton Daily News* will denounce the rich criminal in the same terms that it denounces the poor criminal, and seek at all times to have people understand that 'The name is but the guinea's stamp: The man's a man for a that.'[17]

"Competition was keen and we kept hustling," Cox recalled of these early days. The other Dayton papers "spruced up" and added new equipment and features, but at the end of 1900 the *News* dominated Dayton journalism. The *Mail Order Journal*, a nationally known trade magazine for advertisers, listed the Cox paper among the best one hundred in the country. This endorsement insured the bulk of the advertising done by outside firms in Dayton for the *News*. As readership increased, advertising rates based upon circulation also increased. In the spring of 1907, the three editions of the *News* claimed a circulation of nearly thirty thousand, 25 percent greater than the *Herald*, its afternoon competition.[18]

While efficient management and technology changed newspapers, Cox believed efficiency in government would make the political system more responsive to the needs of twentieth century America. "That which insures the most good to the community should always be the beacon light of guidance to public officials," he editorialized. Broadly conceived, his ideas went beyond the good government clichés of the mugwumps to a plea for an adequate response to changed conditions. Time and again the *News* appealed for more efficient police and fire protection, better lighted streets, safe railroad crossings, underground electric lines, a consolidated traction loop, better garbage service, regulation of saloons and prostitution, schools free of politics, and abatement of industrial smoke. "There is the need for the facilities of a city—not a town," he wrote after a large downtown fire. If urban service did not improve, he warned, "Dayton businessmen might go elsewhere." Cox reasoned that if public officals "efficiently let out contracts" they could offer services at a minimum cost. If "good business methods" penetrated municipal institutions, good city government would then become a reality, Cox claimed.[19]

In the new city the need for diverse forms of recreation seemed obvious. To make

Dayton a first class city, Cox pressed for parks, Sunday baseball, a symphony orchestra, a concert hall, and water recreation facilities. If the city lacked the funds for parks, he suggested the creation of a park corporation, the city guaranteeing a profit. Recalling Paul Sorg's building of the Sorg Theatre in Middletown, he urged "prominent Daytonians" to build a concert hall and assured them that it would return an ample profit.[20] Cox observed the growing Dayton suburbs from the point of view of a downtown businessman. In his view, the suburbs constituted an integral part of the city because they reaped the advantages of the "cosmopolitan life" of Dayton. Suburbanites he argued, earned their livelihoods in Dayton, depended upon Dayton's streetcar service, used the entertainment facilities of the city, and generally garnered high property valuations because of their proximity to the advantages the city provided. The *News* urged its suburban readers to incorporate with Dayton. The city's police and fire protection as well as its schools would prove advantageous to suburbanites while Dayton would gain because annexation would "help lighten the [tax] burden" and make "a bigger and better Dayton."[21] The deterioration of residential areas bordering on the central retail district also concerned Cox. Seeing the slums as a detriment to the community because they fostered crime and disease, the *News* editor believed that as long as landlords continued to rent the decaying tenements to the poor, the problem would remain. If private investors razed the slums and built public housing, the physical and moral health of the entire community would improve. Such action would remove blight, provide jobs, and turn the slum dwellers into "good citizens." The community might thus elevate the poor to the proven level of the middle-class, in Cox's optimistic view.[22]

Though the *News* was "the People's paper," Cox directed his editorials at the concerns of the middle-class on the periphery of the city. In the spring of 1907, the *News* editorial page listed eight essential "Dayton needs" without which, Cox suggested, it could not become a great city. Each of these proposals stemmed from the recognition of a changing city and the need for increased efficiency demanded by the new industrial-technological order. To insure the prosperity of Dayton, the *News* urged the city to give a railroad right of way to the National Cash Register Company in order to keep the firm in Dayton. For safety reasons, Cox proposed that the city insist on overhead rather than grade crossings. To satisfy the recreational needs of middle-class home owners, he proposed a park system in the residential areas that ringed the business district. To accommodate pedestrians using the central business district, he recommended that the city build public comfort stations. For health purposes, the *News* advanced a call for an efficient sanitation department. For the protection of life and property interests, Cox pressed for improved flood control measures. To satisfy the needs of suburban readers (and simultaneously facilitate newspaper distribution), he proposed the construction of a bridge across the Miami River at Fifth Street to give Edgmont residents direct access to the downtown, and recommended that the city extend a number of streets in various parts of the city to promote development. As industry expanded, Cox noted the need for a skilled labor force and suggested the establishment of a manual training school. Finally, the list called for community support for the newly created Dayton Chamber of Commerce.[23]

The population of Dayton doubled between 1890 and 1910, but of more importance to Cox the kind of people coming into the city changed. In 1890 the foreign-born made up almost a fourth of the population, but by 1910 the foreign-born proportion dropped to slightly more than one-tenth of the total. These figures suggest that the greater part of the growth came from the regional countryside. The city experienced only a slight influx of newcomers from the recent immigration, a fact which helps explain the comparative slow growth rate of Dayton when contrasted with places like Toledo, Akron, and Cleveland during this same period. Consequently, the *News* did not try to appeal to eastern and southern Europeans.[24] To the contrary, Cox and his readers received the arrival of unfamiliar groups with disdain.

When confronted by the appearance of eastern Europeans in Dayton, the *News* editorialized that the "Anglo-Saxon is the grandest race that evolution has produced." Cox saw the new immigrants as lazy and unskilled people who would have a negative impact upon the job market once the economy slowed down. He reasoned further that southern and eastern Europeans did not understand politics; hence they posed a threat to political stability and could prevent honest government from becoming a reality. To resolve the dilemma, Cox urged immigration restriction at the national level and recommended that the city enact property and residence requirements for voting rights. For those immigrants already in the city, he called for the establishment of immigrant schools where they could learn American culture.[25]

In 1910 Dayton's black population of 5,000 was increasing. Comparing race relations in the Gem City with other Ohio cities, Frank Quillin wrote in 1913 that he "had found nothing quite so radical" as the system of segregation there. "Hotels," he noted, "restaurants, soda-fountain establishments, saloons and all places of that nature are closed to the Negro." For most blacks, housing opportunities were restricted to the West Side section, while limitations on economic mobility existed as labor unions kept blacks out "except in very rare instances." The situation seemed to grow worse as the city grew, Quillin noted. "The old line white families . . . were dying out," he explained, "and in their place were rising the newly-rich and uncultured families who were ready to take advantage of artifical props to uphold their importance."[26]

The *News* reflected the community's position on race relations. Cox approved of the harsh reality of a rigid economic and social system of racial segregation. The *News* referred to Jim Crow restrictions as immoral but "necessary to prevent a grave reign of terror" because blacks without education could not govern. When the Democrats in Dayton lost the election of 1898, the twenty-eight year old partisan Democrat publisher suggested that the city government disfranchise blacks who "sold their votes." Believing the black workers could not meet the standards of the white mechanic, he suggested that opportunities for black men be limited to agriculture and manual labor. Generally, the *News* disapproved of lynching, but in 1904 after race riots in nearby Springfield, the paper suggested that racial violence could be avoided by speedy trials and the elimination of appeals and new trials based upon technical mistakes. "good Christian people," Cox wrote, "are fed up with the abuses of the law." To justify this position on race Cox, using then current anthropological theories, noted that the brains of Africans did not develop because the skull solidified as a natural defense mechanism to prevent death from hard blows to the head. So Cox, the crusading journalist, attempted to deal with the race question in such a way as to increase the efficiency of the society and promote the well-being of the greatest number in the community.[27]

While contributing to tensions in the area of race, Cox worked towards harmony in labor relations. He disapproved of child labor and strikebreakers and consistently favored legislation to eliminate such abuse. He approved of labor's right to strike, but believed that arbitration would eliminate strikes. The arbitrator, he reasoned, would work in the best interest of the community. The ideas of welfare capitalism served as his guide in the relationship between capital and labor. As Cox put it:

> . . . one is indispensable to the other. Every man who works hard should be paid enough to live comfortably, send his children to school, genteely attired if he is frugal. Capital should receive a fair return on its investment and be compensated for the large element of risk attached to its operation. There is no reason why this condition cannot be created and kept.[28]

In accordance with these views, Cox arbitrated a People's Railway Company strike in 1900. He later urged workers at the National Cash Register Company to settle their differences without a strike, because N. C. R. "is the most humane factory in the world" and the loss of its payroll to the Dayton economy would be "detrimental to all." Recognizing the problems created by inflation, Cox offered no solution other than that labor should act in the public interest. In opposition to the alternative of socialism, he argued that welfare capitalism and labor unions continually improved the lot of the worker. To a local socialist, emphasizing that he was a man of humble origin, the *News* publisher wrote:

> We do not consider people with money our enemies. In our system if we tried for it, we could become wealthy. People become rich because they covet wealth and sacrifice other things for it--even honor, honesty and happiness.[29]

A turning point for Cox in journalism was the failure in 1905 of the *Dayton Press*, his principal competition of 1898. Assured of continued growth in Dayton, Cox proceeded to build a newspaper chain. In the spring he purchased the Springfield, Ohio, *Press-Republic* and the equipment of the defunct *Dayton Press*. On June 1 he changed the name of the paper to the *Springfield Daily News*, made it an afternoon voice, and switched its politics to Democratic.

Within a short time the Dayton News Company became the Ohio News League. Using methods similar to those developed in Dayton, the *Springfield Daily News* gradually monopolized afternoon publishing in Springfield. Years later, Cox reported that:

> It was in 1898 that I paid $26,000 for the *Dayton Daily News* property; it was in 1903 that it turned the corner and became an unquestioned business success; it was in 1905 that this success enabled us to begin accumulating funds for expansion, profits amounting to about my purchase price.[30]

The formula used to build the Ohio News League—crusades, promotions, more news, editorial independence, advertising innovations, a professional staff—derived from Joseph Pulitzer. Concurring with Pulitzer that the modern newspaper needed accuracy, reliability, and "more and greater public service" to "win the confidence of the people," Cox doubted that a newspaper could become a vital force in the community without this confidence. Once the readers believed in the paper, it could achieve its ultimate objective of arousing "public interest and emotion on matters concerning the public good." Cox had come to believe that the newspaper, by informing the public on matters of politics, economic and social situations, commercial and mercantile conditions, attitudes, entertainment, and whatever aspects of life it dealt with, could unite the metropolitan community. As fewer newspapers dominated the metropolitan newspaper zones, Cox's dream approached reality.[31]

Business incentive promoted the new journalistic techniques. Technology kept pace.

Both in turn led to fewer newspapers. Cox continued to tie his sense of duty and desire for power to the profit motive. He hoped to increase circulation and widen his influence by stimulating individuals to support reforms that benefited the community.[32]

After ten years of prosperous operation of the Ohio News League, James Cox decided to turn his attention to politics. He had built the *News* into the pre-eminent paper in the Dayton metropolitan area with a daily circulation of 35,000. With wide readership, public confidence, and financial success, this graduate of the one-room school became a powerful force in the community and in Democratic Party politics. As he shifted his interest, Cox summarized his view of the function of the press. It should willingly tackle any problems it deemed worthy of attention, not to destroy but to use its power positively. The seasoned editor at the age of thirty-eight looked at the paper as an integral part of the power structure and a forum to proclaim what he deemed best for the community. Ten years earlier, Cox had written that the *News* served "as the guaranteeor [sic] of the public welfare without weighing the possible result of such a course."[33] With a philosophy based upon the idea of the greatest good for the greatest number, he now projected an image that ingratiated him with the middling order. He also began to view success in business as a prerequisite for service in government and turned his attention to politics.

III
A BUSINESSMAN TURNS TO POLITICS

In 1908, with the Republican Party in the Third Ohio Congressional District divided, James M. Cox found the moment opportune to run for Congress. Plagued by patronage problems, the Republican organization deserted first term Congressman John E. Harding of Middletown and tendered the nomination to party regular William G. Frizell, a former Dayton Councilman who then was a member of the Ohio General Assembly. In the 1906 Congressional race, Harding had defeated former Ohio governor James E. Campbell of Hamilton by running strongly in Dayton and Montgomery County. The need to counter this strength dictated a Democratic candidate who could run well in Dayton. Known for his Gem City boosterism, the hardworking Cox stood as a likely choice. In addition, Cox had a power base as publisher of the largest newspaper in the Third District, while his support of Democratic candidates and causes during the past decade had accumulated numerous political debts among party regulars.[1]

The Third Ohio Congressional District, with over 257,000 people, consisted of Butler, Montgomery, and Preble counties. More than 80 percent of the population lived in two rapidly growing metropolitan areas. Greater Dayton accounted for approximately 145,000 of the constituents; and to the southwest, in Butler County, Hamilton and Middletown had developed as a separate metropolitan area containing more than 55,000 people. Although native white Americans comprised the predominant strain in the district, first and second generation German, Irish, and eastern European population groups added up to 18 percent of the total residents.[2]

The district, Cox noted, "was teeming with manufacturing industry." Besides the surging annual productivity of Dayton, which increased in value from $39,596,773 to $60,378,376 in five years, Hamilton and Middletown remained centers for the manufacture of paper. Additionally, the Mosler Safe Company in Hamilton and the American Rolling Mills in Middletown grew rapidly. The three cities employed more than 35,000 people in industry. The Hamilton-Middletown complex produced $34,700,478 worth of goods with a value added by manufacturing of 52 percent. With an advanced technology and relatively skilled labor force, the cities did not rely heavily on the products of the countryside for their manufacturing.[3]

The countryside, familiar to Cox, "was rich in agriculture." The Bureau of Census appraised the average farm in the area at $8,175, while the average farm valuation in Ohio stood at $6,994. This difference in value existed even though the farms in the Third district averaged 80.3 acres compared to an 88.6 acre mean for the state. The region produced a rich yield of cattle, hogs, and corn; but a high proportion of the rural population lived a marginal existence. More than two-fifths of the farms in the district were operated by tenant farmers. The overwhelmingly white rural population thus seems to have had a two-tiered class structure.[4]

The National Soldiers Home residents made up another important segment of the population in the district. The Home, located in the Arlington Heights section of Dayton, housed some 7,000 destitute veterans who had fought for the Union during the Civil War. "Waving the bloody shirt" remained a real and emotional issue for most of the veterans and they tended "to vote the way they shot." The Democrats seldom received more than two hundred votes from the Home. His experience with Paul Sorg enabled Cox to understand the virtual hopelessness of this vote.⁵

In mid-September, the third District Democratic Convention met in Middletown to choose a candidate. Cox had organized thoroughly. Ed Hanley, the Montgomery County Democratic chairman, successfully lined up the delegations from Montgomery and Preble counties behind "the live wire of Montgomery County." Judge Benjamin McCann of Hamilton, convinced that Cox could win, pledged the unanimous support of the Butler County Democratic machinery. The party candidate for governor, Judson Harmon, spoke on Cox's behalf at the convention. Referring to the Republican schism, Harmon quipped that "it was the duty of the Democrats to settle the factional squabble by electing James M. Cox." The former Middletown teacher walked onto the stage of the Paul J. Sorg Theatre and received the nomination without opposition. George Burba, a close friend and editor of the *Dayton Daily News*, observed that the businessman turned politician looked "scared and apprehensive" as he briefly pledged his best efforts to the convention.⁶

Two days later Cox launched his campaign. Turning daily affairs of his newspaper over to each respective staff, he appealed to his readers for support. Reasoning that *News* readers functioned as a "community of interest" devoted to similar ideals, Cox declared:

> I have never previous to this time considered a candidacy for any public office. In fact I have been so contrary I never permitted my name to be used with a delegateship to any convention, nor as a member of any party committee.   To represent the third district is an honor of which I should be proud and I will seek it with all my energies.
>
> The readers know my tendencies and predilections. They have gone through the bitter fights with me . . . the character of my service can be measured by the history of the *Daily News* in the the last ten years. Upon this record of newspaper policy and performance I shall stand or fall.⁷

Cox waged an energetic grassroots campaign that formally opened in Dayton with William Jennings Bryan, the Democratic presidential nominee, sharing the rostrum. The Great Commoner, who had built his reputation with ringing appeals to the downtrodden, characterized Cox as having "great force of character in accord with the principles of Democracy" who "through his newspapers has contributed enormously to the Democratic cause." Performing the ultimate political service to a congressional aspirant, Bryan told his listeners, "I personally desire the election of James M. Cox as a member of the next House of Representative." Shortly after the appointment by Bryan, the Dayton Press Club feted Cox with a banquet at which the editors of the *Dayton Herald* and the *Daytoner Zeitung* announced support for their fellow journalist.⁸

The owner of "the People's paper" took his campaign to the countryside with a carefully planned schedule. In spite of the fears of campaign manager Ed Hanley, who believed that rural voters harbored a strong distaste for the automobile, Cox toured a township a day by car stopping to talk to farmers along the way. Holding to his schedule, he battled the muddy roads that led him to nightly meetings in the rural villages.

Again and again, "Jimmy" Cox appealed to the farmers identification with Robert M. La Follette. He charged that the Republicans had spurned agricultural reform when "they rejected the Wisconsin Senator." Cox stood firmly in favor of a low tariff and persuasively reasoned that downward revision would help the farmer by lowering the costs of farm essentials. In concerned tones, he consistently favored guaranteed bank deposits in order to prevent runs on banks and stabilize the financial system, a genuine issue with the electorate so soon after the panic of 1907. Frequently, the Daytonian turned from national issues and stressed the needs of his listeners for good roads and improved rural schools. These programs, he asserted, should receive priority over military spending and "would make American first in more important ways." Generally speaking, Cox projected to the rural populous the image of an earnest and efficient young man concerned about the public good. The main thrust of his campaign, however, was toward the urban areas.[9]

In the cities the campaign had a different emphasis. Ballyhoo and bandwagons still functioned as part of the political arsenal and a number of equestrian parades took place in Dayton and Hamilton. Cox drew upon every available resource: "the Cox Juniors," a drum corps comprised of *Daily News* delivery boys, embellished every parade. The cities provided readily available audiences. The candidate shook hands on streetcorners and spoke to workers as they lunched or changed shifts. He addressed ward political clubs, park and tent meetings, ethnic clubs, and the Soldiers Home veterans. Throughout, the *News* gave its owner full coverage, prodded readers to register in order to vote for Cox, and editorially complimented his stand on the issues.[10]

"The pressing issues today concern the consumer," Cox declared over and over again. "The laborers' prosperity depends upon demands for his labor and the cost of living," he asserted time and again. In keeping with the platform, he argued that free trade would guarantee markets for American goods and simultaneously help keep prices down to the advantage of both workers and management. The publisher told a labor audience in Hamilton, "If reform is to come it will have to come from the masses as ninety percent of the wealth is owned by ten percent of the people." Emphasizing that the Democrats stood as the real party of the people, he pointed out that the platform called for the creation of a cabinet level Department of Labor to give the worker representation in the executive department, and guaranteed bank deposits to protect the savings of hard-working wage earners. Cox approved of both reforms as well as the planks calling for a federal income tax and the direct election of Senators. He contrasted these democratic principles with the "dictatorial Roosevelt" who had "selected his successor."[11]

Although the campaign generally followed the major national issues, Cox geared his style and content to the communities in the district and to a high voter turnout. The votes lay in the cities and this dictated an appeal, in particular, to the working class. Perhaps Cox's strategy simply reflected, on a local level, the rhetoric of the Democratic Party platform which tried to promote a national farmer-worker coalition. Nevertheless, personalities and the specific nature of election districts generally determine the conduct of local campaigns, and such was the case in the Third District. The strategy worked.[12]

For the first, but not the last time, the traditional election night signal lights on top of the *Dayton Daily News* building flashed a victory for Jim Cox. Throughout the country, voters turned out in large numbers for the presidential race. In the Third District, more than 80 percent of the voters went to the polls. In a three way race, the higher voter turnout worked to the advantage of Cox. The interest produced by the presidential campaign brought out the working class voters to whom Cox appealed. Receiving 49.8 percent of the vote, he ran best in the cities. In Dayton and Hamilton, Cox gained pluralities in all sixteen wards and majorities in ten. He successfully worked the periphery against the center in

Dayton, garnering an average 61.2 percent of the vote in the third, eighth, and ninth wards, and large majorities in the second and seventh wards. These wards housed the industrial suburbs and contained the largest numbers of ethnic Germans, eastern Europeans, and were working class wards. In traditionally Democratic Hamilton, Cox carried every ward with majorities. In Harding's hometown, Middletown, Cox failed to win a plurality by only 146 votes out of 3,148 cast. As expected the Democrats lost disastrously in the Soldiers Home—Cox received only 14 percent of the vote, the bottom of his ticket. Similarly, he lost rural Preble County and the farm areas of Montgomery County by wide margins. In contrast, the Daytonian won 56.3 percent of the vote in the rural areas of Butler County. Two factors contributed to this success. The county generally voted Democratic and Cox had grown up in Wayne Township, a fact local politicians and Cox made much of during the campaign.[13]

Cox's victory in 1908 was part of a trend in Ohio that gave the Democratic Party control of the cities. It also reflected a nationwide continuation of a majority surge for Democratic congressmen. In 1908 the Democrats gained twelve congressional seats and had since 1904 added forty seats. The movement of the electorate continued and in 1910, the Democrats became the majority party in Congress, a position they maintained until 1918.[14] A member of the 61st Congress, Cox became part of a coalition of 169 Democrats and 56 insurgent Republicans who generally voted for reform. Of the 119 urban-based congressmen, Cox stood among 58 who consistently supported progressive measures. Among the 88 freshman congressmen elected in 1908, Cox and 53 others joined the progressive coalition. While the vast majority of the reformers had completed college, Cox had barely finished high school. At the age of thirty-nine he was considerably younger than most of the reformers whose median age was forty-eight.[15]

As a new congressman, Cox concerned himself with learning his way around the governmental establishment and serving the interest of his district. He spent most of his time in committee work and took the House floor "as often as seemed useful." To facilitate reelection, he labored assiduously to extend the base of his support by paying particular attention to the legislation he introduced, submitting 800 private pension bills for veterans. In spite of this specialized activity, Cox considered himself part of "the progressive wing of the Democratic party" and the developing progressive majority.[16] On the key issues, Cox smugly recalled:

> I voted consistently for lower tariffs and regarded the Payne Aldrich bill as an outrage. I was an ardent supporter of Canadian reciprocity. Nothing interested me more than the proper control of trusts and the efficient regulation of railroads. On the latter question I accepted La Follette's idea of an honest appraisal of railroad values. I took a keen interest in the alleged frauds in the Interior Department under Secretary Ballinger and sat right beside Gilbert M. Hitchcock when he was conducting the House fight against Ballinger.[17]

For the first term lawmaker insuring reelection became synonymous with promoting the interest of the Third District. Cox quickly learned the ponderous ways of the House when he had to look after the well-being of Dayton industry during the debate over the Payne-Aldrich tariff bill. Circumventing tradition, just two weeks after being sworn in as a member of the House, he asked for floor time assigned to a senior member with irregular attendance. Speaker Joseph Cannon obliged when the lackadaisical member failed to show up at his assigned time. The Dayton booster prefaced his plea for a scientific tariff with the remarkable assertion that he spoke:

> as the representative of a district which not only produces but exports more manufactured goods than any district in America. Our vast industrial concerns not only feel secure from foreign invasion . . . they stand ready to beat any foreign competitor upon his own soil if this government will give them half a chance.

Expressing the concern of leading industries involved in foreign commerce, Cox pleaded for reciprocal agreements to foster international trade. He cited the example of Germany as the principal competition for Dayton machine manufacturers. Buttressing his arguments with letters from key Dayton industrialists, he hammered at the point that without decreased tariffs, these companies would have to establish foreign operations and thus adversely affect American labor. Rather than tax the American public unreasonably, with fewer jobs and higher prices, he reasoned that the administration should "balance the budget." The essence of the position he later said was "economic freedom"; but in 1909, the interests of the National Cash Register Company, the Davis Sewing Machine Company, and other Dayton firms with international markets molded his arguments.[18] The reasoning of Cox and other opponents of the high tariff went begging, and the Payne-Aldrich Tariff became law.

With the same ingenuity, but with more success, Cox manipulated the House rules to get a new post office for Dayton. Congressman Harding had secured an appropriation to enlarge the old post office located on Fifth and Main Streets. In step with the city's growth, the Dayton post office had doubled its receipts during the 1899-1909 decade. Cox, a downtown businessman, foresaw continued development of the central business district and believed that the post office should be an integral part of it. He doubted that mere enlargement of the old building would meet the future needs of the city. To avoid this mistake, Cox had first to secure repeal of the previous appropriation and then get enlarged funds allocated for a new site and building. He introduced the necessary bills, but House rules forbade new legislation in the appropriation bill and a simple call for a point of order would have defeated his scheme. While canvassing the entire House, Cox met opposition from two members, Congressmen Robert Macon of Arkansas and William Stafford of Wisconsin. He skillfully worked around them. When this part of the appropriations bill came before the House Committee of the Whole, Cox pre-arranged to have Macon taken to lunch, and James R. Mann of Illinois, then presiding over the House, asked Stafford to take the chair. With opposition removed, the scheme worked. A few years later, Dayton had a new, ornate, classic revival post office at Third and Ludlow Streets, closer than the old post office to the center of business activity.[19] With the same skill, Cox blended reform and patriotism to promote the interests of the National Soldiers Homes in Kansas, Virginia, and Ohio. Observing that the subsistence allowance in the Sundry Civil bill for the Soldiers Homes had declined from the previous year, he launched an investigation and uncovered some startling aspects about life in the homes. When the appropriations bill came before the House, Cox took the floor and pointed out that prisoners in the Dayton jail and the federal prison at Ft. Leavenworth, Kansas, were better fed than veterans of the Civil War. With statistics in hand, Cox proposed an additional subsistence appropriation of $250,000. Both houses readily approved the addition. Thus, Cox, by combining the skill of a muckraker and the enthusiasm of a patriot, shrewdly promoted legislation beneficial to third district residents.[20]

In the 61st Congress, according to House rules, the Speaker parceled out committee assignments. Speaker Cannon promptly assigned Democrat Cox to the District of Columbia Committee, while he appointed freshman Republicans to more powerful assignments. The District of Columbia Committee hardly gave Cox an influential base to promote the interests of his district. Nevertheless, the position offered him potential weekly floor time in the House and an opportunity to develop the interest in municipal affairs that he brought to Washington.

Of the five committee reports that Cox introduced in this Congress, four dealt with the physical development of the expanding city and transportation lanes in a crowded environment. As in Dayton, Cox concerned himself with tieing newly developed areas to the center of the city. By requesting land acquisition and changes in the District of Columbia Master Highway Plan, he sought to extend streets into new residential areas. Similarly, he recommended to the House that the Washington Terminal Company install elevators in the newly built Union Terminal to eliminate congestion and for the convenience of users. All received congressional approval. The fifth report proposed a minimum wage for workers in the District of Columbia; this measure the House conveniently tabled.[21]

The best known aspect of the struggle for reform in the 61st Congress became the fight for rules change in the House of Representatives. To Cox, Speaker Cannon symbolized "stand-pattism." "I hated the autocratic House management, exercised for the benefit of selfish special interests," he recalled. During caucusing on the issue of House reform, Cox came into contact with the leadership of both sides of the aisle as they vied for votes. He supported the insurgents. To the *New York Times* he wrote:

> I am opposed to the Speaker naming them [committee members] but there has been some question about the most expedient plan to be followed by the House itself. No method has been suggested which meets the same general acceptance as the original theory of having a Committee of the House submit a report on committees to the House for adoption. Therefore I am in favor of it.[22]

Years later, Cox explained that the whole affair resulted from an inevitable "much needed revision of the rules merely postponed for one year." At the end of the 60th Congress, George Norris of Nebraska began a drive for more democratic rules in the House. He proposed a special committee to recommend rules changes for the next Congress. Speaker Cannon blocked the resolution but a point of order vote indicated strong support. In the lame duck session, Norris continued to press for reform. The attack on Cannonism mounted again during the reorganization of the new Congress, but Cannon retained the old rules with the help of southern and Tamany Democrats who also had a vested interest in rules stability. Cox agreed with the Democratic caucus and voted against Cannon, but did not do so dogmatically.

For breaking party ranks on this crucial measure, Representatives John J. Fitzgerald of New York and William Howard of Georgia were expelled from the Democratic caucus. When they applied for readmission, Cox supported their cause and worked for their return. He proposed a secret ballot to protect the members from the wrath of reform minded constituents. It worked. Afterwards, Howard summed up Cox's role when he said, "Well, Fitz, I want to appoint Cox to be my political manager from now on!" But the question of House reform did not abate. Rules revision came up again in March of 1910 when George Norris discovered a weakness in the armor of the Speaker. On a question dealing with taking the census, Cannon ruled that constitutionally privileged resolutions took precedent over House procedures. On March 17, Norris cited the Constitution, which states that "each House may determine the rules of its proceedings," and reintroduced his resolution to exclude the Speaker from the Rules Committee, and deny him the authority to appoint Committees. After that, one historian observed, "the revolution was under way." Two days later, after much furor in the press, confusion in the cloak rooms, and political infighting on the floor, the insurgent Republicans and the Democratic caucus forced a revision of the rules similar to the Norris resolution. Cox again agreed with the party caucus and voted to weaken the Speaker.[23]

Only with tepid enthusiasm could Cox accept Senator La Follette's program for an honest assessment of railroad values; he instead believed firmly in the need for "efficient regulation" of the railroad industry. Since the creation of the Interstate Commerce Commission, there had been persistent efforts made to improve railroad regulation. President Taft promoted the Mann bill which proposed the expansion of the Interstate Commerce Commission's ratemaking power and the creation of a court to handle appeals from Commission rulings. Cox voted with the House insurgents and the Democrats to amend the bill to provide for true valuation of rail properties, to forbid mergers of competing rail lines, to eliminate the court of appeals, and to bring telephone and telegraph lines under the jurisdiction of the Commission. In the Senate, the Taft-supported Elkins bill emerged intact, but in the conference committee the reformers held their own. Although the Senate struck the physical valuation feature and restored the appeals court, the other House amendments remained. On the whole, the Mann-Elkins Act stood as a victory for House progressives.[24]

A political realist rather than an idealogue, Cox deviated from the ranks of the reform coalition on at least two key issues brought before the 61st Congress. Having campaigned for guaranteed bank deposits, Cox voted for the watered down version of the postal savings bank law while most Democrats voted no. Also he did not actively support conservation legislation. On three record votes dealing with conservation, he refused to vote. Perhaps his newspaper holdings put him in a possible conflict of interest since timber was a raw material for paper production. What limited concern Cox expressed about conservation issues involved the Ballinger affair. He later recalled that he was vitally interested in "the alleged frauds in the Interior Department" and in 1910 he was very critical of President William Howard Taft for his dismissal of Gifford Pinchot, the Chief of the Forestry Service.[25]

When Congress adjourned at the end of June, 1910, Cox could look back at his first term with satisfaction. He had consistently and successfully tended to the interests of his constituents and could now face the Third District electorate with a number of accomplishments. The new post office for growing Dayton, better care for the veterans, and a record of promoting the needs of Dayton industrialists and workers, all bid well for his reputation. In addition, and probably most important for his reelection, he had staked out a place in the reform wave sweeping the country.

In 1910 Democratic popularity ran high throughout in the nation, and in the bi-elections the party gained a majority in the House for the first time since the Cleveland era. Campaigning on his record, Cox was the top vote getter in the district. He ran well ahead of Governor Judson Harmon who hoped to run for president in 1912 on the Democratic ticket. His wide margin of victory brought him recognition throughout the state. Defeating George R. Young of Dayton by nearly 13,000 votes, the incumbent received a record 55.8 percent of the total vote. Although he carried every urban ward in the district, as well as numerous rural precincts, Cox again ran best in the industrial suburbs ringing the old city. His support of army veterans paid off handsomely with a 265 vote majority out of 3,000 votes cast at the Soldiers Home. The increased vote he earned in the purely residential suburbs of Dayton pointed to more middle-class supporters, and the large margin of victory during a low turnout election further indicated the friends Cox had made among these voters.[26]

The 62nd Congress opened with the Democratic majority quickly choosing Champ Clark as Speaker and setting the new Rules Committee into operation. The reorganization brought Cox an assignment on the most powerful committee in the House—Appropriations. John J. Fitzgerald of Brooklyn, whose return to the party caucus Cox helped engineer, chaired the Committee. Reform continued to serve as a useful theme on the national level, and Congress enacted a number of reform measures. The areas of concern became tariffs, taxation, political reform, labor legislation, trusts, and railroad legislation. Cox remained a minor figure in the House, and his party regularity continued. Because the Democrats maintained party discipline on reform in this Congress, party regularity meant support for reform measures.[27] (See Table F)

Cox brought his business and urban perspective with him to the Appropriations Committee. As a member of a subcommittee to improve public utilities services for the District of Columbia, he handled the Appropriations Committee bill dealing with the District on the House floor. Three provisions in the bill, Cox said, "marked great progress" that would prove efficient. Citing numerous cities operating municipally owned garbage and asphalt plants, the Daytonian emphasized that such plants would put Washington in step with cities throughout the country. The Great Falls hydroelectric plant would enable the federal government to generate enough electricity for street lights and public buildings to meet its needs until 1935. In addition, it would increase the water supply of the Delacarlia Reservoir, the capital city's principal source of water. Cox pointed out that "great economies can be effected through their adoption." With the District government operating at a deficit, the efficiency aspects of the measure enabled proponents to overcome opposition from Southern Democrats and Republicans. The projects received congressional approval with the entire appropriations package.[28]

This same viewpoint was brought to bear on public utility regulation. On a question involving the construction of a dam on the Black Warrior River in Alabama, Cox spoke of the need for federal controls. "We are the representatives of the people, and since we can in full propriety . . . protect their rights now" he said, "this is the moment to exercise our vigilance." He proposed limiting franchise tenure to twenty-five years and regulating the price charged for the power developed. To buttress his arguments, the Dayton congressman cited the financial plight experienced by the cities because of excessively long term franchises, and pointed out that the increasing urban tax burden made it essential for corporations to pay taxes "in an amount at least commensurate with the value of the rights which they enjoy under the authority of the government." Using the opportunity provided by the *Congressional Record* to advertise his progressive posture, Cox went on to assert that it was "the abuse of public power which is bringing about the demand for more genuine democracy as opposed to representative government." He approved of the initiative and referendum and expounded at length upon the desirability of the innovation for state government. A compromise measure on the dam eventually passed, but Cox had expressed his views for the record.[29]

Over the years, Cox had groped for a formula to unify his thinking on the social issues of the day and his desire to preserve the system. By the latter half of his second term in congress, a unified scheme seems to have emerged.

During the debate over the creation of the Children's Bureau, Cox came to see the measure as essential to the "process of conserving the human race" and believed nationwide information gathering in this area was needed because the states lacked uniform legislation, if they acted at all. Bringing the evidence of experts to bear on behalf of the bill, he cited the ideas of social worker Jane Addams, labor leader Samuel Gompers, and sociologist Charles Henderson of the University of Chicago. An adequate response to the needs of impoverished children, he argued, would eliminate "social and political unrest." He noted further that physicians, juvenile courts, and women's clubs throughout the country approved of the proposed bureau. To counter the position that the bureau would duplicate the work of the census, Cox stated that the new agency would rely on the Bureau of the Census to gather the data. Anticipating a constitutional argument, he pointed out that millions of dollars were ironically allocated to subsidize agriculture and industry while the "sense of right in the breast of man, the sense of justice and equity, the plain common sense view of laymen . . . tell us that these laws are humane and right, and yet they are held unconstitutional."

With a journalist's sense of the value of publicity, Cox saw the proposed Children's Bureau as a way to arouse public sentiment against the worst abuses of child labor by making accurate information available. "There is nothing in our American life," he observed, "which justifies the intolerable conditions in many industrial lines. Corrective measures will only come when the eye of the nation has been cast upon the dark spots." Not only would the bureau uncover industrial abuse, he went on, but it would also reveal the economic waste brought by the abuses. Citing an infant mortality rate of 5 percent, he explained that the problem could not be solved until the causes were known. This in turn would save the lives of "potential contributors to the society." The Children's Bureau met little opposition and soon became a reality.

A few weeks after the debate on the Children's Bureau, the Post Office appropriation came under discussion. On a proposal calling for a pilot project to establish a parcel post, Cox spoke in favor of good roads and prison reform. Citing historical precedents for internal improvements, he rhetorically asked if the railroads received forty-seven million dollars for carrying the mail, "why should not the Federal Government pay to local governments, which keep up the public roads, something for use of these highways in transporting the mails?" That would have tremendous benefits for the nation he explained. Observing that a geographic region functioned as an economic entity, he said the real consumers are the producers in the cities and their manufactured goods are purchased by retail dealers and farmers. Cox reasoned that good roads and a "true parcel post" would tie these interrelated units together. This would work to improve the standard of living by linking producer and consumer and bringing together town and town, and town and country. It would promote education by permitting rural children to attend consolidated schools as well as facilitate outdoor recreational activity by bringing the wilderness closer to the city. To demonstrate further the interaction of the parts of society, Cox took the opportunity to explain that Ohio planned to use its prison labor to help build roads so that "the prisoners through good behavior can gain the privilege of working out in the fresh air and in the sunlight on the highways." Ultimately, an amendment, which Cox co-sponsored, provided funds for local subdivisions to help keep roads in "passable shape."[30]

Cox would also have the Post Office subsidize air transportation. Congressman William Sharp of Ohio offered an amendment to the postal appropriation bill to allocate funds for the development of an aircraft for carrying mail. Former Speaker Joseph Cannon quickly pointed out that the War Department had already begun research. Victor Murdock of Kansas immediately entered the debate. Recalling past experiences with the telegraph and railroads, he charged that for too long Congress lagged behind technology when it came to the mails. Cox then rose in favor of the amendment and took issue with Cannon. Offhandedly, he challenged an assertion by the Republican leader that Dr. Samuel P. Langley developed the first heavier-than-air craft and called attention to two Daytonians, the Wright brothers, as having been first. Favoring the use of technology for peace rather than war, he approved of the Sharp amendment because:

> I believe that by the development of the aeroplane in the postal service its utility will be widened and extended; second, I believe that by this governmental encouragement the biplane will much sooner become the one active, potential force which will make for international disarmament and bring about everlasting peace throughout the world.

The amendment failed, but Cox had boosted Dayton and had promoted the idea of efficient technology as a means to eliminate the problems of man.[31]

By the end of his second term in Congress, Cox had defined the essence of his progressivism as a blend of business and middle-class egalitarianism. He now equated efficiency with social harmony. With the proper data, the experts would provide answers to the nation's problems. Systematic social reforms, he came to believe, would make the system work. Economic interaction, technological development, and efficient communication would provide continued prosperity. This prosperity and harmony, he believed, could best be accomplished by responding to the needs of vocal interest groups.

In addition, Cox had become what one political theorist has defined as a "Lawmaker." He competently dealt with the issues of the period. Aware of political roles, he cooperated with fellow congressman and special interests but still maintained his individuality in performing his tasks. As the representative of a politically competitive district, he looked after the interests of his constituents. Genuinely interested in politics, he decided to make it full-fledged career.[32]

Although committed to the national Democratic reform movement, Cox remained politically tied to Ohio. If ideology conflicted with his conception of his constituents' interests, he sacrificed ideology. While in the 62nd Congress, he served as the congressional representative for Judson Harmon in the Ohio governor's bid for the 1912 Democratic presidential nomination. After his ticket-leading victory in 1910, Cox emerged as a likely successor to Harmon as the Democratic choice for governor. Politically aggressive, Cox turned to Ohio to implement the themes of progressivism. When the 62nd Congress adjourned in the summer of 1912, Cox returned home to campaign for forty-two proposed constitutional amendments to the Ohio Constitution.[33] These efforts became a prologue to his bid for governorship.

IV
CAMPAIGN FOR THE "COMMON GOOD"

By 1912 most seasoned Ohio politicians recognized the need for a political response to the problems of urban-industrial society. For more than a decade, city-based pressure groups had lobbied to make Ohio laws more responsive to the new economic and political realities. Finally, in 1911, the voters approved a call for a constitutional convention and elected 119 delegates to modernize Ohio's constitution. Convening on January 9, 1912, the convention provided an arena to respond politically to the dislocations wrought by industrialism. Representing various interests, the delegates sought order, sought redress of grievances, or sought advantages. By the time the convention adjourned six months later, the delegates had shaped forty-two specific proposals for change to be submitted to the voters. They dealt with the thorny cultural problems of education, liquor, and female suffrage as well as economic and political questions related to taxation, capital-labor relations, political institutions, and the judiciary. James M. Cox also chose 1912 as the year to run for governor of Ohio.[1]

One advisor to Cox in state government remembered him as "a sensitive barometer of the political weather." Little doubt existed that 1912 would be a Democratic year in Ohio. The Democrats had controlled the governorship since 1905, and Governor Judson Harmon now seriously vied for the presidential nomination. At the same time, the Republican Party suffered internal divisions in Ohio as well as nationally. Also, Cox's progressive posture put him in step with the objectives of the constitutional convention. His astuteness, however, went beyond timing, for he adroitly bridged differences within the Democratic Party.[2]

The downstate congressman managed to win the approval of the upstate wing of the party led by Newton D. Baker. The *Dayton Daily News* consistently advanced the cause of the Ohio Municipal League, an organization that Baker had helped to create. Working for the support of the Cincinnati-based Ohio Direct Democracy League, Cox, as early as July 1911, firmly supported the initiative, referendum, and short ballot reforms. Baker applauded these efforts, and assured him that these proposals had strong backing throughout the state. Continuing to promote the initiative and the referendum, Cox called them "an absolute safeguard to representative government." He noted that giving "absolute authority to legislative bodies had often proved a failure . . . in I and R the people take back authority to themselves." As events unfolded, Cox and Ohio's leading urban reformers drew closer and in the spring of 1912, he collaborated with Mayor Baker on a platform for the state Democratic convention.[3]

The Harmon-Hanley faction of the party controlled the state political machine, and Cox had close ties with this group. He served as Ed Hanley's campaign manager in 1911 when the Dayton Irishman tried unsuccessfully to secure the United States Senate seat. When the party caucus instead chose Atlee Pomerene on the first ballot, Cox observing that the Canton senator-elect "will be a credit to the state," returned to Washington. From there, he supported Judson Harmon's bid for the 1912 presidential nomination. He set up a mailing program with congressmen "from all the important states to feel out grassroots sentiment" of key citizens. The program, Cox said, served the dual purpose of "gaining sentiment and acquiring a live mail list." Although a floor leader for Harmon at the Baltimore Convention, he later claimed that his "private hopes were that Woodrow Wilson would gain the Democratic nomination."[4]

Maintaining a modicum of independence and a progressive stance on the vital issues, while party professionals became indebted to him, Cox was not a threat to any of the key Democratic factions. By the spring of 1912, he emerged as the leading Democratic candidate for governor, and on May 16 formally announced his candidacy. Standing by his congressional record on national issues, Cox assured Ohio voters that the state Democratic Party would adopt a progressive platform. Linking the work of the constitutional convention with the business community, he observed that government, like business, should be "receptive to new conditions in order to broaden the benefits of free government." "Efficiency" and "economy," he pointed out, were vital to both communities. From this perspective the Dayton publisher pledged support for the initiative and referendum, the state wide primary, legislation to protect workers, state regulation of saloons, home rule for cities, prison reform; and in general the work of Ohio's constitutional convention.[5]

As the Ohio Democratic Convention approached, the field of gubernatorial candidates narrowed. Hiram Peck of Cincinnati, who had performed distinguished service as a delegate to the constitutional convention, withdrew and the Montgomery County delegation declared its support for him as permanent chairman of the convention. Two days before the Toledo convention opened, Congressman William Sharp of Elyria also withdrew. Cox's nomination seemed assured. From his Hotel Secor headquarters, he predicted a first ballot victory and announced that Herbert Bigelow, the President of the Constitutional Convention, would second his nomination. On the vital question of the unit rule for the Ohio delegation at the National Democratic Convention, Cox announced that he intellectually opposed it, but tactfully urged his supporters to vote as they pleased on the issue. Newton D. Baker soon afterwards announced that he was "satisfied with Cox." As the nominating began, the final obstacle disappeared when Oliver Hughes of the Public Utilities Commission released his delegates. Cox won by acclamation.[6]

With the convention adjourned, a Harmon lieutenant wired his chief: "Unit Rule, Cox, Nichols. Everything right. Congratulations." George Burba, editor of the *Dayton Daily News*, viewed the nomination as a personal victory resulting from Cox's ability as a leader, his progressiveness, the loyalty of his friends, and repayment for "energy, honesty and efficiency in both the private and public sectors." Burba failed to mention Cox's political sagacity. Cox geared his strategy to Ohio's two elections in 1912, the one to decide on the constitutional amendments and then the regular election. The two were not unrelated. Cox and Baker harmonized their proposed platform to the recommendations of the constitutional convention. Their model became the basis for the convention deliberations, and, as Cox predicted, the Democrats adopted a progressive platform. In addition, although he was Harmon's personal choice, Cox successfully avoided the pitfalls of Presidential politics. He entered the campaign with both the regular party and the reformers united behind his leadership.[7]

The Dayton progressive set the tone of the campaign in his acceptance speech. With a brisk and youthful manner, he zealously told the cheering delegates:

> I stand for a progressive charter. . . . This is not an age for laggards.
> It is an age of unrest and why not? It's an ambitious age. The race spurred
> on by the greatest civilization in all history breathes through its nostrils

the air of our free institutions and resolves that our government shall be a help rather than a check to our development.[8]

In spite of opposition from regular Democrats, Cox returned to Ohio when the 62nd Congress adjourned, and aggressively worked for the constitutional amendments. Going into the rural areas to espouse the objectives of the Ohio Direct Legislation League and the Ohio Municipal League, the former teacher performed what he called "a campaign of information." Speaking in urban areas as well, Cox promoted the reforms on a non-partisan basis. In the end, however, he gained a partisan advantage. The campaign introduced him to the state and identified him with the work of the convention. If the amendments lost, Cox would win exposure and friends in the urban communities that promoted the reforms. At the same time, he could adjust his position to the "will of the people." If the amendments carried, he would become the logical gubernatorial candidate to implement the reforms.[9]

While Cox took the initiative on behalf of reform, the Republicans divided on the question. Privately, Cox described the GOP platform as "the most pusillanimous, evasive and cowardly document ever enunciated by any political party." "The dominant note," he went on, "seems to be a declaration in behalf of pure water. There can be no possible difference of opinion on that subject. How they happened to overlook fresh air and the immortality of the soul I do not know." The division within the Republican Party surfaced when the reform wing refused to support Judge Edmund Dillon of Columbus, the GOP gubernatorial candidate. For the sake of unity, Dillon resigned. The party leadership then bypassed progressives and chose Robert B. Brown, a Zanesville newspaper publisher and staunch supporter of President Taft, as a replacement. Involved in internecine strife, the Republican platform ignored the amendments. The Progressives endorsed the work of the convention but the fledgling party lacked the machinery to promote the amendments on a state-wide basis. Local candidates, however, did espouse them.[10]

In a light voter turnout, the electorate approved thirty-four of the forty-two proposed amendments. The voting pattern revealed an urban-rural conflict with rural voters turning out in small numbers and generally opposing the reforms, while urbanites voted in larger numbers and tended to support the changes. Although organized labor endorsed the reforms, wageearners voted sparsely. The most numerous supporters of the amendments were the upwardly mobile middle-class residents of the suburbs. When the results became known, Herbert Bigelow characterized them as not only a victory for the amendments, but for Cox as well.[11]

With the reform momentum high, and with Cox confident of victory, the second phase of the campaign began. At a huge rally in Columbus with Woodrow Wilson, Judson Harmon, and Newton D. Baker on the dais, Cox promised to carry out the party platform to the letter. Interpreting the special election results as a mandate, he pledged to implement all the amendments. As a businessman and party regular, he used the opportunity to defend himself against charges of radicalism. To the contrary, he placed himself between the reactionaries "who resist regulation" and the radicals who "look on personal property with prejudice." He stood as a "true progressive with the common sense idea of moderation, humanity, and compromise." Campaigning vigorously throughout the state, the candidate promised to keep his "contract with the people." Speaking as many as ten times a day, he emphasized both the efficiency and humanitarian aspects of the reforms.

The opposition, rent by schism, battled internally as well as with Cox. The Progressives challenged the two-term congressman's commitment to reform. The regular Republicans scorned their former allies' disloyalty and perceived flaws in the Democratic program.

Cox had widespread support. The state's leading urban reformers, including Henry Hunt of Cincinnati and Brand Whitlock of Toledo, as well as Baker and Bigelow, promoted his campaign. William Finley, who handled patronage during the four years of Harmon's ascendancy, efficiently managed the race and regular party lines held firm. Cox's journalistic credentials helped win widespread newspaper approval, including that of the large Scripps-McRae League and John R. McClean's *Cincinnati Enquirer*. Although Cox failed to gain the open support of the traditionally Republican *Ohio State Journal* and the *Columbus Dispatch*, they did not vigorously oppose him. The Ohio Federation of Labor endorsed Cox and the Democrats capitalized on the praise of labor leaders in their campaign literature. Cox also gained the support of many businessmen because of his image as an efficient manager.[12]

When the polls closed, Cox again awaited the voters' decision in his *Dayton Daily News* offices. Early optimism turned to jubilation as the results indicated a sweeping Democratic victory. In the three-way race, Cox won 41.5 percent, 439,323 votes of some 1,655,000 votes cast. The Republican candidate, Walter Brown, received 272,500 votes, and progressive Arthur Garford trailed with 217,903 supporters.

Cox again ran best in the cities. Fewer people voted in the 1912 gubernatorial race than in the previous governor's contest during a presidential year, which helps explain the basis of Cox's strength. Traditionally in low turnout elections working class voters stayed home. The people most likely to have voted during low turnout years were the middle and upper income urban voters residing in the more affluent neighborhoods and the suburbs. Considering Cox's strategy and the urban middle-class character of the Ohio reform movement, it was more than likely the middle-class who most enthusiastically supported the reform candidate. George Burba viewed the outcome as "a victory for the people" because they wanted "humanitarian laws and progress in government"—the position his boss had "unequivocally stated."[13]

Cox believed the governor should act as both a chief executive and a legislative director. Having campaigned for the election of Democratic legislators to implement the constitutional amendments, he took it upon himself to influence openly the organization of the General Assembly. he launched a trial balloon to make Herbert Bigelow Speaker of the House, but this met with opposition. Charles Swain, also of Hamilton County, was then successfully promoted for the job. To insure leadership from the Cleveland wing of the party, Cox responded to Mayor Baker's request for a direct link with the governor. He chose Carl Freibolin, a Baker lieutenant, as his liaison with the Senate, and promoted the Cleveland senator for majority leader of the upper house. A wise decision, since six Senate and four House committees eventually were chaired by Cleveland Democrats.[14] Reflecting the strength of the cities in the Ohio reform movement, it was no accident that the leadership of both houses came from the state's two leading urban centers.

With leadership team in place, Cox began transforming the objectives of his administration into action. Attracted to the "Wisconsin Idea," he directed a task force headed by party chairman William Finley "to observe, first hand, the execution and administration" of the La Follette reforms. Enthusiastically, Finley reported that the underlying principle of the Wisconsin movement was efficiency, and he stood convinced that Ohio could improve on the Wisconsin model. The task force, Finley noted, had plans for the schools, the state university, an industrial commission, the consolidation of agricultural activity, improved primary elections, and "our big idea . . . a legislative reference library." The Ohio observers affirmed Cox's belief that the key to making government responsive to the needs of an urban-industrial society was efficiency. Cox now prepared his recommendations for the legislature.[15]

In his inaugural address on the following day, as well as in his first speech to the General Assembly, Governor Cox defined his concepts of history, progressivism, and society. "Civilization is simply a relay race," he pronounced, "and unless we take it up with the freshness of spirit with which our fathers began it, the generation is in a condition of certain decay . . . An advanced civilization . . . refines from necessity." Noting the interrelationship between groups throughout the state, Cox commented that reform will foster "a cooperative spirit." Home rule for cities will bring "added responsibility . . . on matters of closer contact, and as we stimulate interest in the plain duty of citizenship, we are, by improved community life, building a state structure of greater strength and usefulness."[16]

Reviewing the responsibility of the General Assembly on constitutional revision, the chief executive suggested fifty-six specific legislative changes. Twenty-nine times he offered efficiency as a rationale; but throughout he used egalitarian rhetoric to blend ideals and self-interest into an attractive reform package. Aware of the pluralistic nature of industrial society, the governor explained that the new order of things puts to the severest test the theory of governmental control over the diversified affairs of the race. . . . " Cox went on:

> This observation prompts the further thought that if every interest exhibited a patriotic co-operation in the legislative task ahead . . . , compliance with changed conditions and public sentiment will be greatly facilitated and the state will enjoy an era of social and industrial peace, unknown in the last two decades at least. He continued:
> Progressive government so called, which means . . . constructive work, along the lines pointed out by the lamps of experience and the highest moral vision of advanced civilization is now on trial in our state . . . If I sense with any degree of accuracy the state of the public mind, I am correct in the belief that a vast preponderance of people of all classes have faith both in the wisdom and . . . results of a constructive progressive program of government . . . . In other days changes such as are made necessary everywhere by our industrial and social conditions, would be wrought by riot and revolution. Now they are accomplished through peaceful evolution. He must be indeed, a man of unfortunate temperamental qualities who does not find in this a circumstance that thrills every patriotic fibre of his being.

Aware of classes and interest groups, he called upon power blocs to promote a new equilibrium for an urban-industrial state. He hoped to eliminate discontent through efficiency in government. Believing in progress, Cox nevertheless recognized that men defined society in their own best interests.[17]

Drawing analogies between the governorship and a corporation president, Cox saw himself presiding over a broadly based community consisting of numerous interrelated special interest groups. (See TABLE G for an overview of the reform program.)

He believed administrative power should reside with the governor, who would make appointments, and the middle-class business community, who would set standards. To make Ohio "a successful state unit," Cox proposed consolidation of the executive branch. He asked the legislature to eliminate duplication in the state bureaucracy through consolidation and restructuring. Explaining the need for experts on state regulatory and administrative boards, he asked for an extension of the police power of the state "where local authority is remiss." These changes were necessary, Cox said, "to insure the enforcement of the same requirements . . . of economy, system, and efficiency that join private enterprise." Cox, then, had come to believe, in spite of his egalitarian rhetoric, that bureaucratic efficiency was the most important aspect of providing for the "common good."[18]

V
ECONOMY, SYSTEM, AND EFFICIENCY: PLURALISM IN OHIO

James Cox became a successful Ohio governor. As an experienced executive, he deftly delegated chores in line with his vision of progressive government. To maintain a tightly knit organization in the General Assembly, he withheld patronage until the predominantly Democratic legislators implemented the bulk of his objectives. This tactic, Cox reasoned, would allow time to clarify what positions would be available, but primarily it provided a lever to keep would-be dissidents in line.[1] Calling upon his congressional experience, he organized steering committees in each house to guide administration bills through the legislative maze. Democratic legislators were arranged in blocs of twelve, each having a whip to deliver the votes. In the executive offices a secretary indexed and charted the movement of every piece of legislation, noting objections as they arose. At such points, Cox would consult with Democrat and Republican leaders and work out a compromise. Here in particular Cox's executive experience proved invaluable for he understood both the use and limits of power. He used organization and persuasion to promote his program as far as the traffic would allow, while still satisfying the basic objectives of the various interest groups. Midway through the first legislative session, he reported "We are having fine support." Cox's program moved through the assembly so smoothly, before long detractors began to apply the sobriquet "Boss Cox" to the Dayton Democrat.[2]

Cox saw a proposed Legislative Reference Bureau as the cornerstone to his program, and once established, he relied upon it heavily. With its experts drawing up the proposed legislation, he was sure that bills would reflect precisely the intent of the legislators and the administration. To win support for the idea, proponents explained that the bureau would function on a non-partisan basis gathering up-to-date information relevant to proposed legislation. When the lawmakers approved the bureau to head it Cox recruited S. Gale Lowrie of the University of Cincinnati, a four-year veteran of the Wisconsin legislative reference bureau.[3]

Similarly, lobbyists were viewed as a source of information. Rather than destroy the lobbies, Cox and the Ohio reformers preferred to make them function "in an orderly manner" on behalf of those interests with "legitimate need for representatives who would confer with members and attend committee meetings to furnish useful information." The legislature agreed and required lobbyists to register with the Secretary of State, name their employer, and pay a three dollar registration fee.[4] With expert legislative draftsmen in place and information available from the lobbies the reformers began to deal with specific issues.

To protect legitimate investment houses as well as unwary investors, the legislature enacted a "blue sky law." In his inaugural speech, Cox had proposed the law in the name of business efficiency. He later guided it through the General Assembly. With the approval of the state bankers association, the governor laid support for the proposed law among nationally based brokerage firms operating in Ohio. At their convention late in January 1913 Cox explained to leading members of the National Bankers Association that if they worked for the objectives of the progressives "no set of people would be more welcome than the business interests. Indeed, in such cases, business interests can help more than any others in framing wise legislation because of their intimate . . . knowledge of actual conditions." Erastus Buckley, a prominent New York banker, referring to Ohio's proposed stock control law, pointed out that

> Present laws do not protect the uninformed investor against the fakirs until after he has lost his money . . . . In my judgement, we certainly should have laws which render impossible in the beginning the sale of fraudulent securities, and the more active and direct interest which the Bankers Association takes in endeavoring to frame up such legislation where the same is being attempted, the better it will be.

The law, approved with little opposition, required stock and bond brokers to be licensed and provide a description of their offerings to Ohio banking authorities.

Additional legislation further helped business put its house in order. Private banks were brought under the purview of state inspectors. Fraudulent advertising became a misdemeanor, the anti-trust code outlawed combinations that controlled food prices, and company officials were held liable if they knowingly acted in restraint of trade.[5]

The public utilities also sought state legislation. During the Harmon administration Ohio cities had gained the right to fix utility rates within their own boundaries. Fearing excessive competition from municipally owned utilities as well as stringent restrictions on profits, gas and electric interests in Cleveland, Dayton, Columbus, and Warren applied pressure on Cox to reorganize the Ohio Public Service Commission. As part of a program to make the utilities commission more efficient, Cox asked that municipally owned companies be brought under the same system of accounting as private firms. He further proposed that the new Public Utilities Commission be supreme in ratemaking, that Commission decisions on rates stand until a court investigation proved them unfair—thus placing the burden of proof on the company, and that all utility company property, tangible and intangible, be subject to taxation. To facilitate this broadened Commission operation, Cox recommended that its staff be enlarged by utilizing Ohio State University faculty and graduate students in part time roles. Designed to meet the needs of the business community, utilities regulation in this form according to Cox, would lead to "satisfactory service and reasonable rates" while generating confidence in the security markets so that utility securities would obtain "better prices and readier demands." The utility companies were satisfied and the investment companies applauded the move. One leading banker predicted "the private corporations would probably have very little to fear from competition from any municipally owned plant." An administration-sponsored bill embodying Cox's proposals became law with little change.[6]

While the privately owned utilities were given more freedom to operate, city governments seeking to improve publicly owned utility services had limitations placed upon the options available to them. The new home rule amendment gave municipalities an opportunity to issue bonds for city owned utility plants in excess of the legal city debt ceiling. Cox, however, vetoed legislation which would have permitted these new debts to be claims against the city rather than against the utility company.

This legislation had significant meaning for municipal ownership advocates generally and the city of Cleveland in particular. From 1902 through 1912, the number of municipally owned power plants throughout the country had more than doubled to over 1500. More than 160 of these changed from private to public ownership. Through annexation, Cleveland acquired two small suburban power plants in Brooklyn and Collinwood. Mayor Baker had hoped to expand these plants to compete with the private sector, and in the process lower power rates, but this required increased capitalization through the sale of bonds. If the city issued the bonds they would appeal, the reasoning went, to a large market. The Mills bill which Cox previously vetoed came up again in the January 1914, special session, but met stiff opposition from the private utility companies and the Ohio Chamber of Commerce. Cox again refused to support it. Instead the legislature enacted, with the Governor's approval, a measure that simply permitted the cities to sell bonds privately in small denominations. Thus it appears Cox willingly promoted legislation beneficial to special interests; but he seldom challenged the private economic sector to benefit the community as a whole.[7]

Turning attention to the interests of labor, Cox saw the needs of labor and industry as interrelated and conceived the role of state government as that of an intermediary. Using the Wisconsin movement as a model, he proposed that Ohio place all state institutions dealing with industry and labor under the jurisdiction of a three-person Ohio Industrial Commission appointed by the executive. The governor described the proposal as an efficiency measure. To help sell the idea, he brought Wisconsin progressives, including John R. Commons, to the legislative hearings where they described the benefits of the commission from an efficiency perspective. The only opposition in the General Assembly came from labor representatives who believed that the law would give the Commission too much power which might be wielded against labor's interests. As finally established, the Ohio Industrial Commission administered the workmen's compensation law and safety regulations, enforced maximum hours legislation for women and children, operated the state employment offices, and encouraged conciliation and arbitration in labor-management disputes. Review of Industrial Commission decisions rested solely with the Ohio Supreme Court.[8]

"No subject was discussed during the last campaign with greater elaboration," Cox reminded the General Assembly, "then the need to implement the compulsory workmen's compensation insurance amendment." He explained that prompt implementation would alleviate animosity "between capital and labor" as well as eliminate the "waste occasioned by the . . . old system." "There is," he continued:

> no characteristic of our civilization so marked as the element of interdependence as between social entities. We are all dependent upon our fellows . . . . Some occupations, however, are more hazardous than others and the rule of the past, in compelling those engaged in dangerous activities to bear unaided the burden of this great risk is not right.

Concluding his plea for strong compensatory legislation, the governor explained that the amendment would force marginal industries to install modern safety devices to keep the cost of their insurance down. Considering the law vital to his program, Cox gave it close attention.[9]

Senator William R. Green, formerly affiliated with the Ohio Mine Workers Union, submitted the administration's workmen's compensation bill. Requiring all Ohio industries employing five or more people to pay the entire premium into a state operated insurance company, the Cox proposal met strong opposition from insurance companies, Ohio industries, and numerous local chambers of commerce. A frequent spectator at the hearings on the bill, Cox became involved in the negotiations for a compromise. Meeting with leading manufacturers, he reached an agreement that enabled the industries to carry their own insurance rather than contribute to the state company, permitted the insurance firms to use contributory negligence as a defense against worker's claims, and prohibited lawyers from soliciting personal injury cases on a contingency basis. In the Senate, Green very reluctantly incorporated the compromises, and the bill passed both houses unanimously.[10]

Labor compromised on other measures as well. The voters approved amendments to establish an eight-hour day for public works employees and gave the state authority to fix and regulate hours of labor, establish a minimum wage, and provide for the health, comfort, safety and general welfare of employees. Although he had a broad mandate to advance boldly the interests of Ohio workers, Cox's instructions to the legislature fell short of the task. He asked for a survey of Ohio industries by the Industrial Commission to determine where the nine-hour day for women and children would be excessive before requesting specific maximum hour laws according to conditions in the specific industries. This, Cox said, would result in better shop conditions since "improvement in sanitation and surroundings . . . is a factor in determining the hours of labor."[11]

Labor accepted the survey idea, but as one scholar noted, "the maximum hours question almost produced a head-on collision between them and the Governor." State Representative Henry Vollmer of Cleveland, a close friend of the AFL, disregarded Cox's instructions and introduced a bill proposing an eight-hour day for women and the extension of maximum hours coverage to hotels and stores. Cox promptly threatened the labor committee with a veto. He won. The legislature extended the survey power to the Industrial Commission and instructed Ohio industries to provide the necessary information. Only after considerable protest did labor resign itself to a nine-hour law and an extension of maximum hours coverage for women working the mercantile business.[12]

The rift between Cox and labor over scientific management widened on an important issue for coal miners. Senator Green hand guided a bill through the legislature which would have paid miners for total coal mined rather than the volume after management screened out the slag. Green had the votes when Cox responded to pressure from mine operators and the Ohio Chamber of Commerce. The governor again proposed a survey commission to investigate conditions in the coal industry. Green charged Cox with subterfuge to placate the coal barons. The governor craftily claimed the survey would avoid repeal of law through initiative and referendum. The report, he added, would educate the public to the injustices in the industry. In an effort to head off discontent among the mine workers, Cox inspected the Ohio coal fields and pointed out to the miners that "there were more users than miners of coal and the failure of the first effort to procure relief would . . . interfere with the whole program." The Commission ultimately recommended in favor of the miners. Their recommendation quickly became law.[13]

The dilemma that confronted labor was reflected in the makeup of the Ohio Industrial Commission. Initially, Cox's appointments took the middle ground since they included Thomas Duffy, a former labor official from the pottery industry; Wallace Yaple, a pro-business attorney; and Matthew Bray Hammond, an Ohio State University economist. Hammond soon resigned, and Cox replaced him with Morris Woodhull, an industrialist.[14]

As with industry and labor, efficiency became the guide when both Cox and the reformers turned their attention to agriculture. After "personal investigations of 25 agricultural activities in the state government," Cox claimed "direct duplication" in fourteen departments and "triplication" in eleven. He asked for the creation of an agricultural commission to coordinate the activities of the State Board of Agriculture, the agricultural experiment stations, the State Dairy and Food Commissioner, the Ohio State University College of

Agriculture, and several other farm related activities. "The present system cannot be justified by any modern method of administration," he said, and added that the commission would "eliminate waste" while creating "a mechanism" for coordinated research and efficient distribution of information and state services. It would lead to greater farm productivity and promote the general welfare. As Cox put it:

> Ohio demands attention the the subject of human conservation, and the police power of the state lodged in the hands of a strong department of agriculture could be exercised for the protection of our citizenship.

Gale Lowrie drew up the bill to establish the agricultural commission and John Cunningham of rural Knox county introduced it. After initial opposition from the Ohio Grange, the bill easily passed both houses after Cox met with agricultural leaders and agreed to compromise language on the makeup of the commission. Cox promoted acceptance of the new law among farmers by persuading farm weeklies, mainly the *Ohio Farmer*, to support and advertise the legislation. The law created a three-person commission with guaranteed representation to the minority party, and stipulated that members should be "directly identified with agriculture or agricultural education." The duties of the Commission fit Cox's broad outlines. It advised local farm societies, promoted scientific farming, coordinated the inspection of farm products and the investigation and prosecution of violations of weights and measures regulations as well as of the misbranding of food and chemicals. Although primarily designed to help the farmer, the Commission was meant also to provide for the general welfare through scientific management. It failed to satisfy the Ohio farmers and the next administration repealed the law.[15]

Special interests and efficiency also came into conflict on prohibition. The liquor question, a tempest in Ohio politics for at least two decades, seemed solved when the voters approved a constitutional amendment to control the liquor traffic by licensing taverns. Cox enjoyed the support of Ohio wets and committed his administration to implement the amendment with a bill drawn up by Percy Andrea and William Hess of the Ohio Brewers Association. In his legislative blueprint, Cox proposed the creation of state and county license commissions appointed by the governor. This would "lift the liquor question from community politics"—which Cox saw as the objective of the amendment. The prohibitionists, however, were far from satisfied with either the amendment or Cox's proposal. Believing centralized enforcement would be lax, they wanted local control of licensing to protect gains previously made by local option.[16]

In the legislative struggle to implement the licensing amendment, both wets and drys, as well as Cox, became active participants. Attending hearings and listening to debates, Cox kept his "public and private offices . . . open at all times to the preacher as well as the brewer; to the anti-saloon workers and also the lobby for the liberal interests." Ultimately, the governor arbitrated the divergent views and forwarded perceived compromises to the legislature, where they were incorporated into the bill. The Greenlund Law provided for a three-person state licensing board, appointed by the governor, which approved or disapproved the actions of the two-person county commissions appointed by the state board. The compromises written into the law required licensees to possess "good moral character," permitted local referendums to reduce the number of saloons in a community, and prohibited individual ownership of more than one saloon. In the end, both Wayne Wheeler of the Ohio Anti-Saloon League and Julius Freiberg, the leading wet lobbyist, gave their approval to the law. Still, it was Cox's law. As Wheeler observed, the governor "had the rare faculty of lining up more representatives and senators for a bill in which he . . . was interested than anyone with whom I ever came in contact."[17]

Aware of the political liability inherent in the new law, Cox determined to make it succeed. To administer it he wanted "high class men" who would establish it with "cleanliness, efficiency, and dignity." Appointed license commissioners had to have stature in the local community and licenses were to be tendered to respectable citizens. Cox wrote to his executive secretary that where it is "the choice as between the worthy and the unworthy, then the county commissioners are censurable if they select the latter." Believing the liquor question could best be dealt with as a law and order issue, Cox hoped to make the commission activities beyond criticism and to eliminate the worst abuses of the liquor industry.[18]

But like so many other well-meaning politicians he failed to defuse this volatile issue. Providing for social control and conciliating the leadership of the interested groups did not take the cultural issue out of politics. Cox's insistence on enforcing Sunday closing laws kept the question in the limelight. In addition, the county unit signally failed to enforce local option laws. Often, either the urban or rural sector of a given county predominated. This left the losers intent upon changing the situation at the first opportunity. In 1915 Cox's successor dismantled the State Licensing Board in favor of county control, and the issue remained alive in Ohio until national prohibition took the question from the states' jurisdiction.[19]

The question of race became entwined with the administration of the liquor licensing law. The constitutional convention had submitted a proposal to delete the adjective white in the voter qualification clause of the constitution. Some 265,000 Ohio voters, a majority, rejected this updating of the law. The Cox administration and the legislature reflected these racial attitudes.[21] These attitudes can be seen in the administration of the liquor licensing law. In view of the governor's guidelines that licenses be tendered to the "worthy," it became easy for administrators to find black men ineligible. In Toledo, after one year of the license law, no black person held a license. Previously, nine black men operated taverns in the city. In response to protests, a Lucas County Licence Commissioner explained that the only black men who had applied had previously operated saloons in Toledo's "Murder District." In addition, "the colored Bishop here was among the written petitioners for the elimination of negro saloons . . . ." The situation went unrectified.[21]

Only unified and articulate blacks counteracted the zealous progressives on miscegenation. When a bill prohibiting the marriage of blacks and whites appeared on the Assembly calendar, the N.A.A.C.P. and other black organizations filed formal protests with the General Assembly and the governor. Pointing out that the proposed legislation degraded black women, they cited William Lloyd Garrison's successful efforts to strike a similar law from the Massachusetts statutes in 1843. They explained that the prohibition of intermarriage was tantamount to Ohio asserting "that black blood is a physical taint, something no self-respecting colored man or woman could be asked to admit." The black press also protested vigorously. In the face of all this, the General Assembly quietly tabled the bill by a two to one vote.[22]

Impoverished women and their children made up another group Cox and the legislature addressed. Following the trend set in other states, Cox recommended a modest pension for widows and dependent children. The legislature complied. Cox also successfully proposed the adoption of a children's code, the fruit of a task force report from the Harmon administration. A comprehensive code, it raised the minimum work age in industry to fifteen and sixteen for boys and girls respectively, and set a graduated maximum hours scale for men under eighteen and women under twenty-one. A newly created county juvenile court system gained the final authority for the legal disposition of delinquents and orphans. Separate detention homes for boys and girls became mandatory, and the emphasis, at least theoretically, for dealing with delinquents was transferred from punishment to rehabilitation. To provide data for dealing with various juvenile situations the code provided for a juvenile research bureau which tested children brought to the attention of the new state board of administration.[23] Although the widow's and children's reforms had humanitarian implications, they also stood as efficiency measures. The pension sought to rectify a social injustice while preserving the family structure. Similarly the children's code, particularly the juvenile bureau, became a vehicle to extend middle-class values.

Cox and the Ohio reformers also sought to impose their values through control of communications. Sensitive to the role played by media in influencing public opinion, the governor requested the creation of a motion picture censorship board. As a former journalist he explained that the film, a new communications medium, should be brought under state regulation during its infancy to avoid future abuses. "The business," he observed, "has many useful functions and under proper restrictions it can become a pleasurable and profitable recreation for people. The youth is entitled to protection against improper presentations. Immoral pictures, in public places, with apparent official sanction, cannot but excite a bad influence." Cox called upon the interest group most directly influenced by the proposal, the Motion Picture Exhibitors League of America, to draft the bill. Representative Thornton P. Snyder of Cincinnati, the home base of the League, submitted the censorship bill. With Cox's prodding and the consent of the exhibitors, the legislature readily created a three-person board of censors to review films submitted for showing in Ohio.[24]

The combination of progressive humanitarianism and interest in efficiency also led to prison reforms. Cox believed the emphasis in penology belonged on "education, reformation, and probation." While Judson Harmon, in this final message to the General Assembly, reaffirmed his belief that prisons existed to punish, Cox told the legislators that

> The underlying desire is betterment of the race, the reform of as many prisoners as possible, aid to their families, with money earned by men confined, and a contribution to the next generation of fewer human shipwrecks.... Over six hundred prisoners in the penitentiary are idle. Their time is doubtless spent in reflection over their own disgrace and the plight of their families back home. The present effort offers no apparent relief from this unspeakable condition. If employment can be afforded for the physical, mental and moral benefit of these prisoners in such a manner as will yield reimbursement to the state for their keep, and an accruing profit to be sent to their families deprived of their support, then this humanitarian consideration must outweigh every thought of continuing the present abominable system....

To achieve these objectives, the governor recommended the creation of a prison farm to supply food for state institutions and the use of convicts to build highways, quarry stone, and work in various industries operated by the state. He called for an indeterminate sentence law, a parole board to supervise parolees, and legislation to assign types of prisoners to specific types of prisons. The legislature responded favorably and the proposals became law. During the next decade prison expenses were dramatically cut.

Convinced that criminals were the combined "product of heredity and environment," Cox believed in prison reform. He frequently visited the penitentiary in Columbus and explained the reforms and the parole system. Evoking cheers from the inmates during one of these visits, he quaintly responded, "the state doesn't want to mint any dollars from your tears." In his personal commitment to prison reform, Cox's progressivism showed through vividly. Individual progress, he believed, could only come through hard work. In an age dominated by business efficiency, Cox emphasized the need for government to apply the standards of efficiency and hard work to attain social progress.[25]

"We are entering upon a new day," the governor had asserted in his inaugural address. He recognized the division of labor and interests in modern urban society and the need for government to promote harmony and respond to specific groups while preserving traditional values. Comparing government to a corporation, he saw the executive branch as the logical arbiter of the divergent interests of Ohio's pluralistic groups.

VI
COMBATING "RIOT AND REVOLUTION:" STRUCTURAL REFORM

The "New Day," Cox's characterization of the Ohio reform program, did more than respond to group interests. The movement also included structural reforms. Amendments for an initiative and referendum procedure, the recall of elected officials, a short ballot, a direct primary, and home rule for cities, had been voted on in the special election of 1912. All but the short ballot were approved, and required implementation.[1] In promoting these political, economic, and social reforms, the Ohio progressives used the rhetoric of democracy and efficiency.

The initiative and the referendum, Cox said, provided a guarantee against "riot and revolution." To avoid abuse of these tactics by "unsavory elements" he asked the General assembly to prohibit the payment of petition solicitors. When advocates from Cincinnati and Cleveland protested that this would make the law inoperable, the governor yielded and the legislature prohibited payment for signing a petition, and required organizations circulating petitions to list their expenses with the Secretary of State. To initiate a constitutional amendment required signatures equal to 10 percent of the electors in the previous general election, and to initiate legislation for consideration by the General Assembly required signatures of 3 percent of the electorate. The reform procedures were ironic. Created to make democracy work, the Ohio Direct Democracy League sought artificial means to be sure the people would rise to the occasion. Cox, on the other hand, viewed the initiative and referendum as a safety valve to preserve traditional governmental techniques.[2]

Opposition to some of the reforms enacted in the 80th General Assembly had been strong, and within a year the compulsory workmen's compensation law and the state's new tax scheme came under attack by way of the initiative and referendum. The chief opponents were the liability insurance interests, especially Daniel R. Hanna's Ohio Equity Association. Dipicting such groups as "scoundrels," Cox gathered information about the opposition, engaged in speaking campaigns against the petition, and used the machinery of the state to uncover procedural abuses. He ordered a full-scale hearing in which Ohio Attorney General Timothy Hogan openly charged the petitioners with fraud, and accused the Ohio Equity Association of perjury. Secretary of State Charles S. Graves, conducting the hearings, rejected the petitions and the courts upheld his decisions. During a special session in 1914, the legislature rewrote the law, broadening the definition of malpractices, and making it mandatory to report the wages paid solicitors. In the process, the new techniques became more difficult to use.[3]

Ohio's recall procedures also proved a very limited form of direct democracy. Empowered to enact "appropriate" recall legislation, the General Assembly passed a weak law. State and local officials could, after 10 percent of the eligible voters in the last election signed petitions indicting the official for moral turpitude or other misconduct, be brought to trial, state officials before the governor and local officials before the common pleas court. Members of the Ohio Progressive Constitution League wanted a more comprehensive law affecting all elected officials, including the governor and judges, and pressed the legislature for a constitutional amendment. Without Cox's support the proposal, as had a similar plea at the constitutional convention, failed.[4]

Although the voters had rejected the short ballot reform, Cox still strongly advocated the change. He reminded the legislature of both the Democratic and Republican platform pledges to simplify voting. Proposing that all state executive and judicial offices except the governor, lieutenant governor, and supreme court judges be appointed, Cox explained this would

> ... insure harmony of action in the state departments and center responsibility in the executive. The several executive department heads could then act in an advisory capacity with the governor, as his cabinet. This is identical with the federal plan, which is conceded to be efficient.[5]

Caucusing with Democratic, Republican, and Progressive leaders, Cox built legislative support to resubmit the Ohio Short Ballot Association proposals to shorten the state ballot and provide for the appointment of certain county officials. Opposition persisted from numerous quarters, not the least of which emerged in Cox's own party. Three of the elected state officials whose positions would become appointive, scorned the proposal for concentrating too much power in the office of governor. Similar cries came from the Republicans. GOP leaders also explained that, although their platform had favored the reform, they had not envisioned such a radical departure. Dissension even surfaced among the short ballot advocates. John Clarke and Mayo Fesler of the Short Ballot Association wanted the ballot shortened for city elections as well as state contests. Cox refused to go that far and explained that opposition from city political organizations would be too difficult to overcome. He asked for unity among short ballot reformers in confronting the upcoming election and Cleveland's Mayor Newton D. Baker interceded for the sake of harmony. Despite good press support and the promotional activities of the the Short ballot Association, Ohio voters again rejected further centralization. Reflecting upon the short ballot issue in his last years, Cox forgot much of what had happened. He blamed defeat on self-seeking Democratic stalwarts who opposed change.[6]

Governor Cox also viewed home rule for cities from an efficiency point of view. At his inaugural he observed:

> In our commonwealth there is now a marked tendency toward a larger measure of home rule for municipalities, and an increased opportunity for involvement in their community affairs. At the same time there is exacted an increased police power from the state in the projects of general human welfare that can only be kept uniform in their beneficence by operation of the state unit . . . . In practice it brings added responsibility with reference to matters of closer contact, and as we stimulate interest in the plain duty of citizenship, we, by improved community life [are] building a state structure of greater strength and usefulness.[7]

The home rule amendment permitted Ohio cities to write their own charters from guidelines drawn up by the General Assembly. It also allowed financing publicly owned utility companies through bonds approved by a referendum, a measure which enabled cities to extend their bonded indebtedness beyond the maximum permitted by state law. To implement the amendment, Cox, after consulting with Newton D. Baker and the Ohio Municipal League, proposed legislation to give cities a choice between the city manager, commission, and strong mayor plans of government. He further urged reliance upon the League's expertise to draft the related laws. The amendment was implemented along the lines advised by Cox, but instead of providing for home rule, it simply defined the scope and process of decisionmaking in urban government. It provided avenues to create institutions at the city level, but real home rule was to be found in providing new revenue for cities. This the state failed to authorize.[8]

Cox believed that businesslike tax gathering would generate financial relief for the cities without political risks. Recalling his efforts at tax reform, Cox explained:

> Since our legislative program had given an unprecedented amount of attention to welfare measures, it seemed not only appropriate but necessary to round out the picture by providing for the financial health of government.[9]

Limited in perception, even with hindsight, as to what was desirable, Cox's efforts fell short of their mark.

Believing Ohio tax laws archaic, Cox planned to update them through administrative centralization. He recommended that city and county tax assessors no longer be elected, but be appointed by the governor and function under the direct supervision of a state tax commission. To promote uniform tax assessment and force intangible property onto the tax lists, Cox wanted to make the state, rather than local government, responsible for annual property assessment. Milton Warnes, the House majority leader, submitted the tax centralization bill, and it became law essentially as Cox had proposed.[10]

Described by a contemporary as "the most radical administrative change in taxation any state had undertaken," the Warnes law aroused considerable opposition. During the drafting of the bill, Chairman Robert Ditty of the Tax Commission was forced to resign because of an unwillingness to promote Cox's objectives. Alfred E. Peckinpaugh, loyal to the administration, replaced him. Almost immediately, leading Republicans attacked the appointive features as part of an effort by Cox to create patronage positions to build a political machine. Courthouse politicians, threatened by a loss of patronage, also condemned it, while farmers and businessmen, fearing increased taxation, criticized the law. These opponents eventually coalesced behind the unsuccessful effort of the Ohio Equity Association to repeal the law by means of the initiative and referendum. Cox defended the efficiency of the law. He pointed out the law actually cut 4,089 positions out of the bureaucracy. He countered that the purpose of the law was to take politics out of taxation rather than strengthen his political position. He skillfully muddled the question of increased taxes by explaining that annual assessment and the techniques of the new system would lead to more revenue, opening the possibility of tax reductions.[11]

Tax centralization proved a mild success. Cox insisted that the assessors be appointed on the basis of "efficiency and integrity." He instructed Tax Commission employees to cease political activities and to enroll in a formal training program run by the state. The tax rolls increased in every county and added $700 million to the tax list. Cox estimated that the procedures saved the state $1.5 million per year. In addition, as a result of separate legislation, $832 million of public utility holdings were added to the tax lists by the assessors. The tax reforms brought an additional $3 million into the state coffers.[12]

In 1914 the financial success of the new tax legislation and Cox's commitment to political expediency led the governor to convene a special session of the legislature to cut taxes. House majority leader Milton Warnes observed that Cox's popularity had sagged and that in an election year the Democrats could make no better move than to cut taxes. Warnes also noted that the example of the state would apply pressure on local taxing bodies to do the same before establishing new budgets.[13]

Cox agreed. He asked Senate majority leader Carl Freibolin to rally Mayor Baker and the Cleveland Democrats behind the special session. Baker, strapped for revenue to meet Cleveland's growing needs, had opposed tax centralization as long as the Smith 1 Percent Law limited taxing power and was, at first, reluctant to go along with the governor. He again sought from Cox a commitment to remove the tax limitation at some time "in the future." Cox refused to budge, and Baker, for political reasons, grudgingly supported the special legislative session of July 20, 1914, to cut taxes. Before the General Assembly, Cox lauded the new assessment system and urged a reduction of the state levy from .961 mill to .45 mill. The legislators responded affirmatively by cutting the education tax from .451 to .15 mill, and the highway assessment from .5 mill to .3 mill. Cox then set about the business of creating "a clamor" for reduced city and county taxes. He privately urged friendly journalists to build pressure against tax increases and "to mount a propaganda for tax reduction."[14]

Convinced that efficient tax gathering and assessment would expand the tax base enough to avoid repeal of the popular Smith 1 Percent Law, Cox also understood that its effectiveness would be contingent upon the state adopting the classification of property for tax purposes amendment. Adoption of the classification system had been the prime objective of the Ohio State Board of Commerce when it led the drive for constitutional reform. Since 1903 the organization, composed mainly of businessmen and corporation representatives, had advocated this change to keep taxation from absorbing the yield of low interest bonds. Defeated by the convention, Cox viewed the measure as an orderly and "just" proposal. He expected it to bring intangibles "out of hiding" once it guaranteed fair assessments based on the knowledge of the nature of the investment. Consequently, Cox urged the General Assembly to submit the classification amendment to the voters.

To gain support from the urban reformers, he coupled his recommendation with a proposal for a 15 mill ceiling on combined state and local property taxes. Cox also hoped this feature would eliminate fears that property would be excessively taxed, while middle-class stockholders received a tax break. Opposition persisted. It somehow became confused with the single-tax movement and many people were repelled by what seemed like an effort to do away with the Smith Law. Cox withdrew his pressure from the legislature, but in 1914, when the Ohio State Board of Commerce succeeded in placing the question on the ballot, Cox openly supported a losing cause.[15]

In the final analysis, Cox's tax program proved unsatisfactory. Centralization could not satisfactorily meet the needs of the cities without classification, a concept unacceptable to many of the reformers and the voters in general. A taxpayers' revolt and special tax interests produced a conflict which would not yield a political solution. The cities suffered the consequences. In addition, other financial measures adversely affected city governments. The state liquor licensing law took away a source of city revenue and the restrictions on financing publicly owned utilities further limited city revenues. At the same time, the authoritarian aspects of the centralized tax commission and appointed assessors alienated a large portion of the population from Cox's financial program. Indeed, the tax question became Cox's Achilles heel. When the Republicans returned to power, tax centralization was among the first "Cox laws" repealed.

The "economy, system and efficiency that join private enterprises," said Cox, were essential to successful state government. With this in mind, he proposed the creation of a state budget system to allocate Ohio's financial resources. Readily adopted, "it put an end to duplication of service." The law created a Bureau of the Budget headed by an expert director appointed by the governor. As his first budget director, Cox chose William O. Heffernan, an efficiency expert formerly affiliated with the New York Municipal Research Bureau. Authorized to review estimates of financial needs of all state institutions and departments, Heffernan recommended cuts and efficiency measures that were later incorporated into the general appropriations bill. In his first year, Heffernan cut Ohio expenses by 10 percent, approximately $1 million. This program also brought criticism for uniting too much authority in the executive department; nevertheless, it remained part of Ohio's administrative system.[16]

Civil service reform also came under the scrutiny of the Ohio progressives. The voters had approved an amendment instructing the legislature to create a civil service system throughout the state's county and city governments. Cox again called for a state commission, and asked Carl Freibolin, who had affiliations with the Civic League of Cleveland, to formulate the legislation. Using the New York and Wisconsin systems as models, the legislature created a three-person commission appointed by the governor for six year terms. The new Ohio Civil Service Commission supervised a state-wide civil service system for the state, counties, and cities. The state commission determined eligibility for the civil list through competitive examinations and established guidelines for tenure and promotion based upon test results and efficiency ratings. To protect patronage, exemptions built into the law included board of election clerks, bailiffs, and laborers. Cox appointed two college administrators and a prominent reformer to the Commission and instructed them to study the intricacies of the Wisconsin system, "reported to be the most efficient in the union."[17]

The constitutional amendments made mandatory several changes in Ohio's judicial structure. Reminding the legislators of their responsibility in this area, Cox pointed out that the prime reason for the changes was to eliminate delay in carrying out the law. He urged the General Assembly to take note of the recent report and recommendations of the Ohio Bar Association. The legislators responded with a bevy of laws that considerably altered the state court system. For example, the children's code provided for juvenile courts in every county with the jurisdiction of juvenile defendents universally transferred to these courts. Considerable refinements were also made in judicial procedures. Prior to a case coming before a grand jury, the prosecution had to gather evidence, and in criminal cases, testimony had to be recorded.[18]

With the mandate of the people and approval of the legislature, Cox revamped Ohio's education system. By a large margin, the voters had approved the creation of a state educational system. Cox asked for authority to create a fact-finding commission to conduct, under the direction of the New York Bureau of Municipal Research, a survey of the state's school system. Data gathered by experts, said Cox, "will enable the state to provide and maintain a modern and uniform school system and bring to every community the advantages wrought by the best thought and research." The task force consisted of a small-town banker, an urban social worker, and a retired University of Chicago professor. Horace Brittain of the New York Bureau of Municipal Research designed the survey. Brittain and more than two hundred Ohioans, including professors, graduate students, and legislators, investigated conditions in some 1,370 schools during the summer and early fall of 1913. Analyzing their data, the commission recommended an updating of all Ohio schools to the level of those found in the cities. In brief, they proposed the efficient administration of every school with consolidation where necessary, improved teacher training, standardized teacher certification, and a standardized curriculum for Ohio schools.

After establishing their objectives, the Commission next sought to promote them. Here, Cox played an important role. Proclaiming November 14, 1913, School Survey Day, he asked every home in the State "to keep a light burning for school progress in Ohio." With Cox's encouragement, granges, chambers of commerce, labor unions, and women's clubs diligently promoted participation. Programmed from Columbus, the format of the day included readings of Cox's proclamation and a summary of the Commission recommendations in every school in the state. The individual schools presented programs featuring children and influential community members demonstrating and lauding the benefits of free public education. When the proper enthusiasm for the reforms had developed, each school district elected delegates to represent them at the December 5 and 6 statewide School Congress in Columbus. Billed as Ohio's "town meeting", Oliver Thatcher of the task force wrote that its purpose "was to keep the public expectant" and described it as a "publicity measure" designed to return the delegates to their communities as opinion molders.

On Survey Day Cox helped keep the question before the people with his observations and thoughts about education in Ohio. Explaining that the vital problems confronting Ohio were tied to the need to revitalize rural life, Cox asserted that "There can be no progressive development in the state without our becoming a greater state agriculturally; so that the question is not one that concerns country folks alone, but the people in the cities as well." Describing conditions in small rural schools, Cox reported unhappy, poorly trained children suffering because of the absence of interpersonal relations found in larger communities. Observing that the rural schools lacked basic facilities, such as libraries, he pointed out that run down "physical plants" diminished the quality of education. Contrasting this situation with schools found in the towns and suburbs, the governor described schools serving as community centers. In these places he noted, "The teachers were more alive; the buildings were in better repair; the attendance was large; and the whole situation was satisfactory."

Cox opened the Ohio School Congress with an address intended to allay the apprehension of rural delegates that the reforms would interfere with the county administration of schools. Nevertheless, some four thousand delegates converged on the capital. Many had reservations about the educational reforms. Throughout most of the two days, Cox and the Commission controlled the School Congress as they explained the proposed changes. The opponents to the changes, however, raised their voices. In the final session, an open forum convened to discuss efficient administration and teacher qualifications. Persistently, the opposition asked how the program would be financed. Finally Cox, the former one-room school teacher, took it upon himself to stymie debate when he shouted out that he would willingly "knock a hole in the state treasury if necessary." At this climatic moment, someone demanded a vote. The delegates shouted their approval and enthusiastically burst into a chorus of "America." In this way, direct democracy and determined governmental social engineering demonstrated to the legislature the need for "favorable and prompt" approval of the School Commission's recommendations.[19]

Convening a special legislative session, Cox asked for implementation of the Commission recommendations, especially those aspects designed to bring rural education up the the level of urban schools. He believed that many urban problems could be solved if the migration into the cities from the countryside abated. He envisioned improved rural schools serving as community centers and intellectual links with the cities, revitalizing rural life.

The legislature promptly enacted a series of laws to promote efficiently administered consolidated rural schools, improved teacher training, and continuing education programs for in-service teachers.[20]

The Dayton publisher deemed transportation, even more than schools, essential to a harmonious relationship between the countryside and the cities. In spite of the defeat of the $50 million good roads amendment, Cox vigorously supported the good roads movement. To the legislature he explained that the amendment lost because counties with good roads feared the expense of providing roads for other counties. In defense of the movement, Cox asserted that:

> Nothing makes for civilization more than good roads. An emphasized community life, improved facilities for school attendance, and better means of traffic in food stuffs are considerations which join to the general welfare of the state. I know of no internal improvement which so widely distributes it benefits. It touches vitally producers and consumers of the farm and city as well.

Calling for recodification of Ohio's road laws, Cox suggested that the legislature heed the advice of the Ohio Good Roads Federation which had long studied the problem. Recommending the construction of a series of interconnected county roads, he proposed providing for their upkeep by adopting the New York automobile tax system which was graduated according to the vehicle's horsepower. Recognizing the persistent growth in automobile ownership, he stood convinced the tax would be an adequate source of revenue.

This commitment to improved highways led Cox to convene the first Rural Life and Good Roads Conference at Columbus in mid-March, 1913. Accepting the commonly held belief that rural voters had provided the margin of defeat for the good roads amendment, Cox believed an educational process could mobilize the population to support improved highways. He created a Rural Life Commission composed of members of the legislature and, among others, Daniel R. Hanna, a well-known good roads advocate. The Commission gathered information on rural life and the road system, arranged the convocation with the avowed purpose of promoting market roads, and in general publicized the idea of revamping Ohio's highways.

Addressing the 1,500 delegates attending the convocation, Cox stressed the positive impact good roads would have on the quality of life throughout the state. A market roads system would help the farmer sell his goods and help stem the tide of immigration from the country to the city. Edith Campbell, the only woman on the Commission, advanced the argument that good roads would promote the development of better rural schools by facilitating transportation of isolated children to consolidated schools. For two days the delegates discussed the various aspects of rural life, and with wide press coverage there emerged the image of a ground-swell of public opinion for the program. The image of grassroots support, plus wide backing from business and industry, the lobbying of the Ohio Good Roads Federation, and the governor's championing of the program brought a positive response in the legislature. The Assembly approved a .5 mill levy for the construction of intercounty and main market roads, and permitted counties to add an additional .5 mill tax to defray their half of the cost.

Ohio's interest in good roads, said Cox, grew out of a

> gradual awakening on the part of the people to the fact that bad roads cost more than good ones. Our farmers are coming to be businessmen in every

> sense of the word, they are capable of figuring out the cost of transportation. They . . . see the financial advantage of good highways.

The governor also reasoned that Ohio's road program would reduce the subsequent "over all cost of goods" to the benefit of consumers.[21]

While appealing to the rural community for support, Cox responded to pressure from the urban centers in weaving the road network. In the spring of 1914, concern mounted from reformers, politicians, and business interests about completing the final stretch of the 130 mile highway connecting Toledo and Cleveland. The Main Market Road #1, from Norwalk to Cleveland, quickly received the highest priority. Justifying this decision, Cox explained that the road "is a main feeder into Cleveland and that city contributes a large sum for the support of roads." To the Mayor of Cleveland, the state's largest city, he observed that it "is but simple justice to make large disbursements for the construction of market roads which are feeders into your city." In addition, Cox divulged long range plans to expend "a great deal of money" for good roads throughout highly urbanized northern Ohio.

Some time later, Fred Rike, speaking for a group of Dayton businessmen, reminded Cox of an earlier promise to complete the Troy-Dayton road with state funds. Explaining the commercial advantages to be reaped by Dayton, the Gem City merchant was quick to point out that the people in Troy and Piqua were also vitally concerned. The governor wasted no time contacting James Marker, the state highway commissioner, and secured a promise that contracts for the project would be assigned shortly. For Cox, good roads became a "bread and butter" issue essential to the interaction of different sectors of the state in an urban-industrial economy.[22] The politics of highways facilitated social control in the interest of efficiency and economic growth in an increasingly urbanized state. It also added a stimulus to the economy in time for the forthcoming election.

A final innovation to emerge during the Cox administration resulted from a natural disaster. In late March 1913, shortly after the good roads convocation, five days of rain brought eleven inches of water down upon the southwestern part of the state and drenched some 8,000 square miles of central and southeastern Ohio with another seven inches. More than one and one-third million people were affected, with 20,000 houses completely destroyed and at least 428 lives lost. Cox estimated the economic cost at $300 million. The entire upper Miami Valley from Hamilton to Sidney was inundated, with Cox's own Dayton most affected by the deluge. The Great Miami River water level in twenty-four hours swelled from three to twenty-nine feet. The levees in the Gem City gave way, putting two-thirds of the city including the central business district and key industries, such as the Barney and Smith Car Works, under twelve feet of water. Throughout the state, telegraph and telephone lines, railroads and highways, were rendered inoperable.

The disaster focused national attention on Ohio and Governor Cox. Acting swiftly, on March 26, Cox declared martial law, took possession of the railroads, and began the process of saving lives. "Wherever we found supplies, food, clothing or what not, we seized them." Cox recalled and "then turned them over to relief authorities . . . . I had given a complete story every day with understanding that the newspapers would render aid in broadcasting the need of funds and supplies." From all over the country, more than $2 million in charity poured into the state, and the governor's office distributed it through the Red Cross. The state provided $250,000 worth of emergency food and medical supplies which the National Guard rushed into the disaster areas. At the governor's request the

Department of War distributed food rations, cots, tents, and other supplies, and established a sanitary commission in the flood plain to combat disease.

As the emergency subsided, Cox took up the task of rehabilitation. After touring the stricken areas of the state, he decided that providing funds was the principal task. To insure an adequate supply of capital, the governor transferred state revenues to building and loan companies in the disaster areas, and increased state deposits in banks in the flood basin. Cox also informally used the influence of his office to loosen the supply of money. When a Columbus bank foreclosed a $3,000 loan of a Dayton savings and loan company, Cox, "in language . . . more emphatic than elegant, but right . . . to the point" forced a reversal of the action. To facilitate rehabilitation efficiently, on April 18, the General Assembly approved Cox's request for the creation of the Ohio Flood Relief Commission. The law empowered cities and counties to establish four-person emergency commissions. They were to operate with the aid and direction of the state commission, to which Cox appointed five prominent Ohio businessmen.

"Ohio has risen from the floods," Cox announced as the rebuilding began. For his work, he won national applause. "The man who has dominated the situation in Ohio," the *New York World* editorialized, "is Governor Cox. . . . James M. Cox excites and is herewith offered assurances of the *World's* most distinguished consideration." On December 10, 1913, for his "prompt, energetic, and wise measures for emergency relief" and cooperation with the Red Cross, the governor of Ohio received the Red Cross Medal of Merit.[23]

The flood and its aftermath made many Ohioans determined to prevent similar disasters in the future and led to the creation of a unique political institution for the purpose of regional planning and service—the conservancy district. A group of Dayton businessmen, headed by Edward A. Deeds, a downtown manufacturer, established the Dayton Citizens Relief Committee and raised a $2 million flood prevention fund. A preliminary engineering survey revealed the need for regional action and called for a series of "dry dams" to the north and west of Dayton. When the plans became known, cries of opposition arose in the cities and farm districts to the north of Dayton. The Citizens Relief Committee organized an advertising campaign to sell the project and a lobby to enact the necessary legislation.

From the beginning, Cox approved the regional plan. The Dayton publisher personally contributed $5,000 to the flood prevention fund. As governor, he was brought into the writing of the bill, and provided political advice to limit opposition. Guiding the bill through the legislature, "was one of the heaviest tasks imposed on me," Cox recalled. To insure party support, he labeled it an administration measure and he personally helped line up the votes. Finally approved, the Vonderheide Act, established a conservancy board composed of three representatives from each county in the district. The board had the authority to sell bonds, levy taxes, and administer the flood prevention program. The Miami Conservancy District project, consisting of six dry dams costing $39 million, was completed in December 1922. Edward A. Deeds wrote of Cox's efforts, "Without you as Governor we would not have had the law under which we will be able to work out the salvation of the whole valley. . . . "[24]

Bringing business efficiency to government, Cox proudly noted "every mandate of the constitution had been carried out and the major reforms promised in our party platform had been adopted." "The progressive movement in our state had come from the needs of the day" and was completed "long before the time expected by the public," he recalled. Using the rhetoric of egalitarianism and the mentality of Taylorism, Cox had helped to create a government that intrenched the middle-class values of economic individualism and efficiency in an urban-industrial state. Now Cox, "the public man," submitted his work for the verdict of the people.[25]

VII
DEFEAT AND VINDICATION

Although Cox had appeared to honor his "contract with the people," by July 1914, when the legislature cut taxes, it had become apparent that Cox had failed to win popular support. Cutting taxes represented a last ditch effort to maintain power under the banner of efficiency. Cox had erred when he thought the leaders of the various groups would be satisfied with compromise and that the general public could be educated to accept a progressive model of government. He experienced his first electoral defeat in 1914.

Opposition to Cox's reelection came from numerous sectors. The gubernatorial campaign for all practical purposes began in the summer of 1913, when the insurance interests mounted their attack upon the workmen's compensation law. Since Cox successfully resisted these efforts to destroy the mandatory features of the law, the insurance companies openly worked to defeat the Governor. The Anti-Saloon League also opposed the incumbent. Dissatisfied with the regulation of liquor, the League used the initiative and referendum to challenge the licensing law by proposing two amendments. One called for outright prohibition, and anticipating failure, the second proposal establishing the township or the city as the unit to determine local option. Correspondingly, restrictions in the area of saloon licensing made enemies of former tavern owners who no longer held licenses, as well as of the brewers who were in the same position.

In addition, numerous old line Democrats experienced alienation from the new order. Harvey Garber, who closely identified with the Bryan forces in Ohio and who expected to become party chairman, typifies this group. Likening the Cox Democrats to Tammany Hall and charging the governor with excessive centralization of power, Garber brought discontented Democrats into an organization known as the True Democracy League of Ohio. Congressman John J. Whitacre of Canton, disturbed over patronage questions and the allocation of highway funds in his district, decided to take advantage of the discontent and challenged Cox in the state's first direct primary.[1]

Facing the challenge, Cox spent the spring and summer defending the efficiency of his program and pressing county tax commissions to cut taxes. In rural areas, he responded to attacks made by Whitacre on centralized schools, appointed assessors, the agricultural commission, and the liquor licensing law. Answering charges that he had created a political machine, Cox explained that he had made the legislature keep its promises to the people. Placating urban leaders, especially Newton D. Baker, Cox appointed a commission to investigate municipal financial problems and to determine what legislation was needed. Supported by the financial power of the True Democracy League, Whitacre waged a campaign that seriously threatened Cox in the rural areas. Nevertheless, the well organized regular party machinery garnered Cox a two to one primary victory in a light turnout of some 200,000 voters. Carrying the state's five largest cities by margins ranging from seven to one to ten to one, Cox ran poorly outside the cities. Whitacre won a majority in eleven rural counties including two of those affected by the Miami Conservancy Law. Victorious in the primary, Cox quickly set the tenor of the campaign by announcing that he intended to protect the "New Order" from Republican "standpat" opposition.[2]

Congressman Frank B. Willis, a former teacher at Ohio Northern University and the darling of the Anti-Saloon League, secured the Republican nomination by 20,000 votes in a strong Republican turnout of more than 230,000 voters. The Progressive Party had virtually disintegrated. James R. Garfield, son of the former President and a personal friend of Theodore Roosevelt, won the Progressive nomination with only 7,081 votes. Most Progressives had returned to their traditional party loyalties, but differences between the Republicans and Progressives still persisted.

The Progressive Party's platform criticized the Republicans for bossism and Cox, in particular, for usurping legislative power, weakening home rule, overlooking the needs of labor, and favoring the liquor interests. It approved the proposed prohibition and woman suffrage amendments, the eight-hour day and minimum wage for women, and an extension of workmen's compensation. While the strong dry position of the Progressives won them the endorsement of the Prohibition Party, the liquor question split the recently reunited Republican Party. Willis favored a strong platform statement on the issue, but leading wet Republicans from Cincinnati, Cleveland, and Toledo threatened to leave the convention if the document attacked the wets. To preserve unity, the liquor plank lamely pledged not to take a backward step to solve the wet-dry question. Silent on women's suffrage, the rest of the platform condemned Cox for authoritarianism.

The Cox-dominated Democrats had little trouble defining the issues. Characterizing his administration as "promises fulfilled" and "rooted in justice," Cox stressed the need for the "New Order" to be tested by friends rather than enemies. To heal rifts within the coalition, the governor called attention to the breadth of the reforms, noting that

> . . . the most conspicuous phase of the whole program of legislative progress seems to be its freedom from a provincial spirit—it reflects the very essence of co-operation between the elements in city and country life so much dependent upon each other.

If reelected, he pledged a period of "legislative rest" and promised a short legislative session dealing only with matters of "direct concern" to various "communities". The platform committee ignored arguments for female suffrage and the pleas of the Ohio Federation of Labor for support of the eight hour day for women and extensions of the Workmen's Compensation Law. Short and inoffensive, the document defended the "Cox Laws," especially the liquor licensing and tax assessor systems, both under serious attack, and called for a federal workmen's compensation law.[3]

Although Theodore Roosevelt entered the state on behalf of the Progressives, the campaign centered around Willis and Cox. Not even Roosevelt could stop the decline of the third party. The sparse turnout in the primary indicated the lack of voter interest and the major parties denied the Progressives an audience when they sidestepped the women's suffrage and prohibition referendums. Beset by financial difficulties, the reform party waged a poor campaign. By the end of October, even Roosevelt had given up hope for the party as a viable third force in American politics.[4]

In a hard fought contest, Willis and Cox criss-crossed Ohio answering each other's charges. A Delaware County native and popular in rural areas, Willis stumped the state promising to undo the misrule of Cox and "to turn the government back to the people." The rhetoric of the True Democracy League worked to Willis' advantage. He equated Cox with boss rule, and charged him with conflicts of interest while a member of congress. Revealing that as a congressman Cox had operated a consulting firm which negotiated the consolidation of two Dayton power companies, he charged that for his services Cox received a considerable holding in the Dayton Gas and Electric Company. To this charge Cox replied that it was simply a business venture as a private citizen and that he "would do it again." Although failing openly to support prohibition, Willis near the end of the campaign announced he would "vote dry." The GOP candidate criticized the failure of Cox to support labor on key issues, and along with leading Republican newspapers emphasized the traditional theme of the "full dinner pail" to win the labor vote.[5]

On the defensive in rural counties, Cox devoted most of his personal attention there. The appointed assessors, centralized schools, highway taxes, the agricultural commission, and the conservancy act were all viewed as a form of urban imperialism in the rural areas. This situation made the rural districts Cox's nemesis, hence he geared his campaign to convince rural and small-town voters of the desirability of his program. Using the arguments initially advanced to implement the reforms, the former teacher again sought to educate the voters. The charges of bossism were categorically false, said Cox. He defensively explained many times that he had simply insisted that the legislature "keep its promise to the people." The incumbent moved his campaign to the cities in the last part of October, and there emphasized the improved conditions brought by the workmen's compensation law, regulation, and decreased taxes. Pointing to attacks on the insurance law by the private insurance interests, Cox depicted Willis as a friend of business and the insurance companies and as a foe of labor. Referring to Willis' dry tendencies, Cox and the Democrats defended the license law as the only reasonable alternative. It was not a question of wet or dry Cox argued, but one of law enforcement and the need to eliminate the "worst evils associated with drinking." To bolster Cox's image among rural voters and prohibitionists, William Jennings Bryan again came into the state and described the governor as one with "untiring devotion to the people's interests."[6]

In addition to the struggle over images, alternative administration systems, and group interests, nativism marked both camps. In a close primary in which the predominantly Protestant suburbs and rural areas provided the margin of victory, Warren G. Harding won the Republican nomination for the United States Senate. The Democrats selected Timothy Hogan, an Irish Catholic from rural Wellston who had come into prominence prosecuting the referendum scandals. Anti-Catholic feeling was visible throughout the state in graffiti, posters, and journalism by way of a whispering campaign. Rumors developed that Cox was Catholic, a story the governor's staff spent considerable time discounting. While the Republicans made gains because of the anti-Catholic sentiment, the Democrats exploited prejudice against blacks to hold the partisan ranks together. Rather than associate with the black community, Cox decided not to contribute to the 1914 Emancipation Day booklet. In addition, the governor's staff repeatedly ignored communications from pro-Democratic blacks who offered to work for the reelection of Cox.[7]

As election day approached, Cox reviewed the main reasons why he should be returned to office. He deemed it imperative to keep "efficient business organization in the affairs of the state" and to have the workmen's compensation law administered by friendly hands. Further, the implementation of the good roads program had just begun, as had the school, prison, and agricultural reforms. In addition, he pointed out that decentralization of liquor regulations would be inconsistent with efficient law enforcement. In sum, his reelection was essential to protect the work of the previous two years.[8]

Certain of the path to follow, Cox and his organization were optimistic by election day. With the support of leading big city newspapers, including some traditionally independent and Republican dailies, Cox's staff released speeches and supplied editorial information to answer the charges of the opposition. Party strategists felt secure in the belief that middle of the road positions on the liquor and tax questions satisfied the majority of the electorate. During his administration, Cox had conciliated numerous groups and now secured pledges of support from their leadership. For two months the governor had defended and explained the reforms from the back of his touring car in rural areas and before organized crowds in the county seats and larger cities. In addition, the party had carried out its pledges. From an organizational point of view, what could go wrong? When the returns came in, however, it soon became apparent that the reformers had failed to do enough to maintain power.[9] (See Table H)

Both Cox and Willis defined the dominant issue of the campaign as the repudiation or endorsement of the current administration. In this respect, the outcome must be viewed as a personal defeat for James M. Cox.[10] A long term analysis of Ohio gubernatorial elections supports this interpretation. From this point of view, 1914 emerges not as a critical election that signalled the end of Ohio progressivism, but rather as a deviant election in which the dissatisfied voters were interested enough to "turn the rascals out." Cox, retracing the steps of his defeat, demonstrated his political sagacity when he wrote

> This brings us to a curious phase of human nature . . . in political affairs. Most of those in opposition were not moved by principle. With them it was grievance, and they remained militant until Election Day. There was no need of hauling them to the polls. This type votes early. On the other side, a certain portion, in support of the movement such as we were maintaining, accepted what was done as a matter of course. Believing it was the plain duty of the administration so to do, they held their political lines. When the polls were canvassed it developed that we had polled a tremendous Republican vote. Labor was well nigh unanimous because of the compensation laws. The teaching force of the state was actively with us. Many adherents of the dry cause approved the workings of the liquor licensing law. Even the tax law, although it was decidedly a debit in the situation, brought us more than partisan support.[11]

Proud of his stewardship, Cox went before the General Assembly prior to leaving office, with no regrets. "The mandates issued by the people have been respected," he asserted with his usual self-confidence. Assuming the role of President of the Board, he underlined the benefits of his business-like conduct of the governor's office. Emphasizing that Ohio finances were now on a business footing, the outgoing governor described the tangible benefits of efficient management. Buildings for the university, normal schools, state hospitals, and a new prison all stood as monuments to progressive government. Although the bureaucracy had grown, he pointed out that "every department with regulatory authority, is self-supporting," while the entire society as well as the institutions regulated "share the benefits." Cox asked that the direction established be followed in the future—especially good roads and schools, business efficiency, and a balanced budget. After two years of residence at the Neil House he tried to ease the burden of his successor and recommended the purchase of a governor's residence. Satisfied to have been governor and proud of his achievements, Cox concluded:

> Altogether, at the beginning of a new year and a new governmental regime in the state, we should all felicitate ourselves as proud citizens of a great Commonwealth that our fiscal condition is healthy beyond precedent; that industrial justice and peace have been wrought by the Workmen's Compensation Law which has removed the courts from the zone of distrust and re-established them in the confidence of the people; . . . that the boy and girl in remote locations back on the mud road see the manifestations of interest on the part of . . . government in their educational and material welfare; that taxes on the average, were lower . . . in December than ever before.[12]

After six years of public service, Cox graciously returned to private life. The years of apartment living in Washington and hotel dwelling in Columbus had left their mark on his personal life. In 1912, after seventeen years of marriage, the Coxes amicably separated and were divorced. Establishing successful newspapers and public service led to neglect of family affairs. Cox won custody of the two children on an equal time basis. The former Mrs. Cox married shortly after the divorce while Cox remained single until 1917 when he married Margaretta Blair of Chicago. In 1915, however, the forty-five year old divorcé sought stability and decided to build a residence befitting a prosperous publisher and former governor. Desiring a country estate, he chose a wooded site five miles east of Dayton overlooking the Miami Valley. He built a great stone and brick mansion in Georgian architecture which bore a remarkable resemblance to the White House. He called it "Trailsend" because, as he later wrote, local legend reported that it had been a favorite campsite of a group of Miami Valley Indians.

With his newspapers prospering, Cox turned to the promotion of innovations in journalism. Foreseeing the rise of weekly news magazines, he urged Kent Cooper of the Associated Press and John N. Wheeler of the North American Newspaper Alliance to offer more diversity in their wire service news. Recognizing New York as the urban center of the nation, he suggested that the wire services provide more background news as well as reviews of plays and motion pictures and editorial excerpts from leading New York newspapers. The wire services were not interested, but by the 1920's weekly news magazines, using these concepts, had earned a secure place in journalism. Re-adjusting to private life proved difficult, and before long, Cox again turned his energy to politics—"keeping close watch on the trend of things in the State House."[13]

Governor Willis emphasized economy and the need to undo the "executive usurpation" of the previous administration. In his inaugural address, the former Republican congressman noted, "As the human organism requires seasons of inactivity for assimilation and rest, so does the state require periods of legislative recuperation." Little that was new emerged during Willis' tenure, although some Cox administration laws underwent restructuring. The most significant changes were a return to the elected tax assessors, abolition of the State Liquor Licensing Board in favor of district licensing boards, and the creation of a ten-person agricultural board in place of the Agricultural Commission. These changes were a response to the wishes of the constituency that had helped elect Willis. The State Militia was reorganized into the National Guard, and on several occasions Willis called the guard out to end industrial disorders. For the most part a weak governor, Willis undid little of the bureaucratic super-structure that had emerged in the previous administration.[14]

While watching events in Columbus and tending to his newspapers, Cox still maintained considerable control of the Ohio Democratic Party. As early as July 1915, party leaders urged him to repair his political fences for the 1916 gubernatorial race. Eager for the political interplay, Cox began inviting prominent Democrats and journalists to visit him at Trailsend to spend some time in "pleasant" conversation. After the bi-elections of 1915 when several referendums to repeal legislation passed during his administration were defeated, Cox found the thought of a return to politics irresistible. He interpreted the results as a vindication of his program and the "Cox laws." Letters began to pour into Dayton from county politicians, influential labor leaders, and business groups congratulating him on his "personal victory." He responded with typical pride that the "Cox laws will live in this state. These laws were suggested by public necessity and being born of good purpose, it is always safe to hold to the doctrine that they were entitled to a trial."[15]

The ex-governor became convinced that Frank Willis, his rival of 1914, could not win in 1916. From this point on, despite the impression of reluctance for the benefit of fence sitters, Cox was a candidate for reelection. Responding to the first formal resolution endorsing his candidacy for 1916, he emphasized uncertainty about running but guaranteed to support whomever the party chose. To those elements whose backing Cox deemed essential, his posture appeared less diffident. When William Green promised that labor would rally behind him against Willis, Cox enthusiastically confided that all indications were that the incumbent would be beaten next fall. To another political ally he confidently promised that none of Ohio's state Democratic machinery would endorse Alfred P. Sandles of Elyria for the nomination. To weld progressives to his candidacy, he used support tendered by the business community. The Dayton publisher announced to the progressive Cleveland wing of the party that his business friends now urged him to run, but that his decision would be determined by whether or not "it would help Ohio's progressive movement."[16]

Skillfully lining up such supporters, Cox avoided alienating them while making inroads among those agricultural, dry, and business groups who had opposed him in 1914. To the farmers his posture became that of a wounded idealist who stood up for what had been right in the past, even though it had lost him votes. Cox explained that he was encouraged by the results of the last election. To prohibitionists he continued to assert that the licensing law had been a result of a mandate from the people, and should prohibition become the law, he would be equally satisfied. On questions of business reform, he maintained silence. By mid-March he still played the part of a reluctant candidate, but opened the door a bit more by announcing that he would head the ticket if his "services were needed."[17]

Before formalizing his candidacy Cox wanted a united party. By April, eighty-five county organizations had passed resolutions of endorsement and he stood assured of the party nomination. Lacking only the support of the Wilson administration, Cox depicted himself as a "Cincinnatus" who would run to help President Wilson carry Ohio. To create the image of administration approval and gain the support of Newton D. Baker, who still wielded considerable power among Cleveland Democrats, Cox asked Wilson to allow the newly appointed Secretary of War to serve as chairman of the Ohio Democratic Convention. Wilson replied that he preferred to stay out of state politics but would yield to Baker's judgment.

Administration support seemed desirable from several standpoints. During a presidential year, the President's coattails could make the difference. In addition, Baker had informed Cox that some Wilsonians doubted the loyalty of Cox because of his dissatisfaction with Secretary of War Lyndley Garrison's proposed continental army reorganization and they were now considering a draft of Judson Harmon to help carry the state. The then Cleveland Mayor explainded that he agreed with Garrison that the defense program ought to be federalized because the militia system would be ineffective if the country went to war. Wilson's confidant stated that the President would have to compromise with Congress to get any preparedness legislation at all. Baker undoubtedly knew Wilson's objectives, for a short time later he was confirmed as Secretary of War and carried out a compromise preparedness program. When a Cox supporter complained about the Garrison proposal, the Daytonian expressed the hope that a compromise could be worked out that would not "smack of militarism." Just what Cox's position really was is difficult to discern. Later, however, he worked to keep the Ohio National Guard intact and it seems that his ultimate concern was to keep control over the state's armed forces for political purposes. Baker ultimately accepted the task of convention chairman, an act that reflected administration approval of Cox and a belief that he could best help carry the state in what guaranteed to be a close election.[18ep]

In the spring of 1916, his candidacy still unannounced, Cox began to develop a platform. Ohio State University economist Matthew Bray Hammond pointed out the need to continue the direction of social legislation begun in the first administration. Planning a campaign based upon denouncing the Willis administration, Cox asked Hammond to develop his ideas. In the area of social reform the Ohio State professor recommended a compulsory medical insurance program with employers and employees contributing equally, a minimum wage for women and minors—to be established by wage boards in the various industries, an increase in workmen's compensation death benefits, and extension of coverage to all industrial workers. Cognizant of the political necessity to maintain the Smith 1 Percent Law, the economist urged a tax on mortgages and graduated inheritance and income taxes as new revenue sources for improving educational, charitable, and correctional institutions. To provide money for the cities he suggested a business excise tax. The former industrial commission member undoubtedly recognized the unpopularity of his proposals in some quarters and indicated no surprise when Cox failed to reply.[19]

Rather than restoke the reform fires, Cox told the Scripps-McRae chain of newspapers that "honesty with the voters" stood as the leading issue in 1916. Answering questions on what would be new in a Cox administration, the ex-governor asserted that his chief objective was to give the laws of his first term a chance to operate under efficient administration. "In the main," Cox observed,

>we have enough fundamental laws for the present. The general welfare of
>the state will be conserved if we retain a sympathetic executive and legis-
>lative attitude toward the things accomplished after the new constitution,
>and then refine the laws that have been passed as experience suggest.

He had some specific "refinements" in mind. Death benefits under the workmen's compensation law should be increased to $5,000 and additional money for medical expenses should be provided. To solve the shortage of revenue experienced by the cities, he proposed returning to them the inheritance tax and a portion of the liquor and automobile license proceeds. A restoration of the appointed tax assessors, he said, would make the Smith Law operable.[20]

With few controversial issues and the parties unified, the state Democratic and Republican conventions met to endorse Cox and Willis. Secretary of War Newton Baker urged the delegates to support Cox and advised extending the power of the cities "to determine affairs that concern them alone without imposing burdens upon others not members of the municipal unit." "All the virtues needed for its accomplishment," he observed, "were shown in the two great constructive years of 1912-1914." Committed to "legislative rest," Cox flayed the Willis administration for inefficiency and a failure to make the most of the new constitution. After endorsing Cox and Wilson, the delegates adjourned to attend the National Democratic Convention in St. Louis. There, the Ohio delegation headed by Cox, Judson Harmon, Senator Atlee Pomerene, and former Governor James Campbell, routinely supported the nomination of Woodrow Wilson. Returning to Ohio, they reconvened the state convention in September and adopted a bland platform that condemned Willis and promised financial relief to the cities.[21]

In an effort to bring all the Progressives back into the party, the Ohio Republican Convention adopted a reform platform. Endorsing Willis, the document called for a six-day work week in industry and a strengthening of the Workmen's Compensation Act. Additionally, it proposed permitting the cities to modify the Smith Law by referendum, called for the continuation of the good roads program, and promised to eliminate needless jobs in the bureaucracy. The Republican platform and the decision of Theodore Roosevelt to endorse Charles Evans Hughes for President brought an end to the already disintegrating Progressive Party. Having failed to gain enough votes in 1914 to be listed on the ballot in the 1916 primary, most of the Progressive leadership returned to the GOP, although a few obstinately switched to the Democrats.[22]

Alfred P. Sandles, a former Agriculture Commission member, challenged Cox in the August primary, but Cox, well known, organized, and confident, won an easy victory. Rather than debate Sandles, the party's choice used his time and energy to attack Willis. In one of his few primary speeches, Cox affirmed the work of his administration and called for "refinements." Defending regulation, he claimed that no established business had been "disturbed" and the role of insurance companies had only been "altered." In the best tradition of popular rhetoric, he accused the insurance companies who opposed him of seeking to "re-establish their harvest of dollars made off the injuries of workers." "Let us redeem Ohio" became Cox's slogan as he campaigned on his record as an efficient administrator.[23]

With political and social reform de-emphasized, the questions of preparedness and war and peace became critical in state and local politics as well as in the nation. On the eve of the Democratic national convention, the *Dayton Daily News* editorially praised Wilson for keeping the country out of war. Seeking to return to office, the leader of the downstate Democratic Party recognized the importance of this position among the large German population of the Miami Valley. As leading Republicans such as Theodore Roosevelt came into Ohio calling for intervention on the allied side, this position took on added significance. On the state level the *News* tied preparedness for war to efficiency by attacking Willis for failing to make the Ohio National Guard a crack fighting force. In a series of exposes, George Burba scorned the shortage of equipment, the inefficient use of training sites (particularly the use of a Columbus site rather than Camp Perry), and unsolved logistics problem. The *News* pointed out that the failure of the incumbent to encourage absentee ballots for the guardsmen and charged administrative negligence. Questioning the gratitude of the Republicans, Burba criticized Willis for failing to stop rent evictions of the families of soldiers activated during the Mexican border crisis—"something Ohio owed the troops who were willing to sacrifice for the state."[24]

Having been a prime exponent of good roads for Ohio, Cox was disturbed with the de-emphasis of the movement by Willis. With the possibility of war at hand, he chastised Willis for neglecting the construction of a unified highway network. Pointing out the national commitment to good roads, as evidenced by the 1916 federal road program, the *News* explained that it took the efforts of the National Highway Association to keep the Republicans from dropping the program completely. Urging acceptance of the matching federal funds provided by the federal legislation, Cox pledged to continue the movement if reelected.[25]

In the shadow of the presidential campaign, the gubernatorial contest lacked excitement and issues. In August, Willis and Cox confronted each other before an estimated 10,000 people at the Miami Valley Chautauqua. Defending his stewardship, Willis focused on the need to protect individual freedom. The return to elected tax assessors, he claimed, was a step in the right direction. Other bureaucratic institutions, such as the Board of Censors, should also be destroyed. Anticipating Cox's charges on good roads, he pointed out that the return of road control to county officials represented a return of government to the people that kept taxes low. With Willis on the defensive, Cox pounded home the need for efficient government. Returning roads to the counties, he charged, represented a patronage ploy that actually increased government costs by $75,000 monthly, while the essential good roads movement languished. The Warnes Law, he asserted again, kept taxes down and insured revenues for essential services. The censorship board was, he said, a positive progressive step to save Ohio's youth from obscenity. The reform laws, he stressed, needed progressive administration. Relying upon President Wilson's popularity, Cox asked his listeners to vote for "the man of peace"—vote Democratic.[26]

In September and October, Cox went to the people. Over and again, he emphasized the need to redeem Ohio through efficient management. Promising a short legislative session that would not disturb business, the defeated reformer pointed out that few of the Cox laws "had been overturned during the Republican administration." He stressed the need for "refinements," and to insure continued success of the reforms, he called for proper administration. With Ohio considered essential to a Wilson victory, national Democrats and Republicans stumped the state. Theodore Roosevelt, in particular, thundered the need for American entrance into the war on the allied side. Cox, Newton D. Baker, William Jennings Bryan, and others, stressed preparedness and the theme that Wilson "kept us out of war." With few state issues, the theme of peace emerged as the central issue of the 1916 contest.[27]

Cox won reelection by the slim margin of 6,616 votes, representing 48.4 percent of the vote and an increase of 2.8 percent over his 1912 vote (See Table H). In 1914 Cox had failed to win widespread support of the urban middle-class while losing considerable rural backing. The reforms of his first term had come too quickly. Aware of this, in 1916 he rejected programs to meet pressing needs in favor of values that mirrored the interests of the urban middle-class by stressing efficiency, honesty in government, and a sympathetic attitude. This position, plus Wilson's coattails, returned Cox to power. Although he regained some rural support, it was Ohio's urban centers that provided Cox the margin of victory. The state's twelve urban counties gave Cox a 27,015 margin over Willis.[28]

For the first time since 1856, the Democrats swept Ohio in a two-party presidential race. The President led the ticket with a majority of some 89,000 votes, and his coattails helped elect Cox, Senator Atlee Pomerene, and thirteen of Ohio's twenty-two congressmen. The only other state east of the Mississippi and north of the Ohio carried by the Democrats was New Hampshire. Alluding to the long term significance of the results, Cox predicted "Not only the West, but all sections of this broad country will be dominant for Democrats in the future . . . The East will catch the spirit of things . . .

VIII
WAR GOVERNOR

Woodrow Wilson won reelection on the slogan "He kept us out of war." On April 6, 1917, the United States declared war on Germany. The state and national governments proceeded to direct their bureaucratic structures to promote the war effort. With considerable opposition to the war, violations of civil liberties were rampant as individuals and organizations joined the government in forcing conformity to foster efficient prosecution of the war. In the process, the economic might and ideological persuasion of the nation were drawn together to create maximum military participation, and the wartime relationship between the federal government and states was transformed. At the onset of American involvement in World War I, the United States lacked a nationally organized war machine. Consequently, state governments initially maintained a free hand in coordinating their efforts with those of the national government. This loose relationship eventually tightened as the war continued and fears of possible defeat grew during the winter of 1917-1918. By the spring of 1918 federal guidelines over the states began to dominate as the war effort was nationalized. In July 1918, Secretary of War Baker considered the national effort completely organized.[1]

But early in 1917, most Americans were cautiously optimistic that the United States would not be drawn into the conflict. Reflecting this euphoria, Cox failed to mention preparedness in his address to the Ohio General Assembly. He concentrated instead upon keeping his campaign pledge of a short legislative session. Believing efficient administration essential, he asked the legislature to "go no further in this session" than to provide for "accruing necessities." He called for revision of the Workmen's Compensation Law and changes in Ohio election laws. The legislators responded by establishing provisions for absentee voting, providing for separate ballots in state and national elections, creating a nine-hour work day for women, and by increasing death benefits under the workmen's compensation law. In response to Cox's prompting, the General Assembly accepted matching federal funds for highway construction and vocational education. The trend toward bureaucratic centralization continued. A state health commissioner and a four member Public Health Council replaced the State Board of Health, and offices of Superintendent of Public Instruction and Commissioner of Securities were established. Before adjourning late in March when the possibility of war was becoming more real, the legislature allocated a quarter of a million dollars for possible emergency war use.[2]

On the national level, preparedness had been an important question for some time. Early in 1916, Congress approved the Army Appropriations Act, part of which created the Council of National Defense to coordinate "industries and resources for the national security and welfare." Designed to serve as an advisory group to the government, the Council played a vital role in early mobilization efforts. Secretary of War Baker relied heavily upon it since the Council was the only organization specifically created to coordinate the resources of the country. Composed of leading representatives from industry and business, the Council served not only as an advisory body, but also as a communications link that gave government administrative departments almost immediate contact with industry. The Ohio Branch of the Council performed these roles and several others as well.[3]

On May 2 and 3, 1917, the Council of National Defense met with representative of the states. Recognizing the need for state cooperation, Secretary of War Baker, as council chairman, asked for the voluntary establishment of state and local councils of defense to coordinate wartime activities with those of the national committees of the Council. Cox responded. On June 1, 1917, he created by executive order the Ohio Branch, Council of National Defense, to mobilize the state's resources with the war policies of the national government. Conceived as a "war cabinet," the Ohio War Council had no legal status but functioned as an advisory group. The council and the governor nevertheless acted to promote maximum military participation. They dealt with labor and industrial relations, food conservation, Americanization, transportation, propaganda, and in other areas that appeared to require government pressure and control.[4]

Power would have to be used, Cox believed, to make Ohio function in the interest of the nation. This often meant further extending influence to already established pressure groups. The governor, a progressive with an unabashed faith in experts, created numerous "Blue Ribbon" committees composed of leading members of business and industrial groups to promote the war effort. The technique was extended to the grass roots level through local war councils, when the state council finally set guidelines for the formation of county councils. The proposed model explicitly asked for leaders from "important interest groups of the community."

Committee membership lists of the Ohio Branch, Council of National Defense, thus consisted of recognized leaders in their fields. The Committee on Labor and Industrial Relations contained such industrialists as Harvey Firestone of Firestone Rubber Co., Samuel Bush of Buckeye Steel, as well as Daniel J. Ryan of the Ohio Manufacturers Association and Thomas J. Donnely of the Ohio Federation of Labor. The Committee on Food Conservation and Supply called upon the resources of Ohio State University President William O. Thompson and the influence and marketing ability of Barney Kroger of the Cincinnati based Kroger food chain. Raymond Moley of Western Reserve University, head of the Cleveland Americanization office, became director of the state Americanization program while numerous industrialists and educators became committee members. Cox believed the factory was a natural school for immigrant groups, and emphasized the need for interaction between education and industry. For publicity and propaganda, Cox recruited the well known political analyst, James W. Faulkner, of the *Cincinnati Enquirer*. The Transportation Committee drew upon leading railroad and commodity industry executives. Party affiliation was not a critical factor in determining membership on the state council which consisted of eighteen Republicans and ten Democrats. Cox also established a Women's Committee with departments paralleling the major council committees. Separate women's committees were also created to deal with nursing, child welfare, and other service projects. Leadership within these groups reflected social status and visibility.[5]

The organization mirrored the urban-industrial complex of the state. A preponderance of committee members came from large urban communities. Hardly accidental, it grew out of the realization that modern warfare required the mobilization of urban resources, which included the media, transportation centers, educational facilities, and warehouses as well as heavy industries and the urban based service industries. Cities provided the bulk of the essential human resources. Not simply manpower, but more importantly, urban living, generated the necessary technological expertise needed for the war, i.e. the mechanics, machinists, stenographers, and other skilled workers.[6]

Cox demonstrated his awareness that the cities represented the foundation of the war effort in the coal crisis during the summer and fall of 1917. High prices and the short supply of coal made the fuel situation acute in Ohio. To meet the situation, he established a state Coal Clearing House which attempted to regulate retail coal prices and coal distribution, functions soon assumed by the Federal Fuel Administration. The Fuel Administration allocated six million tons of Ohio-produced coal for state consumption. Fearing the amount would be inadequate, the Clearing House surveyed eighty-two cities and towns, as well as the public utility companies, hospitals, and schools. Severe shortages, especially in vital service areas, seemed certain. Cox appealed to the Federal Fuel administration for a release of Ohio produced coal, but had no success. By the end of September, city governments began distributing coal reserves to meet claims of emergency household needs. The possibility of shortages led to public protests and threats by local governments to expropriate coal passing through their communities. Acting quickly, Cox confiscated coal shipments enroute to Great Lake ports on the theory that the lakes would be frozen and the coal would not be used before spring.

With the controversy at a peak, Senator James Reed, Chairman of the United States Senate Committee on Manufactures, asked Cox to come to Washington to discuss the shortage of coal. Aware of the hostility between President Wilson and Reed, Cox replied that government control of vital resources was sound and efficient in wartime. He refused to lend support to Reed's opposition to regulation. Cox explained that the problem was with the inefficiency of Harry Garfield, Chairman of the Fuel Administration, and pointed out that Ohio received relief when President Wilson became aware of the situation.[7]

Years later, Cox recalled the coal episode and said that he "acted to further the war effort rather than impede it." He sought to alleviate public distress and to promote harmony between local-federal authorities and the irate population. Cox recognized that without coal the public utilities would have collapsed and Ohio industries would have come to a standstill. A breakdown in essential services or the hardship of a severe winter, he believed, would have provoked demoralization and alienation from the war effort as well as the possibility of civil disorders.[8]

In mid-June 1917, the Ohio War Council held its initial meeting with Governor Cox and defined its immediate objectives. The agenda set by Cox called for the development of methods to stabilize employment, provide adequate labor for the fall harvest, secure highway construction workers, and establish policy to deal with industrial disputes and vagrancy. Rather than prohibit the mobility of labor by fiat, the committee on labor and industry decided that each firm should stabilize its own labor force. Since much of the rural labor force had moved to the cities, Cox's advisors developed a plan to tap industrial labor for farm needs by asking industry to promote short-term factory leaves of absence to bring in the harvest. Emphasizing the need to keep the highways up to par in anticipation of military needs and to insure the availability of supplementary transportation arteries should the railroad system prove inadequate, the committee approved Harvey Firestone's recommendation to use vagrants, "slackers," and draft dodgers for highway work. Fred Croxton, Vice-Chairman of the council took charge of resolving industrial disputes. Cox assured the council that his office was watching closely the influx of blacks into the state and Croxton spoke against industry recruiting rural blacks "for fear that a million of them might come to Ohio." Cox's chief industrial relations advisor reasoned that no action should be taken until the entire labor picture crystallized. Some council members pressed for a relaxation of labor regulations to meet contracts, but Cox insisted that existing regulations remain intact. Rather than seek special favors, he asserted that industries experiencing difficulty should sublet their contracts. Before adjourning, the War Council recommended that each urban center be organized down to the precinct level for the purposes of recruiting labor, operating the food and conservation programs, selling bonds and stamps, and developing Red Cross activities.[9]

The most crucial aspect of the Ohio Council's work involved the Committee on Labor and Industrial Relations. This committee maximized production by solving labor disputes and expanding the state labor exchange system. Dividing Ohio into twenty-one labor markets ranging from two to seven counties, the Committee located free employment agencies in the central city of each region. Cox requested and received the cooperation of mayors and representatives of labor and industry in the twenty-one cities. To establish the employment offices on a systematic footing, Cox recruited experts from the academic community, private planning agencies, and the state bureaucracy. Croxton, on loan from the Ohio Institute of Public Efficiency and the former director of the Ohio public employment offices for the state industrial commission, took charge of the overall Committee on Labor and Industrial Relations and the labor exchange system. Chester H. Mayhugh and Wilbur Maxwell were relieved of their duties with the Ohio Industrial Commission and established a central administrative network that tied government, industry, and labor into a compact for efficient use of Ohio's labor supply. Matthew Hammond of Ohio State University and William M. Leiserson of the University of Toledo contributed ideas and organized the regional employment offices. Organizing ability was the key criteria in the selection of employment office directors, but regional committees from labor and capital submitted mutually acceptable recommendations. Croxton chose the director from the list. These local committees also advised the employment service about day to day operations.[10]

Throughout the war the industrial committee performed its tasks with vigor. Fearing a disequilibrium in the labor supply, many of the small industrialists criticized the exchange program. They reasoned that natural laws of supply and demand would fill essential jobs. Approving the program leading industrialists launched an educational campaign on its behalf. They explained that maximum use of the labor force dictated flexibility in matching workers with jobs. They also pointed to the increased opportunities for workers provided by the wider job market. As the system evolved, "it was very clearly shown that the men who were out of employment in one place might be badly needed in another . . . ." The regional employment offices registered available workers in the district and tried to place them where they could be the most help according to their qualifications. A statewide clearance system issued daily bulletins listing job openings and prospective applicants. In emergencies the clearing house telephoned or telegraphed lists of available personnel to the area office concerned. For one project, the construction of housing at Fort Sherman near Chillicothe, the labor exchange recruited 3,000 workers in forty-eight hours.

In the first month of the program 20,000 workers were matched with essential jobs. During its entire existence, the employment offices received 840,904 job openings for 980,646 job requests and successfully matched 564,570 jobs with applicants. Many of the openings developed because of job mobility stimulated by wages not keeping pace with the cost of living. To prevent labor transience and unrest, chambers of commerce in cities like Canton and Springfield resorted to blacklisting. On balance, the labor exchanges facilitated wartime production and assisted industry in keeping costs down by providing a ready supply of labor.[11]

At the end of May 1918, Secretary of War Baker returned from France gravely concerned about manpower needs. He instructed Provost Marshal General Enoch Crowder to issue a "Work or Fight" order to meet manpower demands on the front, and to insure an adequate labor supply for essential industries. Although the order was never issued, in mid-June President Wilson and the War Labor Policies Board proclaimed that all industrial labor for either public or private work tied to the war effort should be recruited through the United States Employment Service. To promote acceptance of the national service, Secretary of Labor William B. Wilson and the President publicly urged all employers to recruit even their unskilled labor needs through the federal system. Organizers of the Ohio labor exchange, with numerous other employment experts, came to Washington to systemize national recruitment and placement practices. After a three-day conference, the experts approved the basic idea of the Ohio system of regional community labor boards representing industry, labor, and the employment service. Croxton along with key members of his Ohio staff spent most of July in Washington devising a plan that designated each state as an operating unit to follow federal guidelines for placement and recruitment.

The federal regulatory guidelines represented tacit recognition of the need to synchronize the state systems to promote the nation's war objectives. At the same time, the organization reflected the federal government's acceptance of the pluralism in American society. The community labor boards consisted of leaders from vital groups. The regional concept demonstrated awareness of spatial considerations and the interrelationship among city, town, and country. On August 1, 1918, the state employment services became part of the federal system under the auspices of the War Labor Policies Boards, but the United States Employment Service hardly had time to go into effect because the war ended abruptly.[12]

Through effective cooperation, the Ohio Branch, Council of National Defense, the United States Food Administration, and Ohio State University successfully directed Ohio's food production and consumer activities toward national objectives. During the first year of the war, Cox's War Council directed Ohio programs to meet broad federal food goals, but in 1918, when the national bureaucracy reached full momentum, the United States Food Administration assumed the dominant role. The joint appointment of Fred Croxton as Vice-Chairman of the Ohio Council and as Federal food Administrator for Ohio, eased the transition from state to federal control.

Maximum use of Ohio food resources required that the bureaucracy take into consideration the interrelated roles of the city and farm. To do so, governmental interference, pressure, and propaganda were extended to deal with food production and acreage utilization, conservation, consumption habits, and marketing procedures.

The pooling of labor for agriculture conflicted with the industrial effort. Consequently, the state tried to alleviate competition while efficiently using available labor. Industries promoted short-term leaves of absence for the 1917 harvest and 1918 spring planting. The Agricultural Extension Department of Ohio State University appointed regional representatives who reported the farmers' labor needs to the employment offices. Similarly, Governor Cox made grass roots appointments of township Food Crop Commissioners who maintained contact with the regional labor exchanges while the employment directors established communications with local farmers. With the Ohio State school of agriculture involved, students from the campus were recruited for farm work. Also Professor H. C.

Ramsover established a statewide farm recruitment program to draw labor from all of Ohio's colleges and high schools. The schools cooperated by permitting early dismissal and by registering students for the program, which placed the young workers primarily in agricultural work, but also offered some industrial opportunities. Because in many cases the farmers took individuals into their households, the employment offices used "discretion" in assigning farm workers. Blacks were thereby largely excluded from the Ohio agricultural work program. Between May 1 and December 31, 1917, more than 12,000 people registered for farm work, but Ohio farmers accepted only 5,937 out of 8,696 referrals.

Agricultural needs for 1918 loomed large. Early that year the United States Department of Agriculture organized to take an active part in state farm programs. In Ohio this simply meant taking over the existing organization and co-ordinating it with federal objectives. Under the auspices of the United States Food Administration, Ohio farm representatives and employment superintendents surveyed the state to determine farm labor needs. With the survey complete, the Food Administration in conjunction with the labor exchanges launched an extensive recruitment campaign. The United States Boy's Working Reserve program filled a large part of farm labor needs. With the 1917 student experience to draw upon, Chester Mayhugh, Director of the Boy's Working Reserve, successfully mobilized Ohio school boys and young men for the 1918 planting and harvest. Advertising the need for "boy help," county school superintendents and principals of public and parochial schools in the cities enrolled 18,000 boys for the spring planting. As in the previous year the schools and employment offices worked closely, releasing students early and placing the young men on farms requesting labor. In addition, efforts developed to establish boys' farm labor camps, but a lack of funds for supervision and maintenance of the camps kept this program from going beyond the planning stages. However, a derivation of the camp program evolved in the onion and beet fields. The state employment offices organized boys' labor gangs and transported them to the fields daily. The labor exchanges continued to place adults in farm jobs. Generally, the procedure proved efficient. At war's end, Fred Croxton reported, "that no appreciable percentage of the year's harvest was lost because of the lack of farm labor. This was accomplished in spite of the tremendous shortage of labor and the more attractive inducements offered to workers in the cities."[13]

A number of programs emerged to increase agricultural production. Governor Cox appointed county War Food and Crop Commissioners to report farm needs to the Farm Council. To facilitate communication and provide scientific advice, Ohio State University more than doubled its county advisory staff to increase farm output. These efforts contributed to more grain output in 1917 than during the previous year, and in 1918 the state sought further to improve production through mechanization. Cox launched these efforts with a conference of representatives from the farm equipment industry to promote tractor use in Ohio. From the industry representatives, Cox learned that tractors were plentiful but that farmers lacked the capital for investment. The governor proceeded to establish more farm credit by directing the State Superintendent of Banks to urge bankers to cooperate by extending loans for tractor purchases. He simultaneously instructed the Ohio Industrial Commission to invest $1 million of its funds in rural banks for 6 percent tractor loans. To interest farmers, the Agricultural Commission set up a series of tractor schools throughout the state. At the Columbus school Cox explained:

> Because our boys have gone from the farm—have been called to the colors, we must add by mechanical means as best we can to our agricul-

tural energy . . . . We must replace by machinery what we have lost by having our boys go to the front.

By March, with Cox's prodding, the tractor manufacturers established service operations throughout Ohio's agricultural areas. By the end of the war, more than two thousand tractors had been added to the Ohio farm economy. In addition, the state provided seed during shortages, tested soil and seed, and found markets for the surplus products of individual farmers to guarantee maximum land use and eliminate waste.[14]

The Ohio Council, following national council suggestions, also influenced urban living. Through city gardening projects, the agricultural committee encouraged city dwellers to grow their own produce. Representatives from Ohio State University spoke to chambers of commerce, factory workers, service clubs, and school audiences in seventy-six cities and towns, urging listeners to plant backyard and vacant lot gardens. Various service organizations distributed seeds and garden tools. In the spring of 1918, the program became part of a nationwide effort with the creation of the United States Garden Army.

Trying to alter urban diets, with the cooperation of the Home Economics Department and the Agricultural Extension Service of Ohio state University, the council coordinated an education program in home food processing techniques in schools, service clubs, and factories. Also, under the auspices of the United States Department of Agriculture, home demonstration agents began making individual contact during the summer of 1918. The combined efforts of the state council and the federal food agency led to more than 375,000 personal contacts on the efficient use of food resources. The publications of the council, a war cook book and a canning manual, brought efficient food use techniques to another 180,000 households. Hundreds of thousands of pamphlets, urging and demonstrating the use of meat and wheat substitutes in connection with meatless and wheatless days, further added to the total war effort. In 1917 alone, the Ohio Branch, Council of National Defense, distributed over two million pieces of printed material related to the food program. The transition of the food program to the United States Food Administration accelerated the process affecting virtually every household in the state.[15]

With industry and agriculture striving for peak efficiency, transportation loomed as a vital part in the Ohio war effort. At the onset, Cox's war cabinet established a transportation committee to ease the flow of goods within and through the state. Chaired by M. J. Caples of the Hocking Valley Railroad, the committee in August 1917 devised a three-phase program to help solve the nationwide problem of railroad car shortages.

The first phase, conditioned upon agreement by the Railroad's War Board of the Council of National Defense, proposed regional pooling agreements within the state. Calling upon local producers to serve each zone, the committee reasoned that rail equipment would then be used for shorter hauls, lessening maintenance requirements and speeding the flow of traffic. The limited supply of cars would then be more systematically utilized. The second part of the program urged Ohio railroads to ship all freight in full carloads. Estimating that the full carload program would free 5 percent of Ohio railroad company cars for the use, the Committee additionally recommended that all service be cut in those areas where traffic regularly flowed with trains not completely full. Phase three of the transportation program called for increased use of the state's more than 3,000 miles of inter-urban electric transit lines to ship freight to fill the void created by the full carload policy. Committee member S. D. Hutchins of the Central Electric Railway association guaranteed the suitability of electric lines for freight purposes, especially farm products. No national decision came on pooling agreements which involved a rescinding of Interstate Commerce Commission regulations, but the Railroads War Board and the I.C.C., relying upon authority under the Preferential Shipments Act of August 1917, did recommend full carloads and priority use of certain railroad cars.[16]

Heavily burdened, the nation's railroad system limped along without a uniform program and with six different authorities claiming control of at least some phase of the 260,000 mile network. By the fall of 1917, congestion plagued rail facilities as coal, iron, lumber, food, and finished products were shipped. To relieve the burden, in November the national council began experimenting with highway transportation. Cox's War Council announced that it planned to improve the Lincoln Highway through Ohio as an experiment to move freight by truck and to ship newly built government trucks and automobiles under their own power. Cox pressed the county and city governments across Ohio's northern tier to put the road in peak condition. In December 1917, the Ohio transportation committee, with the help of Ohio automobile clubs, tested the roads and quartered and entertained the drivers as they moved from Detroit to the east coast.

Concerned with congestion on the railroads and aware of the flexibility the automobile offered the national transportation system, the War Department, in April of 1918, decided to move 40,000 trucks from Detroit to Baltimore under their own power. To a request that the National Road through Ohio be completed for the caravan, Cox urged private contractors to give up longstanding contracts in favor of state labor gangs. Reasoning that efficiency dictated the change, Cox explained that while the contractors lacked labor Ohio had a ready supply available in the prisons. To tap this labor source and remain within the law, the state had to perform the work. Cox recalled that:

> There was one link covering twenty-seven miles in Muskingum and Guernsey Counties . . . which provided a real obstacle to the transportation in question. The job had to be done not only quickly but thoroughly . . . the thoroughfare had to be built along modern lines.

Hoping to avoid delays, Cox met with local officials.

> We had there the judges of the courts, the county auditors, the county engineers and surveyors and the county commissioners. They all . . . pledged their cooperation. The real problem was not machinery nor supplies but labor. I consulted Warden Thomas of the penitentiary in Columbus and suggested that we assemble 250 prisoners . . . Without much delay 250 Negroes were assembled . . . . The state bought materials and placed the whole operation in charge of a brick manufacturer of good repute. The state auditor assigned a competent accountant and the disbursement of money was carefully supervised. How the red clay flew in those hills of south-eastern Ohio! The countryside shook from the explosions of dynamite that were tearing away rock and hardpan soil. Nothing interfered with the expeditious carrying out of the project and in a surprisingly brief time the automobiles and trucks were rolling eastward.[17]

Truck transportation proved effective and the Council of National Defense urged the various states to organize transportation subcommittees to deal specifically with the development of highway transport. Responding systematically, in March Cox appointed a highway subcommittee consisting of chamber of commerce representatives from regional population centers. As part of Ohio's "return road bureau" system, the local chambers became clearing houses for manufacturers, merchants, and truckers in each city and became quasi-public agencies. Relying heavily upon business expertise the subcommittees had difficulties in establishing priorities.

In August 1918 the Council of National Defense requested the creation of separate state highway transportation committees. On September 5, Cox replaced the subcommittee with a Highways Transport Committee, taking the system out of the hands of the chambers of commerce. The committee in turn established regional highway committees, continued the return load bureaus, cooperated with the Federal Railroad Administration, advertised the value of trucking, and gathered information on the utility of mass truck transportation to meet national objectives. In operation less than three months at the end of the war, the committee continued to gather highway usage information for some time after Cox dismissed the Ohio Branch, Council of National Defense.[18]

A maximum war footing would have been impossible without propaganda. Convinced of the educational value of the newspaper, Cox appointed James W. Faulkner to chair the council Publicity Committee. Designed to support Ohio's wartime activities and to promote successful prosecution of the war, this committee functioned as a coordinator for the various council propaganda activities. From early August 1917 through December 15, 1918, the publicity bureau controlled news of state wartime activity by daily bulletins to every newspaper in Ohio. In most cases these items, which emphasized the day-to-day activities of the council, became standing features in the large urban dailies. In addition to press information, the publicity committee distributed posters and pamphlets issued by the various state and federal committees.

Throughout 1917, much of the information provided by the Ohio publicity committee represented responses to requests from the Council of National Defense and from the federal Committee on Public Information. For the most part Ohio performed the task well and received commendations from various sectors of the national council. As the year came to a close the directives of the governmental wartime agencies, reflecting the consolidation of authority by the federal government and the phasing out of the Council of National Defense, became more precise. Nevertheless, propaganda remained important throughout the wartime program of Governor Cox.[19]

To "educate" Ohioans to support the war effort, Cox early in November of 1917, appointed a Patriotic Education Committee headed by President Willianm Oxley Thompson of Ohio State University. Beginning with a circular letter to some 1700 "select patriots," by mid-November the Committee had created a speakers' bureau. Organized down to the grassroots level, Professor Carl Perry, also of the state university, categorized several hundred speakers according to their interest and locality for ease of assignment. Local bureaus were developed in regional cities. At every opportunity, the speakers saturated their region with wartime doctrine through appearances in the schools and before organizations. When national speakers from the Four Minute Man organization or from the speaker's division of the Committee on Public Information came into an area, the local bureaus developed the itineraries. With the emergence of the local councils, the role of the Public Education Committee vis-à-vis the speaker's program was limited to providing information for speakers to meet the needs of the hour and to serving as a clearing house for national speakers.

Originally intended to tap the expertise of the academic community, the ranks of the speakers bureau quickly swelled to provide a podium for virtually anyone who wanted to speak for the war. Consequently, the calibre of speeches met with protest from certain academics. Gale Lowrie of the University of Cincinnati soon resigned from the propaganda committee. Other academics complained bitterly about the "flag waving" nature of the program because it undermined the activities of a unified statewide war effort.[20]

Propaganda emerged as an important aspect of the Americanization program. On April 3, 1918, the eve of a national conference of representatives from the state war councils, Secretary of the Interior Franklin K. Lane appealed for active state Americanization programs. Addressing the representatives on the following day, Josephus Daniels claimed there was a need to end treason. Discussion followed and gave birth to proposals ranging from elimination of German language teaching in the schools to vigorous prosecution of disloyal Americans. The representative from Ohio, Fred Croxton, returned home and recommended the creation of an Americanization Committee—a long time idea of the governor. Surveying Americanization efforts in the state, Cox discovered that, aside from the cities of Cleveland, Cincinnati, Akron, and operations in a few large industries, little activity took place to assimilate the foreign-born population into the society. In addition, Cox learned that some 600,000 foreign-born or mixed parentage people resided in Ohio with a large portion being of German heritage. Citing these facts as proof of the need to homogenize the population, Cox created a statewide Americanization program and based upon Croxton's recommendation put Western Reserve University Professor Raymond Moley in charge.

Rooted in the belief that the foreign-born population maintained loyalties to European nations, the Americanization program endeavored to educate immigrants about American values and institutions. The Committee published a number of pamphlets as guides designed to standardize methods of teaching English and citizenship, to promote industrial Americanization programs, to encourage community recognition of citizens completing naturalization, and to guide volunteer agencies in efforts to improve living conditions of immigrant families. One leaflet defined Americanization as an attempt to unify America through "mutual understanding and trust, and to make America a vast fellowship of free men," while another offered "practical suggestions" for teaching English, citizenship, and the "necessity of naturalization." "Americanization in Industry" appealed to employers for programs that would "assimilate their foreign-born employees into the ranks of intelligent, efficient, and thoroughly American wage earners." "Americanization Through the Public Library" described how the library could be used to promote loyalty. By the end of hostilities, twenty-five cities in Ohio had organized local Americanization committees and were busily involved in carrying out the objectives of the Ohio War Council. Moley's committee maintained close contact with the local groups and by the end of the war had begun organizing programs in the Ohio Department of Public Instruction.

In addition to pamphleteering and coordinating local activities, the Ohio Americanization Committee became active in censorship. At the end of June 1918, the Council of National defense circulated a list of "pro-German" books to the state councils. The Americanization Committee distributed the list to libraries throughout Ohio with the statement that the books, in the opinion of many critics, should "be withdrawn temporarily from circulation." The list contained volumes described as having anti-war sentiment, socialist leanings, or favorable attitudes toward Germany, with many of them having prewar publication dates. Moley's committee also circulated an approved reading list.[21]

Under the guise of forestalling sedition and treason, the nation on a war footing harassed groups outside the mainstream. In the days between President Wilson's request for a declaration of war and the ensuing congressional action, the *Dayton Daily News* had editorialized that socialists, by opposing the war, were undermining the well being of the country. Two weeks later, to forestall a railroad strike, Cox announced that

> If labor and capital are unpatriotic enough to engage in a grapple of strength which will result in a paralysis of transportation that would endanger our food supplies and keep from President Wilson the supplies he needs in his hour of crisis, I will place the state under martial law and suffer the consequences.

With the strike averted Cox activated the National Guard and placed them in strategic locations throughout the state to combat possible sabotage. When the country entered the war, Cox continued to issue statements reflecting his belief that opponents of war were involved in treasonable activities.[22]

Ohio police action during the war, either through regular channels, the state council, or private activities, generally reflected the views of the governor. At the outset of American intervention, the National Board of Fire Underwriters volunteered their inspectors to help protect food and industrial supplies. Accepting this nationally distributed expertise, the Council of National Defense alloted the underwriters to their respective states. Cox assigned them to the office of the State Fire Marshall and instructed them to report to the War Council. This act put 257 men in the field to serve not only as efficiency experts, but simultaneously to guard against sedition and root out pro-German activity. Ranging from informing employers about alien guards, or the lack of guards, to reporting what they conceived as pro-German activity, the volunteer inspectors made over 6000 investigations. The official history boasted that they had unearthed a large number of seditious plots which resulted in numerous convictions.[23]

In addition to this rudimentary police force, the state council relied upon the tyranny of opinion to promote conformity. When a local council in a given community found individuals deviating from the efficiency and conservancy guidelines of the state, the process began. If pressure from the local council failed, upon request the state council denounced publicly the individuals for lack of patriotism. These actions generally sufficed to arouse significant public indignation which in turn coerced the recalcitrant. When public opinion failed, the American Protective League, a vigilante group tolerated by the United States Department of Justice, badgered the supposed deviants.

The case of Herbert Bigelow serves as an example. Bigelow opposed American entrance into the war and after involvement stood against conscription. Early in October 1917, with Bigelow attending an anti-draft convention in Chicago, the American Protective League raided his Cincinnati office in the People's Church. They uncovered a petition proposing an old age pension, but no antiwar material. Still, the Cincinnati press characterized Bigelow as a traitor, and the superpatriots waited for an opportunity to punish him. President Wilson had asked clergymen throughout the country to pray for victory on October 28, 1917, but Bigelow led his congregation in a prayer for peace. Afterwards he planned to attend a socialist meeting in Newport, Kentucky, but while entering the hall was kidnapped and spirited into the northern Kentucky backwoods. There, "In the name of the women and children in Belgium," he was beaten and left to find his way out. When the episode became known, President Wilson characterized the terrorism as a "manifestation of the spirit of lawlessness" while Secretary of War Baker condemned the act and declared "no rebuke is too strong nor any punishment too swift for those who mock our Republic."

However, Mayor George Puchta of Cincinnati noted, "If a man misbehaves he gets what's coming to him." Governor Cox expressed concern and asked the United States Department of Justice to investigate. A young investigator, J. Edgar Hoover, reported to Cox that since the incident occurred in Kentucky, Ohio could do nothing.[24]

By June 1917, the American Protective League had local units in over 600 cities and towns and claimed more than 100,000 members recruited from various commercial, service, and church organizations. Generally composed of upwardly mobile, middle-class citizens, the Ohio League's activity centered in Cleveland, Cincinnati, and Dayton—cities with large ethnic German and socialist populations. The Cleveland group, at its peak claiming more than 1500 members, rooted out pro-German sympathizers, made loyalty investigations and harassed the general population about adherence to food, fuel, light, and gas regulations. According to Emerson Hough, the official historian of the League, the gathering of evidence and helping with the arrest of Eugene Debs represented the crowning achievement of the Cleveland "Web."

Extensively involved in the same activity as their cohorts to the north, the Cincinnati branch infiltrated socialist clubs and boasted having made over 14,000 "visits" to the homes and places of business of "alien enemies." These activities led to the requirement that twenty-eight aliens report to League "supervisors" on a weekly basis. The Dayton branch boasted of similar activities. They also claimed to have made 269 "persuasions" during the Liberty Loan drives. With less activity, the work of the League followed similar lines in other Ohio cities. To carry out its work the League received financial support from local defense councils, which in turn raised funds through the Victory Chest and Red Cross Drives.[25]

Concerned that numerous areas of the country had not achieved a war footing, the Council of National Defense in the fall of 1917, asked every state to organize county and community defense councils. This request flew in the face of existing realities in Ohio, since Cox had organized the state according to regions and functions. Recognizing that counties represented political subdivisions that did not necessarily reflect functional geographical systems, Cox and his war cabinet refused to alter their organizational scheme. This failure to comply with the Council of National Defense precipitated a conflict with Washington officials. In March 1918, Fred Croxton attended a national conference of state council officials and heard charges that Ohio had failed to organize fully. Returning from Washington, Croxton pressed Cox to establish a program for county organization. Reluctantly, the governor consented. Pleased to learn of the decision to organize "community councils" President Wilson wrote Cox that "by extending your organization to small communities . . . every citizen of the nation can be touched with the inspiration of common cause." Wilson explained further that the process represented a "fusion of energies, now too much scattered and at times somewhat confused, into one harmonious and effective power."[26]

Chagrined by the assertion that Ohio had not organized, Cox and the War Council reviewed their accomplishments a week after receiving Wilson's letter. Presiding at the meeting, the governor recommended a "uniform policy" of county organization that would eliminate overlapping work and promote efficiency. Without legal existence, the Council had a difficult time deciding upon a formula for organizing the counties. A proposal by Cox to establish a six-member County Council Section, to give organizational advice and to promote co-ordination of activities between rural and urban areas, fell short of the mark. After discussion, Cox appointed a committee to devise a method for county organization. A month later, in a meeting with the heads of various Ohio war projects, Cox insisted that the state have nothing to do with organizing the county councils. Instead, he planned to issue a general proclamation asking the counties to organize along the lines recommended by a Committee on County and Community Councils. This, Cox explained, would "avoid the criticism that the governor would boss the organization," while preserving the role of the sate council as a planning and co-ordinating agency. Pressure from Washington must have been great, for on June 17, 1918 Cox issued a proclamation directing all counties to organize county councils of defense and urged extending to the federal agencies in the counties a "co-operative" rather than a "subordinate" role in their activities. The final aspect of federal dominance of the war effort in Ohio was now operation.[27]

The guidelines set up by the new Division of County and Community Organization demonstrated Cox's belief in the necessity of working through community power structures. People already engaged in war activities formed the nucleus of the new county councils, and new members came from "important groups." A county council of twelve people (none was to exceed fifty) could act on all matters. Where large councils were desired, the mayors and county commissioners chose representatives from each township, town, and city in the county and recruited leading citizens from the Chamber of Commerce, labor, capital, farmers, Protestants, Catholics, political parties, and "any other interest group of importance." At the end of the war, Ohio had sixty-one county organizations only "satisfactorily organized" because Cox failed to support the efforts.[28]

The only available case study of an Ohio local council demonstrates the interaction that resulted from Cox's organizational approach between pluralistic organizations and the state. In Cleveland, Mayor Harry Davis had created the Mayor's War Board "for the purpose of taking care of any extraordinary matters which might arise during the period of the war." The board served as an umbrella organization by appointing numerous quasi-legal regulatory organizations and "possessed the power to encourage work which it deemed wise by liberal appropriations, and to repress others not considered wise or soundly organized by withholding endorsement or subsidies . . . ."

Taking charge of the Liberty Loan and Savings Stamp drives as well as the Victory Chest drive which financed its activities, the Board extended varying degrees of support to over sixty organizations. Among the most active operations was the Chamber of Commerce Committee on Military Affairs which became the Mayor's Committee on War Activity. It "represented the community in a general oversight of the interest of soldiers and sailors . . . ." The committee helped enforce conscription, took charge of military parades, drilled men briefly before induction into the service, and provided military escort at soldiers' funerals. The Military Training Camp Association, part of a national association founded at the outset of the war, recruited men for training as officers until the draft began to provide an adequate supply of officer material. The association then helped the War Department recruit men for special services like the motor, aviation, and tank corps. The Committee on Housing and Sanitation found housing for workers and served as a rental adjustment board. Initially it also existed as a Chamber of Commerce committee. Americanization and patriotism committees were created to solidify public opinion behind the war effort and "strengthen the morale of the community." The local Red Cross and numerous church related organizations cooperated with the United States Commission on Training Camp Activities to provide for the physical and spiritual needs of troops while on leave. The 1500 member

Cleveland branch of the American Protective League was also financed by the Mayor's War Board. The District Manufacturers Committee, initially the War Industries Board of the Cleveland Chamber of Commerce, advertised government manufacturing needs and worked to enlarge Cleveland industry.

The Cleveland Chamber of Commerce represented the nexus of power in the local war effort. The historian of Cleveland's wartime activities observed that from the Mayor's War Board and the Chamber of Commerce "sprang many committees of business and professional men, often closely related and even identical in personnel and function, to meet the exigencies as the directors saw them." The business community set the values used to rally the people to mobilization. With local councils serving as the mobilizing force throughout the state, similar patterns emerged, although not necessarily through the Chamber of Commerce, in the other Ohio cities. Ideologically, the reliance upon local councils represented an awareness of Jeffersonian principles, but functionally the procedure was a use of political, organizational, and spatial realities in order to promote efficient mobilization along regional lines on a statewide basis. The official state report on wartime activities concluded that Cox's war council program had best been carried out in "groups of counties which were most densely populated." Estimating that it effectively reached 90 percent of the population, the Ohio Branch, Council of National Defense claimed to have successfully mobilized the state in spite of its tardy and incomplete county organization.[29]

As war governor, Cox relied upon his war cabinet as an advisory and planning organization in those activities considered essential to efficient mobilization. Labor utilization, food production and conservation, publicity, and transportation were all centrally planned and directed by the war council. With great faith in public opinion as reflected by local organization, Cox preferred to let local councils determine policies wherever they proved effective. But programs necessitating interaction between town and country, such as food, labor, transportation, fuel, and publicity, were regionally organized. Thus, Cox failed to organize Ohio along county lines, but instead organized on a metropolitan regional basis. A structure which reflected functional realities. At the end of 1918, James M. Cox declared the work of the Ohio Branch, Council of National Defense, completed. Disbanding the council, the governor explained that with the end of the war the main purpose for its existence had disappeared, but pointed out that some of the council's work would continue in permanent agencies of the state government. In particular, Cox hoped to retain the Americanization effort and a demobilization - adjustment program for returning soldiers to civilian life, both of which the federal government had not assumed during the war. Reflecting upon the work of the council, Cox felt that one lasting contribution was the "awakening of interest and responsibility in human welfare and the achievement of public good by organized effort." He might have added, and directed from above.[30]

In placing Ohio on a war footing, Cox had strengthened the ties between the leadership of Ohio's various groups and the state government for the sake of efficiency. If efficiency represents a key to understanding the progressives, then Ohio progressivism did not die or even slacken during the war. The efficiency movement simply continued with the government and the established powers of state, region, or community efficiently mobilizing the economy, culture, and social life for war. Probably the best sociological study of the impact of war on society points out that the survival of ruling groups depends upon their ability to convince the people that they are fighting for themselves. In Ohio, this meant appealing to the prevailing patriotic attitudes and beliefs of the people who for the most part resided in the metropolitan areas. Similarly, it was in the urban areas that the deviants from the mainstream resided, that is, the immigrants, socialists, ethnic Germans, blacks, and unemployed. Perceived as deviants, these people in some way posed a threat, real or imagined, to the established order and its archetypical view of America. Hence, community power structures with the sanction and help of Governor Cox sought to create "100 percent Americanism" through maximum military participation. When the war ended, the significance of its military, economic, political, and intellectual impact confronted the nation. Cox realized there was no turning back. Perhaps his perception was too limited, but it is doubtful that societies can turn back, and the postwar years seem to bear this out.[31]

IX
THE EMERGENCE OF A PROGRESSIVE PRESIDENTIAL CANDIDATE

When Ohio, the state of Presidents, chose James M. Cox for a third gubernatorial term in 1918, he automatically emerged as Democratic presidential material. Unchallenged in the primary, Cox had run on his war record, announcing "the duties of the hour are more important than my reelection in November, and I cannot in conscience . . . leave my desk to make a campaign." In a primary devoid of issues, the Democrats emphasized the importance of winning the war.[1]

The GOP nominated ex-governor Frank Willis and in contrast to the Democrats subordinated the war to prohibition and women's suffrage in their platform. With a strong pro-German image, the Republican nominee hoped to capitalize on the large Ohio German vote. Prior to American wartime involvement, Willis as governor had openly opposed the sale of arms to England and France and had discreetly neglected to condemn the sinking of the *Lusitania*. In addition, he had committed the indiscretion of writing several pro-German letters which his opponents exploited fully in the press. Although Willis received the backing of the Anti-Saloon League and the Prohibition Party, he soon came into conflict with leading Republicans who refused to support him. The Ohio Manufacturers Association endorsed Cox, and many traditional contributors to Republican coffers lined the campaign chests of GOP congressional candidates, but ignored Willis. Despite a period of Republican ascendancy, the questions surrounding Willis' patriotism caused his campaign to languish.[2]

Ignoring his own plea for an adjournment of politics, Cox vigorously promoted the war cause before enthusiastic crowds. Simultaneously, the state Democratic Party mounted an extensive newspaper and billboard campaign calling attention to the patriotism and efficient war record of the incumbent. This statesmanlike posture helped Cox win the support of the Patriotic League of Ohio and business groups, as well as the continued backing of the Ohio Federation of Labor. Cox's generally "wet image," carefully cultivated in this campaign, won him the approval of the liquor interests and perhaps even some of the German vote. With such varied support and a well organized state party, Cox could afford to adhere to his pledge not to campaign formally. In the process he denied Willis the audience provided by debate.[3]

Throughout the nation, 1918 emerged as a Republican year and Ohio proved no different except for the reelection of Cox. The Ohio GOP elected fourteen of the twenty-two congressmen, twenty-one of the thirty-three senators, and seventy-seven of the one hundred and twenty-four representatives. With a slim majority of 10,944 votes, Cox saw the result as another personal victory. Aware of the effect of ticket splitting on his success, he analyzed the outcome as

> . . . a tribute to service rendered that mere words cannot phrase. Political lines were forgotten in the state contest and toilers and businessmen joined in a common concept of what the suffrage obligation was.

Carrying only twenty-nine of eighty-eight counties, Cox's margin of victory again came from the six most heavily urbanized regions—Cuyahoga, Hamilton, Franklin, Montgomery, Lucas, and Butler counties. With the exception of Franklin County, these districts also opposed by wide margins a state prohibition amendment which carried by 26,000 votes. With support for the war and opposition to prohibition high in Ohio urban centers, Cox successfully reflected the pressing concerns of the people in the cities to secure his reelection.[4]

World War I ended abruptly after the election and in his third term, Cox developed a program designed to cope with postwar problems. Emphasizing efficient management and giving priority to issues with a distinctly urban coloration, the governor told the Republican-dominated legislature that financial relief for the cities stood as the most pressing need. He called attention to situations in Cleveland and Cincinnati that demonstrated the broad dimensions of the urban crisis. Explaining that these cities would lose $900,000 and $600,000 respectively in liquor revenues, he pointed out that Cleveland alone would be forced to operate with a $1.7 million deficit. The two largest cities of Ohio had cut their service and improvements expenditures to a bare minimum, and Cox predicted that the situation could only deteriorate as costs spiraled and as more people came into the urban areas. Public safety in the cities stood imperiled as old improvements fell into disrepair and public servants became disgruntled. The governor pointed to the Cincinnati police strike which resulted from the inflation and financial squeeze in the Queen City. In addition to rising costs and needed improvements, the reform governor called attention to the ever increasing city indebtedness resulting from the 1 percent tax ceiling that middle-class and rural Ohioans had imposed. He urged the legislature to provide new revenue sources for the cities, but, instead of burdening property owners with higher taxes, Cox suggested a city income tax, a graduated automobile license tax, and an inheritance tax as possible alternatives.[5]

Following the model advanced by the National Tax Association, the General Assembly did establish a state inheritance tax that classified heirs and graduated rates. Dividing receipts equally between the local municipality and the state, the law provided new urban revenues but continued the tax drain from the large cities by expanding the tax base of the emerging suburbs as the affluent moved to the urban fringe. In addition, the Republican dominated legislature refused to approve the administration's Hopple bill which was designed to eliminate existing city indebtedness through five year bonds to paid off with an income tax. Cox conceived this measure to avoid tampering with the Smith Law. Rather than consolidate the debts, the legislators approved a series of emergency tax laws, over the governor's veto, that permitted cities to levy property taxes outside the legal limitations if the money was used to pay sinking fund charges and interest rates.[6]

Financial difficulties also afflicted the school districts of the cities and the growing suburbs. As in other governmental subdivisions inflation created increased costs for the maintenance of existing facilities and services. Simultaneously, population growth produced demands for more teachers and facilities. Cox gave the school crisis an added dimension. Urging financial relief, he emphasized the need to continue the Americanization programs through the schools to eradicate many social problems in the cities. Asking for "new sources" of revenue, Cox was partially rebuffed. Instead, the legislature approved the School Relief Bill, an emergency measure which permitted county school districts to add three mills to the school property tax without voter consent and an additional three mills with voter approval. Continuing the trend toward efficiency the bill eliminated state aid to weak school districts as a lever to promote consolidation.⁷ Cox ultimately gave his approval.

Cox continued to believe that the state universities had an important role to play in solving the social problems growing out of urban industrial change. Forseeing a great influx of students to Ohio State University during the postwar years, Cox petitioned the legislature to build dormitories for women. This seemed logical since the barracks built to house pilot trainees during the war would now be used for male student housing. Columbus was becoming a large city and Cox reasoned that university controlled housing would shelter the students from the "evils" of the city while insuring a "healthy" college experience. Inherent in this proposal was help in alleviating the housing shortage experienced in the expanding capital city.

Not only would Cox have the state protect young people from the evils of the city, he also viewed Wilberforce University, the African Methodist-Episcopalian university, as having the potential to help slow the process of black migration into Ohio cities. Noting that blacks had served the war effort valiantly, the governor urged the legislature to allocate funds to buy agricultural lands to model Wilberforce after Tuskegee Institute. Cox explained that:

> Practically all the colored population in Ohio is resident in the cities. No part . . . has drifted toward the countryside where labor conditions have at times become more or less acute. Out of this situation comes the proposal of an agricultural course, based upon the physical facilities accruing from additional land.

Agreeing with the objectives of these proposals, the legislature financed the dormitories and authorized the governor to appoint a committee to investigate conditions at Wilberforce.⁸

During the last quarter of 1918, the nation experienced a severe influenza epidemic which focused attention on the glaring weakness of health facilities throughout the country. Pointing out that Ohio had more than two thousand health jurisdiction, Cox claimed that fewer than twenty met local needs and that only—five Cleveland, Cincinnati, Akron, Dayton, and Springfield—had full time health officers. Declaring that political institutions must keep up with scientific advances, Cox, once again as after the Miami Valley flood of 1913, called for the creation of a new political entity—the regional health district. For management purposes, he explained that areas adjacent to cities should be brought into a single public health unit and that predominantly rural county units should be consolidated. He insisted that every urban district should be forced to have full time officials. The legislature agreed and approved the Hughes Health Code. Placed under the jurisdiction of the State Department of Health, the new districts and health officials were brought under civil service regulations. Passing costs down to the local level, the Hughes Health Code met with resistance, and the legislature pulled away from the law and revised the code before it adjourned. The new version did away with the requirement of full time officials and eliminated the civil service provision, thereby gutting the nascent law.⁹

The idea that a relationship existed between the foreign-born population and the problems of Ohio persisted and intensified in the postwar years. Now wartime xenophobia took on a different coloration. As part of his postwar program, Cox told the legislators "the statute books must be purged . . . . Every germ of Prussian poison must be squeezed out of the organic law of Ohio." He urged the General Assembly to ask Congress, by a joint resolution, to permit people detained in government camps to exercise their right of appeal and then have them deported! The Ohio solons responded with a bevy of loyalty laws, including an anti-German language law and a criminal syndicalism statute.

To extend the concept of orderly Americanization, Cox played a central role in creating the anti-German language law which prohibited teaching and using German in Ohio elementary schools. Disturbed that the Comings bill, when it came out of committee, failed to include private schools, Cox in a special message to the legislature, described the bill as "artful, insidious and apparently deliberate in its attempt to deceive the people of the state." Explaining that he proposed the bill because "the teaching of German to young people was a menace to the ideals of the republic yet it protects only those children in public schools," Cox noted that the bill as it stood "would leave places of refuge for breeding treason." Unwilling to face the wrath of German Catholics, the legislature continued to avoid the question.

Five weeks later, Cox sent another message charging that the teaching of German stood as a barrier to Americanization and "was part of a conspiracy formed long ago by the German government in Berlin." With a detailed compilation of statements taken out of context from German language publications, histories of Germany, nationalistic German songs, statements by German-American organization leaders, and wartime charges, Cox relentlessly depicted a German conspiracy against the United States. He insisted that his version of German language restrictions become reality. Convinced of internal threats to the nation, the governor called for legislation requiring teachers to sign a loyalty oath to protect "our children from the wolf in sheep's clothing." With increased pressure from the governor and the heightening of xenophobia throughout the nation, the Ohio General Assembly approved the anti-German language law suggested by Cox, and made teacher loyalty oaths mandatory.

Set on a cultural revitalization course, the Assembly established a committee to investigate German propaganda, created a state Americanization Department, forbade the publication of official election results in German language newspapers, and required all Ohio schools to teach American government and citizenship in the seventh and eighth grades.[10]

As the postwar economy began to slow and inflation continued to mount, labor unrest increased. Law and order developed as an issue and the question of whether Ohio should establish a state police force emerged. The main impetus to create the force came from the Ohio Grange and the Ohio Manufacturers Association, while the principal opposition came from labor leaders who cited the Pennsylvania experience and characterized the Pennsylvania State Police as "American Cossacks."

Opposed to a state police, Cox tactfully avoided the issue in his address to the General Assembly by pointing out that the 1916 National Defense Act permitted the reestablishment of the National Guard. Favoring this course, the governor explained that this would give Ohio the cost of a separate police force. Nothing came of the constabulary bill, but pressure for a state police force persisted as Ohio industries were plagued with strikes that sometimes erupted in violence, and the nation became engrossed in the "red scare."[11]

Responding to the economic and social unrest, the Ohio legislature unanimously joined eighteen other states in passing a criminal syndicalism law. Although not openly supporting the law, Cox generously sprinkled his address to the General Assembly with references to the Bolshevik revolution and the threat of disorder at home. This supposed threat was advanced as the prime reason for the law. Patterned after the California statute, the Ohio law defined criminal syndicalism as "the doctrine which advocates crime, sabotage, . . . violence, or unlawful methods of terrorism as a means of accomplishing industrial or political reform." A felony conviction resulted in a fine up to $5,000 or imprisonment for up to ten years or both.[12]

As in the other states, the labor unrest continued in Ohio in spite of the syndicalism statute. Ohio accounted for 15 percent of the nation's 3,630 strikes in 1919. Cox nevertheless felt secure in his position that no need existed for state police action to keep industrial peace.

During the nationwide steel strike in the fall of 1919, business leaders throughout Ohio urged state officials to act forcefully to control the strikers. Calling a conference of Ohio mayors and sheriffs, Cox insisted that local authorities keep order, particularly in those cities with large numbers of "alien residents." At the mass meeting, the governor recognized the problems presented by language differences, and alien legal concepts, but maintained "that the individual conscience tells every man that violence is both a moral and legal wrong." Refusing openly to help industrialists transport strikebreakers in and out of plants, Cox, however, insisted that picketing "go no further than moral persuasion." To preserve order among the workers, he instructed:

> All officers must act with care. It will be found that trouble can often be avoided by an open, frank and firm contact of public officers with both the representatives and employers. No call that I have ever made on either side of these controversies has ever gone unheeded. We are in the midst of unprecedented conditions, but if we devote ourselves to the single thought of making government the agency of justice and the instrument of bringing swift punishment to those who violate the laws of this commonwealth, we will pass through the storm safely. No man must be permitted to define the rules of his individual conduct. The law is supreme. When they have rendered their utmost effort and failed to meet conditions, then the state will act promptly.[13]

Industrial violence continued in the Canton steel industry and Cox demonstrated his determination to restore calm without direct state intervention. A week after the meeting with the Ohio mayors, officials of the Canton Alloy Steel Company and the Canton Retail Merchants Association demanded state help to keep peace between "foregin-born" workers and strikebreakers. On October 26, the governor's office replied that Cox would not "be stampeded into action in the matter of ordering the state troops into Canton." Discerning that the Mayor of Canton refused to mount a sufficient police force to control the strike situation, after meeting with the Mayor and fifteen leading Canton businessmen, Cox suspended the Mayor. Immediately he ordered the Vice-Mayor to assume executive duties and insisted more local police officers be added to restore calm. Several days later, with these steps taken, officials from the Ohio Industrial Commission and the State Board of Mediation reported that peace prevailed and that the mill guards were restricted to company property. Two days later, with strikebreakers through the picket lines, Cox was satisfied that order had returned. He left Ohio to campaign for the Democrats in Kentucky.[14]

Another area where social control gained added impetus after the war was prohibition. Ohio had long been a center of dry activity. Organized in Ohio in 1894, the Anti-Saloon League emerged as a political pressure group to elect dry officials. Quickly, the "Ohio Idea" caught on throughout the country and the liquor question became an important issue in state politics. In 1913, the League lobbied the Webb-Kenyon Act through Congress. The

Act forbade the transportation of intoxicating beverages into dry areas. By 1919, the League had successfully advanced restrictive legislation in twenty-six states.

National restrictions on the use of alcoholic beverages first appeared in 1917 in the Food Control Law, which as a rationing measure prohibited the manufacture of whiskey. When the war ended, the Anti-Saloon League continued lobbying for national prohibition and in December 1918, Congress sent the prohibition amendment to the states for ratification.[16]

Cox had tried to walk delicately between the wet and dry interests. But by 1918, as thinking polarized on the liquor question, the Daytonian was forced to side with the wets. Recognizing that the questions surrounding the control of drinking were cultural, and that opposition to drinking was rooted in urban middle-class reactions to the changes wrought by industrialization as well as rural antipathy to urban dominance, he defined the issue as one of law and order. The unregulated saloon was seen as a symbol of corruption, a source of poverty, and a detriment to industrial efficiency. With the insight that time provides, Cox later wrote that

> If liquor laws on the statute books of the states had been properly enforced, doubtless there would have been no prohibition amendment to the federal constitution.

"The [Ohio licensing] law," he explained,

> ... worked very well and undesirable persons were denied licenses. Enforcement matched the letter of the law. Certain elements were shocked when the saloons were closed tighter than a drum on Sundays, but I had many letters at that time from wives and mothers who approved the new order. Too many of them to be counted expressed their satisfaction, substantially in the words of one communication . . . . "things are different in our house. Time was when there was hardly such a thing as the Sabbath. My husband went to the saloon in the morning, came back in due time filled with liquor, pretzels, liver and onions, and our whole day was spoiled."

But when prohibition replaced temperance and regulation, Cox personally could not be pushed beyond control by regulation. He pledged himself to uphold state and national laws.[17]

These law and order positions won Cox widespread recognition, but it was his concern for the postwar economy that placed him squarely in the national limelight. With the Wilson administration lacking any plan for demobilization and conversion to a peacetime economy, fears of massive unemployment began to mount. Concerned but optimistic, Cox told Ohioans that

> Our industrial status has become disjointed . . . . A great opportunity is at hand. The warehouses are empty—the shelves of the merchant, so far as peace essentials are concerned, are quite bare. Part of the world is to be rebuilt. The great momentum in ship building is to go on and the genius and industry of labor, combined with the wealth of our natural resources, should guarantee a golden age for America.

Faith and confidence, however, are very necessary elements. Suspended effort, in the hopes that wages and prices will lapse to the standards prevailing before the war would be dangerous. The far-seeing manufacturer recognizes that labor is to participate more in profits than it once did and accounts are to be balanced first by recognizing the fundamentals of justice and reducing the overhead expenses by more scientific methods.

> . . . Let us all, therefore, join together in this state—let governmental agencies cast doubt to the winds and build the essentials for tomorrow. Let the banks recognize the importance of their cooperation and let public opinion be the prescription for fanatical agitation on the one hand and despairing skepticism and close fisted industrial justice on the other, then there need be no fears as to the future.[18]

In this spirit the governor asked for continued funding of road construction to match federal grants in aid provided by the Federal Highway Act of 1916. The road construction, Cox explained, would provide immediate jobs for thousands of demobilized troops while helping manufacturers and farmers efficiently distribute their goods. Cox believed the latter benefit would lower the cost of living and enable Americans to compete more readily on the European market. When finally approved, the Busby-Fouts Highway Act provided over $20 million in state and federal funds to be spent in three years. In addition, the highway program made the maintenance of improved highways mandatory and extended the main market road idea to every county.[19]

By early March 1919, Cox's efforts to provide immediate work amounted to $41 million worth of public programs and furnished jobs for 25,000 men. Yet, these efforts fell short of the needs. At the end of January, Fred Croxton told a conference of mayors and county commissioners that the state had 150,000 men and 20,000 women out of work. Cleveland alone had some 50,000 people unemployed. To meet the situation, Cox called upon prominent businessmen urging them to put money in the economy and encourage local officials to call local conferences with regional business interests. The governor also prodded local governments to begin public improvement programs and promised to release Ohio funds for state projects as soon as possible. Giving top priority to veterans, the Ohio Labor Exchange processed applicants for the bulk of these jobs. Through residence requirements of one year in the state and six months in the municipality, the registration procedures discriminated against blacks and other recent arrivals.[20]

Despite these efforts at least 150,000 Ohio workers were unemployed as the President's Conference on Unemployment and Reconstruction opened at the White House. Representatives from one hundred and five cities and forty-three states attended. Undoubtedly, Cox saw an opportunity in the meeting to tie the postwar economic situation to his personal ambitions. Just four days before President Wilson told a meeting of Democratic National Committeemen that he would not violate the two term tradition.[21]

If any delegates came to the conference expecting help from the administration, their hopes soon were dampened. Opening the conference with a brief address, Wilson told the mayors and governors that

> The primary duty of caring for our people in the intimate matters that we want to discuss here, of course, falls on the states and upon the municipalities, and the function of the federal government . . . [is to] draw the executive minds of the country together . . . [to exchange ideas].

On the following day, Wilson left on his second trip to Europe.

Almost unnoticed by the press, Cox openly disagreed with the President and criticized the federal government for not doing enough to solve economic problems. He urged the

Department of Commerce to investigate inflated prices in the building industry and to publish a fair price guide. To stimulate the economy, he pleaded for government rehabilitation of the railroads because "the railroads and related industries buy approximately 30 percent of all the industrial necessities of the country." Cox went on:

> We should all become bulls in the future of America, and whether the railroads are turned back this year or five years from now, what the government shall have expended now will, of course, be reimbursed to the fullest extent.

Programs such as these, said Cox, represented the middle ground between those who wanted wages to fall to prewar levels through a depression and those who wanted the government to serve as the employer of last resort. Viewing the latter as wasteful, Cox believed the former path would "guarantee a regime of bolshevism in America." Other spokesmen took similar positions, including Mayor John Hylan of New York City, Mayor Charles Jewell of Indianapolis, and George Foster Peabody, who represented New York Governor Al Smith. [22]

The conference closed on a note of controversy with Cox directly involved. When Mayor James Rolph, a Republican from San Francisco, proposed a petition to Woodrow Wilson to reconvene Congress to establish federal make-work legislation and machinery for collective bargaining, Cox as Chairman of the Resolutions Committee refused to consider the measure on the grounds that it was "partisan." Instead, the Resolutions Committee proposed, and the delegates approved, statements that urged railroad improvements to stimulate the economy, criticized the dissolution of the federal wartime employment agencies, approved wage reductions only if matched by reductions in the cost of living, and asked that governmental wartime restrictions on industry be removed.

Although the conference accomplished little, Cox had strengthened his political position among the urban leadership in the Democratic Party. The propositions approved by the delegates bore a striking resemblance to the program suggested by Governor Cox. Openly critical of President Wilson as many eastern Democrats were, Cox opposed Mayor Rolph rather than become involved in a direct confrontation with the President and pro-Wilson congressmen. By offering a postwar economic program and identifying himself with the forces of law and order, Cox emerged as a national figure. Convinced of the need for government to cooperate with business, much as business had cooperated with government during the war, his point of view reflected an urban business perspective.[23]

In spite of the rising unemployment, the economy continued to boom, and by March 1919, had surpassed the wartime peak. Inflation haunted urban leaders. During the President's Conference, Mayor Hylan had accused meat packers and coal producers of profiteering and asked the Justice Department to prosecute. In July, Cox launched an attack on spiraling costs. Believing that the problem resulted from artificial restrictions in supply, he asked the federal government to market its wheat surpluses. A few days later, A. Mitchell Palmer suggested that the sale of government food holdings would decrease the cost of living and simultaneously alleviate much of the labor and racial unrest in the cities. To control prices in the food industry, at the end of August, Cox instructed the Ohio Attorney General to begin prosecuting violators of the state Cold Storage Law which limited the length of time meat could be stored.[24]

By autumn, wages for coal miners emerged as a major problem. The soaring cost of living and wage gains of other industries provoked the United Mine Workers to seek a contract adjustment before November 1, 1919, in spite of a standing agreement with the United States Fuel Administration not to strike before April 1, 1920. As rumors of impending coal shortages developed, Secretary of Labor William B. Wilson brought the miners and operators to the conference table, but the talks soon broke down when the owners insisted upon limiting discussion to a small wage increase. The mine workers, in violation of a federal restraining injunction, walked off their jobs on November 1. The strike lasted until December 10; in the interim, coal prices skyrocketed, public utility companies cut back services, and schools and factories closed. To avert the crisis in Ohio, Cox had earlier requested the Fuel Administration to permit the state to fix coal prices, but federal authorities rejected the idea. When the strike came, Cox succeeded in bringing the Ohio Mine Workers and owners to the conference table to discuss an 18 to 25 percent wage increase, and established an arbitration commission to investigate other grievances. A month after the strike ended, John Moore, President of the Ohio Mine Workers, told the International United Mine Workers convention that Cox's action in Ohio had compelled the President to reopen talks with the miners.[25]

The theme of collective bargaining was crucial to Cox's program for postwar America, but it was part of a larger design to deal systematically with the quality of life in the cities, and hence the nation. During the peak of the labor unrest, Cox's newspaper voice characterized Americanization as the best means to eliminate urban unrest. When the ethnic populations became educated in American ideals, the *News* editorialized, they would earn higher wages, gain better working conditions, and become a useful part of the nation. Two weeks later, Cox told the Ohio Building Association convention that the threat of a Soviet regime and the failure of industrialists to cooperate with Americanization and to pay cost of living wages, ranked among the key problems confronting America. The revolutionaries should be deported and industry should be compelled "to pay more attention to Americanization" Cox insisted. The governor assured the International United Mine Workers that collective bargaining and Americanization would resolve the unrest permeating the nation. Cognizant of the continued impact of migration into the cities, Cox told the Community Millers Association of America that bringing rural living conditions up to urban standards would alleviate congestion in the urban centers. To help solve the postwar housing crisis, Cox, along with Governor Al Smith of New York, called for rent controls. Though his various proposals were feeble and had little impact, Cox emerged as the most prominent national Democrat of 1920 who conceived the problems confronting the nation from an urban perspective.[26] Americanization, collective bargaining, government intervention, and law and order, all represented systematic efforts to deal with the complex problems of an urbanized society.

Cox continued to stress the need for efficient management of governmental funds. The Ohio budget system, he told the Scripps-McRae newspapers, put government on a business footing. After six years of operation, he applauded the success of the system but recommended the legislature be prohibited from enacting programs unless they provided the essential revenue. In a prepared statement for the national Budget Committee, he urged Congress to adopt the Ohio system, with proposed reforms, as its model. This approach, Cox explained, fixed responsibility for action as well as inaction. Recalling his experience as a member of the House Committee on Appropriations, the governor charged that Congress failed to adopt a more efficient system in the past simply because "congressional committees vested with the powers of appropriating money have been unwilling to surrender them." The budget system, Cox believed, would bring business efficiency to the executive branch of the federal government.[27]

Viewing postwar America from the perspective of an urban businessman, Cox looked at foreign policy from the same vantage point. Reasoning that United States foreign policy should promote American pre-eminence in commerce, his thoughts in this area changed little over the years. As a young editor and publisher, he believed that lower tariffs would promote the interest of American industrial workers. Dayton industrialists, he had instructed in 1899, should exploit international markets. Critical of the Hague Peace Conference on treaty arbitration, in 1904 Cox asserted, "It is useless to talk about universal peace as long as great nations are holding weaker people in subjugation—while injustice and wrong is perpetrated by the strong against the weak. The only way for universal peace is to negotiate a pact of universal justice." Opposed to colonialism, on the floor of Congress Cox stood among the forces favoring a scientific tariff and reciprocal trade agreements to promote American business. As governor of Ohio, Cox gradually became sensitized to the movement for an international peace keeping agency. In June of 1914, he attended the Philadelphia conference creating the League to Enforce Peace, but out of office for the next two years he demonstrated scant interest in the organization. Reelected in 1916, and with the advent of World War I, Cox supported President Wilson, and the *Dayton Daily News* on numerous occasions called for a "peace without victory" and a League of Nations.[28]

During the 1918 political campaign, Cox saw support for the President as the principal issue but he seemed to misunderstand Wilson's vision for the postwar world. He wrote of the war a short time before the Armistice that

> . . . we are not contemplating a peace in the sense as it has been regarded in the past. Wars have been fought because of disputes over boundaries, domain or racial conflicts, and when the belligerents had fought themselves out, or one side or the other had met with complete defeat, the terms were written. This is not the case in the present war. Civilization will be called upon to consider a crime. The war didn't start because of a falling out of nations. It was a deliberate conspiracy. A brutal and bestial bully ran amuck in the world—violated the honor of nations and ignored the prohibitions which civilization has been two thousand years in establishing. The criminal will be at bay—the prisoner will be at the bar of justice, and he will have nothing to say about the sentence. Now that's precisely my view.

But several months later, as chairman of the Ohio League to Enforce Peace, Cox actively began mounting support for the League of Nations. Throughout the summer of 1919, the *Dayton Daily News* urged swift ratification of the Versailles Treaty and asserted of the controversial Article X that there "is nothing mysterious about it that would draw America into every continental brawl in Europe." Instead, Cox's newspaper claimed the League would "guarantee" peace and prosperity, and "promote security." Referring to business and the League, the *News* editorialized:

> There is not a single legitimate industry in this country that would not feel immediately the quickening impulse of a restoration of normal conditions on the other side of the Atlantic. Out trade with European countries is heavily reduced because of the ruinous rates of foreign exchange and these rates can not be stabilized. France and Italy can not get

their finances in order until financiers know what the future of Europe is to be. To us it means less foreign demand for our industrial and agricultural output, less profits out of which to maintain our higher wages which in turn leads to more labor troubles, with a greater number unemployed. In Europe it means much the same.[29]

Journeying to Washington to address the Jackson Day Dinner in January 1920, Cox consulted with Gilbert Hitchcock, the minority leader in the Senate. After two hours, Cox and Hitchcock, a moderate on the League agreed that the Democrats should take a strong position supporting Wilson and the treaty. In an address characterized by Oswald Garrison Villard as "ideally and satisfactorily boresome," Cox praised the conduct of the war and assured party leaders that he firmly supported Wilson and the treaty.

Returning to Ohio, Cox addressed the Duckworth Democratic Club in Cincinnati and won a standing ovation from the large Irish ethnic audience, when he promised, if elected, to "appoint Thomas R. Noctor the first Ambassador to the new Republic of Ireland." Discounting stories that the party had divided on the League, Cox noted "a unity of desire for peace" and said the League would guarantee "world peace and world prosperity." A few days later, the *Dayton Daily News* explained that Article X represented the "very heart of the treaty . . . if it is emasculated or amended so as to rob it of its sustaining and protecting influence, the League itself is nothing more than a collection of phrases, purposeless and impotent."[30]

The traditional debut for potential Democratic presidential candidates, the Washington Jackson Day Dinner, marked a turning point for Governor Cox. It openly signified his availability for the party nomination and represented his definition of the 1920 campaign issues. Committed to the two-party system, his speech emitted partisanship. In addition to defending Wilson with pot boiling rhetoric, Cox charged the "old guard" Republicans with seeking to "purchase the presidency" with a huge "slush fund." This Cox considered irresponsible, especially since the nation was badly divided between radicals and reactionaries. The Ohio reform governor reasoned that the Democratic Party must remain committed "to vigilant evolutionary progress" to forestall "revolution." He called for the restoration of confidence between capital and labor and noted, "if we are going to preserve America as a bastion of self-government and human rights," law and order remained essential. Portraying himself as a modern liberal, Cox placed himself between the forces of revolution and reaction.[31]

Though considered one of the frontrunners for the nomination, Cox maintained a low profile. Enroute from Washington, he commented:

> I have no delusion whatever and have never assumed to take seriously the mention of my name in connection with the presidency . . . [nevertheless] considering the responsibilities and the conditions how can anyone else take himself seriously in this connection.

Three weeks later, Cox formally entered the presidential sweepstakes. Reiterating his Washington address, the governor added a new dimension when he stated that the most pressing problem confronting the nation was the relationship between capital and labor. Adopting Republican slogans from the days of Mark Hanna, Cox promised "a full dinner pail." He declared of the President's conduct of the war, "We are proud of the fact that the American dollar is the only symbol of national value on earth now selling at a premium." Of the senate refusal to ratify the Versailles treaty, Cox contended that "the purpose of the whole fight primarily is to have the country reach the fall of 1920 with commercial affairs dismembered and to lay it all down at the door of the Democratic Party." Quickly momentum began to build. The American Federation of Labor announced formation of a political action committee and President Samuel Gompers stated that the A.F.of L. would actively campaign for those candidates who favored the cause of labor. Cox was assured of twenty-six Ohio convention votes when Senator Atlee Pomerene withdrew from the presidential race and Secretary of War Newton D. Baker declared of Cox that

> His effective administration as Governor and his splendid sympathy and cooperation with the national government during the war, virtually entitle him to the honor at the hands of Ohio.[32]

At the end of March, the "Cox For President" headquarters opened at Columbus with Ohio National Committeeman, Edmond H. Moore, as campaign chairman. In a prepared statement characterizing Cox as "a practical and a successful businessman, a natural leader, and a constructive progressive" Moore portrayed him as the logical choice. In addition, 1916 had demonstrated that Ohio represented a pivotal state essential for Democratic success. Cox could win Ohio. Describing Cox's affinity with labor, efficient fiscal management, crusade against the high cost of living, and progressivism which made government "effectual as well as orderly and efficient," Moore explained that the problems solved in Ohio were "similar to many that now confront the federal government." De-emphasizing foreign policy, the statement concluded

> We believe that the great domestic problem of the next four years will be to establish a new understanding and confidence between capital and labor. They must be brought together to gain for the country that which it is due; and to this end a leadership is demanded such as has been demonstrated in Ohio.[33]

X
WINNING THE NOMINATION

The choice of James M.Cox by the Democratic Convention at San Francisco reflected the determination of many Democratic leaders to select a standard bearer unaffiliated with the Wilson administration. The governor's selection also represented an effort by urban Democrats to assume control of the party. The move of Ohio and California into the Democratic ranks in 1916 was a harbinger of a new urban base in the party. Cox could win in Ohio, and his career in journalism and politics gave him a claim to national urban leadership. The postwar xenophobia grew out of problems experienced in the cities, and Cox had developed a program to deal with some of these issues. Consequently, he offered something besides availability to the Democratic leaders. Viewed from this perspective, the election of 1920 and the role played by Cox assumes new significance.[1]

By the spring, a host of personalities, including the incumbent but disabled Wilson, sought the 1920 Democratic mantle. The frontrunners included Attorney General A.Mitchel Palmer, the wartime railroad director William G. McAdoo, and Cox.

Palmer had catapulted himself into prominence during the economic and political unrest of 1919. Leading the dramatic "red hunts" against socialists and labor radicals had made the former Alien Properties Custodian the best known cabinet member. His anti-radical program offered the American people simple solutions to complex postwar problems. Palmer briefly tried to use the Department of Justice to combat inflation, but failed. The Pennsylvania Quaker skillfully used governmental ties and membership on the Democratic National Committee to enhance his position. Through discriminating distribution of patronage, the Attorney General claimed the loyalty of numerous lower echelon party stalwarts as well as the seventy-six Pennsylvania convention votes. Palmer was the national party professional and the favorite of the national committee.[2]

Linked to the New Freedom as the Secretary of the Treasury, to the war as the railroad director, and to Wilson in an awkward role as the son-in-law of the President, McAdoo symbolized the administration candidate. Reputedly the ablest Wilsonian administrator, his association with the Federal Reserve Act, the Federal Farm Loan Act, War Risk Insurance, high railroad wages, as well as efficient railroad management, represented political assets. The first choice among the Wilsonian establishment, the Georgia-born, Tennessee-bred lawyer reportedly had the financial backing of Bernard Baruch and Thomas L. Chadbourne for up to $10 million. His friends also included a number of second-line administration people and a few party professionals. Robert Woolley, George Creel, and Daniel Roper actively worked on his behalf, while Texas National Committeeman Tom Love became his campaign manager and assured McAdoo the Texas convention votes. Failing to seek delegates publicly, McAdoo appeared willing to accept the nomination if offered it. Working indirectly, he undercut the Palmer movement by promoting favorite son candidacies or supporting uninstructed delegations in states where the Attorney General sought delegates. Publicizing his position on major issues, he expressed concern over infringements of free speech, praised the farm loan program, called for middle-income tax reductions coupled with higher taxes on unearned incomes, and suggested a two-year moratorium on the payment of the war debt. As the convention neared, McAdoo had the support of the largest number of delegates.[3]

Both McAdoo and Palmer looked to Wilson for a signal of his intentions in 1920. In mid-February after conferring with Cary Grayson, the presidential physician, McAdoo withdrew his name from the Georgia primary. Again in June, just before Louis Seibold published a sensational article in the *New York World* which described Wilson as on the road to complete recovery, McAdoo five times tried to discuss convention plans with the President. Wilson refused to see him. After the Seibold article, McAdoo announced he would not allow his name to be placed before the convention. Wilson regretted that McAdoo's statement did not include a categorical refusal of the nomination.

Twice, before formally entering the nomination derby, Palmer tried to determine Wilson's position. He even hoped for a presidential endorsement. Pennsylvania National Committeeman Vance McCormick approached Wilson on behalf of Palmer, but Mrs. Wilson curtly told him that the President might feel obligated to run again. When Palmer sent word to Wilson that he planned to seek the nomination, but would defer if the President objected, Wilson replied that Palmer was free to do as he wished.[4]

On April 20, Wilson decided to run again, if necessary, to salvage the Versailles Treaty. Informing the cabinet, he said he could not

> . . . retreat from conscientious duty. I may not talk as well but I can still use the English language and if the people do not see the issue clearly, I will put it so plain they must see it.

Launching a public relations campaign to convince the public of his good health, Wilson began to preside at cabinet meetings on a regular basis, and now appeared in public for long periods without his physician. On April 26, officials at the White House announced that the President now tended fully to his duties. The four-hour interview granted to Louis Seibold of the *World* seems to have been part of the plan. The President developed a strategy to be available for the nomination if and when the convention deadlocked.[5]

After announcing his candidacy, Cox did not campaign vigorously. "My friends," he explained in May,

> . . . are urging me to open up a vigorous campaign. But I prefer to wait. If, when the convention opens, they finally turn to Ohio, all right. We either have an ace in the hole, or we haven't. If we have an ace concealed, we win; if we haven't, no amount of advertising can do much good.

An astute poker player, Cox had an ace. Early in May a group of Democratic leaders gathered at the French Lick Springs resort of the Indiana Democratic Party chairman and former mayor of Indianapolis, Tom Taggart, to discuss convention strategy. In addition to the host, the group included Charles Murphy of Tammany Hall, George Brennan, the newly recognized leader of the Illinois Democrats, Ohio National Committeeman Ed Moore, and leaders of the pro-Cox factions from Kentucky, New Jersey, and Pennsylvania. They represented 386 possible convention votes, more than enough under the two-thirds rule to keep any candidate from being nominated. This coalition stood determined to block the nomination of McAdoo, a dry southerner, and to prevent the convention from turning to Wilson. They rallied behind the candidacy of Governor Cox. The big city bosses believed that with Cox's position in favor of light wines and beer, or a redefinition of the Volstead Act, his candidacy would negate the need for a messy convention confrontation on the question of prohibition.[6]

In late June, the leadership of the New York and New Jersey delegations began a leisurely trip to the west coast and enroute refined strategy with Cox in Columbus, Taggart in Indianapolis, and Brennan in Chicago. After the Chicago meeting, Brennan told reporters that the withdrawal of McAdoo indicated President Wilson wanted a third term. Simultaneously, Murphy and his traveling companion, Governor Alfred E. Smith, announced that they were "interested" in the candidacy of Governor Cox.[7]

Other factors operated in favor of Cox. Since McAdoo and Palmer were determined to unite the Wilsonians behind their candidacy, they split the administration ranks and inadvertently helped the Cox effort. As long as they vied for the nomination, Cox, unaffiliated with the administration, represented the obvious alternate choice. With deadlock imminent, Ed Moore diligently cultivated second choice support. Recalling Moore's role, Cox wrote ". . . he was not disturbed because he knew that neither one (Palmer or McAdoo) could get the necessary two-thirds vote and that they would never join forces."[8]

Switching to Cox also meant turning to the Ohio progressive's program. Soon after the French Lick Springs strategy meeting, Cox prepared a lengthy policy statement on the pressing issues of the day for the *New York Times*. Continuing to tie foreign policy to commercial interests, he believed America should join the "international community" through the League of Nations to promote "stability in foreign commerce." Citing the loss of a traditional Italian market by remote Kentucky tobacco growers, Cox claimed that every American industry suffered in similar ways. The League, he explained, "with the cooperation of the five or six wealthiest nations," could provide the vehicle to stabilize the international foreign exchange system. The League "was far from perfect," but, "would put the loose ends of civilization together now and do more for the restoration of normal conditions in six months time than can the powers of the earth acting independently in ten years time." If elected he would place two restrictions upon United States entrance—the purpose of the League should continue to be maintenance of peace, and "the government of the United States must at all times act in strict harmony with the terms and intent of the United States Constitution which cannot in any way be altered by the treaty making power." Believing "territorial disputes and racial aspirations" among the leading causes of war, he reasoned that the League could best promote peace by emphasizing "self-determination of peoples."

Cox vowed continued efforts to end domestic turmoil. The solutions he offered bore the imprint of the Ohio experience. To prevent revolution and industrial unrest, he proposed a national Americanization program. He suggested federal pilot projects and surveys to establish a basis for cooperation between the states and national government to deal with urban tensions. "We need have no fear," Cox explained,

> . . . if we take the simple precaution to educate to our ideals the alien groups which they [the radicals] seek to mislead. Where Industrial controversies in the middle west were maintained by alien elements, we were enabled to observe the foreign-born, once he talks our language, reads our newspapers and comes into intelligent contact with the currents of our life . . . he rejects irresponsible leadership.

To handle labor disputes systematically, he proposed the creation of a permanent presidential commission, under the commerce clause, to report to the nation and the government, the facts surrounding strikes. This, Cox explained, would facilitate negotiations and arbitration if "public opinion" demanded it. Taking note of the new fundraising techniques of the Republicans, a quota system in metropolitan centers relying upon business contributions,

Cox charged the GOP sought to "establish a reactionary government which will force industrial peace."

Continuing to express his concern about population pressures in the cities, Cox suggested federal programs to improve the quality of rural life which would encourage people to stay on the farms. As part of this proposal, he urged federal aid for education in the outlying areas and a rural life survey to provide a blue print for further action to end the trek into the cities. To meet the increased revenue needs of the cities, Cox would reserve the inheritance tax for state and local governments.

In the realm of fiscal matters, the Dayton businessman urged a repeal of the excess profits tax. He offered instead a "1 to 1 1/2 percent tax on the volume of business of going concerns," in essence a value-added tax, and increased income taxes in the higher brackets. To control government spending, he called for the adoption of a federal budget system and a reduction in military expenditures. To stimulate the economy, Cox suggested the establishment of Federal Reserve Bank branches in major foreign ports.[9] Ambivalence on the prohibition issue, and identification with the big city leaders, soon led to the labeling of Cox as the wet candidate. William Jennings Bryan characterized his campaign as a "disgrace," observing that

> It is becoming everyday more and more apparent that he is the man about whose standard the wet forces will gather . . . . His nomination would make the Democratic party the leader of the lawless element of the country and his election . . . would turn the White House over to those who defy the government and hold law in contempt.

Wayne B. Wheeler of the Anti-Saloon League, similarly charged that "Cox was the last hope of the wets in their program of nullification."

As deliberations on the party platform opened in San Francisco, it became clear that Cox could not escape the polarization over the prohibition issue. To counteract the detrimental effects produced by both Wheeler's and Bryan's presence in the Bay City, former Ohio governor James E. Campbell issued a statement asserting that Cox did not believe the platform "was the proper place for treatment of the wet or dry issue." The question was one of law and order and Ohio's favorite son stood on his record for law enforcement. Taking the middle ground on the issue, this position was consistent with his record in Ohio politics.[10]

On the question of women's suffrage, Cox stood on firm ground. Any candidate in 1920 who had failed to support it earlier might have to face the consequences if the proposed nineteenth amendment went into effect before the election. Cox had been a proponent of extending the vote to women and the activist National Women's Party approved of his candidacy. Shortly after his election to a third term as governor, one Ohio suffragette reported that Cox had

> . . . been helpful in the suffrage campaign ever since he came into public life. His newspapers have been open to us and we have always had his support in everything we have asked . . . . Governor Cox was one of the principal forces in securing the passage of the presidential suffrage bill in Ohio.[11]

Broadly conceived, James Cox addressed most Americans in 1920 from the perspective of an urban businessman. Willing to promote efficiency in international affairs through the League, he would simultaneously use the League to advance American foreign policy objectives. Fearing both revolution and reaction, the former teacher had no qualms about taking the national bureaucracy into the uncharted area of Americanization to develop national loyalty through systematic use of propaganda. To promote industrial peace, the efficient administrator would bring industry and labor under the watchful eye of the government and force arbitration when desirable. To curb the growth of cities and alleviate urban tensions, he would extend the values of the city throughout the nation but stem the flow of population into the metropolis. In fiscal affairs, Cox advocated using the tax system to stimulate industrial growth by permitting businesses to pass new taxes on to the consumer, and would promote international commerce through an extension of the Federal Reserve System. With government cooperating with business, Cox would also bring business techniques to government through an executive budget system. As the convention opened his views were well known and Cox stood among the leading candidates.[12]

President Wilson had drawn up the model for the platform deliberations and the resolutions committee was stacked with Wilsonians. Aware the national convention would be an administration affair, the Cox coalition knew it could not set the tenor of the platform, but opposition did develop. The urban coalition and some Wilsonians wanted a condemnation of the Volstead Act and an Irish independence plank. William Jennings Bryan, on the other hand, proposed a strong dry statement and a resolution calling for ratification of the Versailles Treaty with any necessary reservations. The administrative people stood firm in support of Wilson's League and prohibition. However, the persistence of Massachusetts Senator David I. Walsh and the fear of appearing too rigid in defense of the President produced the additional phrase that the Democrats "do not oppose the acceptance of reservations making clearer or more specific the obligations of the United States to the League associates." By reenunciating the principle of self-determination of people as "one of the chief objectives for which this country entered the war" and expressing sympathy for "the aspirations of Ireland for self government," the platform satisfied some of the concern about the Irish question. Not far from the views of Charles Murphy and the positions taken by Cox, these alterations represented victories for the anti-administration Democrats.[13]

Nevertheless, opposition to the platform continued and surfaced before the entire convention, when William J. Bryan in an eloquent forty-five minute address recommended a series of platform additions. Beginning with an assault on the wets, he called for "effective enforcement" of prohibition without "any increase in the alcoholic content of permitted beverages." He concluded with a direct attack upon the administration by recommending ratification of the Versailles Treaty "with such reservations as the majority of the senators may agree upon . . . ."

The urban coalition responded with Bourke Cockran, a well known Tammany personality, advocating a statement favoring light wines and beer for home consumption. If Bryan had not submitted his proposal, said Cockran, he would have left the question dormant. A further counter to Bryan came from the administration. Secretary of State Bainbridge Colby defended the League resolution and asked that the issue be made "a national referendum" so that the people in "their own rough and ready and honest fashion . . . could decide the issue." Resolutions Committee Chairman Carter Glass, a dry, explained a committee decision to ignore prohibition because it was already the law of the land. Edward L. Doheny, a California oilman, presented a minority resolution in favor of a strong statement on Irish independence. Glass responded by reiterating the already expressed sympathy for Ireland in the platform and explained the need to recognize "our international obligations."[14]

The issues of prohibition enforcement, the legalization of wine and beer, and Irish independence, were controversial enough to demand roll call votes. On enforcement, the urban coalition and the administration joined forces to defeat the Bryan proposal by an eight-to-one margin. The Cockran amendment suffered a similar fate but analysis of the vote reveals that 300 of the 356 votes for the proposal came from ten states with 384 total delegates, enough strength to block any candidate. With the exception of Pennsylvania, they were all decidedly in the Cox camp. These same ten states, with the addition of Missouri, represented the mainstay of the Irish independence plank which went down to defeat by a much closer vote of 676 to 402$^1/_2$. The bulk of the support for the wet proposal and Irish independence resolution came from the heavily urbanized and industrialized Northeast and Midwest. Approved without change, the platform was basically an administration document acceptable to the urban coalition.[15]

Calling for a return "to the fundamental progressive principles of social, economic and industrial justice" curtailed by the war effort, the Democrats urged systematic control of international affairs, the national economy, the transportation network, and the various groups in American society. Praising President Wilson, the party urged "immediate ratification of the treaty without reservations which would impair its essential integrity" and criticized Republican obstructionism. To stabilize the economy they hoped to increase production, prosecute profiteering, continue the scientific "tariff for revenue only," and bring economy to government through the budget system. On transportation they proposed extensive federal aid for highways, an efficient railroad system without subsidies, and the development of port facilities and inland waterways where feasible. They promised the farmer expanded farm credit and collective bargaining for farm cooperatives. Against compulsory arbitration of labor disputes, the party observed "Labor as well as capital, is entitled to adequate compensation. Each has the indefensible right to organization, of collective bargaining . . . ," but actions of "either class" had to be in the "public welfare." To match workers with jobs, the platform asked for the reestablishment of the wartime federal-state employment offices. Concerned about unemployed veterans, the Democrats tried to provide them with jobs in step with technology through vocational education programs. To help combat unrest in the cities, the party recommended an Americanization program paid for with federal aid to local education.

While the above aspects of the platform stood couched in reform terms, certain aspects of the Democratic position paper were openly reactionary. Asiatic exclusion was considered the "true expression of the judgement of our people . . . . " In addition, the Resolutions Committee refused to consider the pleas of the National Association for the Advancement of Colored People for statements condemning civil rights violations against black people and calling for anti-lynch legislation. Diplomatic recognition of Mexico would be given when that country realized "the propriety of a policy that asserts the right of the United States to demand full protection for its citizens . . ." and when "its statute books [had] just laws under which foreign investors shall have rights as well as duties . . . ." Free speech did not imply "toleration of enemy propaganda or the advocacy of the overthrow of the state or nation by force or violence."[16] This platform, the longest in Democratic Party history, was ready made, in view of his past record, for Cox.

When the first day's balloting ended on July 2, McAdoo, Palmer, and Cox led the field of twenty-three candidates. The South and West provided most of McAdoo's strength. Palmer relied heavily upon Pennsylvania and Georgia. The delegates for Cox came from

Ohio, Kentucky, and Mississippi with clusters of votes from various northern and southern states. Caucusing went on throughout the night and included a meeting between Palmer and Moore. Palmer admitted he could not win, and agreed to oppose McAdoo. On the next day, the frontrunners maintained their relative strength until the seventh ballot when New York and New Jersey left their favorite son candidates, Al Smith and Edward I. Edwards, for Cox. The drive to nominate Governor Cox had begun; by the twelfth ballot he led McAdoo, but by the fifteenth loyalties had stabilized. Cox had 468 1/2 votes, McAdoo followed with 344 1/2, and Palmer, who had lost nearly 100 votes, stood at 167. With the Cox drive stymied, the convention seemed deadlocked. Little change occurred until the twenty-second ballot when Woodrow Wilson received 2 votes. The injection of Wilson as a candidate was an omen of possible disaster for Cox and McAdoo, consequently the convention adjourned for the Fourth of July holiday.[17]

Vieing for delegates and sharpening tactics, left the leaders little time to celebrate. Among themsleves the somewhat rudderless McAdoo managers conceded defeat. Discovering that Ed Moore had secured the second choice pledges from most of the pro-McAdoo delegates, they decided to move, at the right moment, for Cox. Arthur Mullen of Nebraska and Mrs. Antoinette Funk, a McAdoo organizer, met with Moore and agreed to stop any attempt to nominate a dark horse [meaning either Wilson or John W. Davis]. Simultaneously, Wilson's friends held several meetings and concluded that nomination of the President would be disastrous both for him and the Democrats. Bainbridge Colby notified Wilson that the anti-administration bloc would stop any effort to nominate him. Palmer, still hoping for administration support, stayed in the contest. Murphy, Brennan, and Taggart urged McAdoo to accept the vice-presidential nomination, but McAdoo refused. The urban coalition decided to stay with Cox to the end.[18]

The recess failed to break the deadlock. To force Palmer out of the voting, Indiana switched 29 votes to McAdoo. This triggered McAdoo's last and biggest drive. He gained a majority on the thirtieth ballot, but the McAdoo forces could not crack the veto power of the Cox bloc. Believing the deadlock insurmountable, party leaders called for a three-and-a-half hour recess after the thirty-sixth ballot and met with Palmer. Convention Chairman Joseph Robinson of Arkansas urged him to spare the party further disruption and some of his staunchest supporters threatened to desert. On the thirty-seventh ballot, the Pennsylvania Quaker's strength began to fade and after the next ballot he withdrew.

"This was the turning point," Cox wrote. On the next roll call Cox gained 83 1/2 votes, 61 1/2 from the Palmer bloc. McAdoo picked up 56 1/2 new votes but lost 19 from Indiana and 3 from Kentucky, which returned to the Cox column. The return of these 22 votes had the effect of inflating the gain of Cox and depressing McAdoo's strength. Both grew stronger, but Cox outdistanced McAdoo. Winning 15 McAdoo votes from Alabama on the forty-first ballot, the Cox people soundly defeated a move to adjourn and maintained the momentum. On the next ballot, Cox had a majority. Beneath the speaker's platform during the forty-third ballot, Moore and Joseph Guffey of Pennsylvania caucused. Guffey committed most of the Pennsylvania votes to Cox for the next roll call. During the forty-fourth ballot, with numerous states turning to Cox, Samuel Amidon of the McAdoo contingent moved to suspend the rules and nominate Cox unanimously. Amidst great applause and ballyhoo, the motion carried and James M. Cox of Ohio became the 1920 Democratic candidate.[19]

Once the platform had been adopted, the San Francisco convention became a wide open affair. The only administration interference came after the twelfth ballot, in the midst of the first Cox drive, when Carter Glass told the press that Wilson opposed Cox. Moore sensed the deteriorating effect the statement would have on the Cox momentum and urged Cox to counter it. Immediately, the Governor telephoned the White House from Dayton and requested a denial of the assertion. Wilson, playing his own game, would not act but Joseph P. Tumulty, on his own initiative, issued a press release stating the President "has expressed no opinion to anyone either in favor or in opposition to any particular candidate . . . his attitude has been one of strict impartiality." For the most part Cox gave Moore a great deal of flexibility and to a large degree the Ohio National Committeeman was central to Cox's victory. With the nomination secure, Cox wired Moore:

> Rarely, if ever, has the magnificent fight which you made been equaled in a National Convention. Your generalship matched support from the ranks, and that is saying much for both.[20]

After learning of his nomination, Cox received a telephone call from Judge Timothy J. Ansberry of the Chicago delegation and a personal friend of his and Franklin D. Roosevelt. Explaining that many members of the coalition electing Cox believed it essential to concentrate on the East because Cox was the wet candidate, he suggested Roosevelt for a running mate. Roosevelt, he reasoned, would help carry New York and his links with the administration as Assistant Secretary of the Navy would be an asset among Wilsonians. Cox agreed. Leaving the *Dayton Daily News* building, Cox arrived at Trailsend at dawn. Ed Moore telephoned to discuss the vice-presidental candidate. Cox said he wanted Roosevelt because "he met the geographical requirement . . . was recognized as an independent and . . . was a well known name." If Charles Murphy disapproved, Cox's second choice was Secretary of Agriculture Edward Meredith of Iowa. Put in a position of dismissing his personal animosity for the Dutchess County maverick or losing the reward of having New York and the East represented on the ticket, Murphy approved. He told Moore "I don't like Roosevelt. He is not well known in the country, but, Ed, this is the first time a Democratic nominee . . . has shown me the courtesy. That's why I would vote for the devil himself if Cox wanted me to. Tell him we will nominate Roosevelt on the first ballot as soon as we assemble." Symbolizing homage to the new urban orientation of the Democratic Party, Roosevelt was chosen by acclamation.[21]

Without the tenacity, skill, and votes provided by George Brennan, Charles Murphy, and Tom Taggart, Cox could not have been chosen. Similarly, the support he received in the South was essential. Senator Pat Harrison of Mississippi joined the urban coalition, seconded the nomination of Cox, and became Moore's chief lieutenant on the convention floor. From the peak of the first drive on the twelfth ballot, the states of Mississippi, Arkansas, Louisiana, and Kentucky became an integral part of the Cox bloc. Cox also consistently had pockets of support among the Alabama, Tennessee, Missouri, and Florida delegations. Georgia was central to ending the deadlock. On the forty-second ballot the Peach State left Palmer and cast 28 votes for Cox. In the final analysis, Cox benefited from an open convention while his program permitted the formation of a new north-south coalition around him rather than a member of the unpopular outgoing administration. So the Democrats chose an urban personality for their candidate at a time when, as Oswald Garrison Villard of the *Nation* wrote, "nobody except Mr. Wilson himself should have been asked to shoulder the burden of the mistakes, the follies, the wrongs, perpetrated by the President and his subordinates, but no Democrat could have won."[22]

XI
COX AND THE ELECTION OF 1920

Just before the Democratic National Convention opened, a visitor to Trailsend predicted that 1920 would be a Republican year and asked Cox why he bothered with such a dubious opportunity. Cox, then also weighing the value of the nomination, replied "Well, after all it is a great honor to be named a candidate for president by either of the great parties."

Confronted by the problem of widespread discontent after eight years of Democratic leadership, the party's dilemma intensified because of its inability to unite at the San Francisco meeting. Rather than heal differences, the open convention broadened the fissures within the ranks. Consequently, Woodrow Wilson stubbornly tried to keep control of the party machinery in order to make the election "a solemn referendum" on the League. In contrast, leading urban politicians jockeyed to have Cox campaign on domestic issues, while many drys including William Jennings Bryan, sat out the election or deserted the Democrats. To win required getting control of the party machinery, uniting the diverse forces, and waging a vigorous campaign; the situation appeared impossible. Nevertheless, with the nomination in hand, Cox permitted his aspirations to soar and let his determination take command. He turned to the task of running for president.[1]

Woodrow Wilson had promised to "take off his coat" and "roll up his sleeves" for the Cox-Roosevelt ticket. Responding to this pledge the candidate made plans to confer with the President, but simultaneously let it be known that he preferred to keep high administration officials "in the background during the campaign." Despite this effort to play down the Wilson meeting, opposition developed among Cox's close advisers who wanted complete separation from the administration. Intent upon waging a unified effort, Cox made the highly publicized visit to the White House. Afterwards, the Ohio governor announced that he and the President stood agreed on "the meaning and sufficiency of the Democratic platform and the duty of the party in the face of threatened bad faith to the world in the name of America." More specifically, Wilson stated, "he and I were absolutely at one with regard to the great issue of the League of Nations" and promised the support of an "absolutely united party." The stage appeared ready for the Cox coalition to take control, but agreement was more apparent than real.[2]

When the Democratic National Committee met at Columbus on July 20 to reorganize, the Wilsonians wanted to retain Homer Cummings as chairman. Cummings, at the President's insistence, offered to continue as chairman but Cox formally supported Ed Moore. To thwart the administration's efforts, George Brennan and Charles Murphy engineered the creation of a subcommittee to work with Cox to select a chairman with broad based acceptance. Cox finally recommended George White for the job, an old friend in Ohio politics and his traveling companion on the recent trip to Washington. The urban based leadership won its second victory when the Committee quickly approved White as chairman. As events unfolded, White served as chairman but Moore directed the campaign.[3]

Much of the inner party conflict centered around the degree of prominence the League of Nations should receive in the campaign. Late in July, Senator David I. Walsh of Massachusetts, after conferring with Cox, was confident the candidate would emphasize domestic

109

issues. Party chairman White in his first press conference, explained the Cox-Wilson meeting as an indication Cox stood for "the spirit of the League," but "Progressivism was the principal issue of the campaign." This apparent drift away from the Wilsonian League quickly produced pleas from independents and Wilsonian Democrats for Cox not to forsake the League. Robert Woolley, a Wilsonian, tactfully warned that independent voters were concerned about White's remarks. Supreme Court Justice John H. Clarke referred to White's comments as "an amazing indiscretion" and urged Newton D. Baker to use his influence to dissuade Cox from campaigning on domestic issues. The effect of the pressure is difficult to measure, but after completing his acceptance speech, Cox sent copies to numerous League stalwarts including Wilson. Joseph Tumulty, probably with Wilson's approval, added two short paragraphs on the League which Cox delivered virtually unchanged.[4]

In his formal acceptance of the nomination on August 7, delivered over an electronic public address system, Cox identified the main problem confronting the nation as the need for "confidence in government" and saw implementation of the Democratic platform, "a contract with the people," as the best way to restore confidence. His address was a critique of Republican politics and a plea for continued progressive measures. Convinced that domestic policy and foreign affairs could not be separated, he characterized the League of Nations as an expansion of progressivism into world affairs and United States membership in the League as the surest way to end "world anarchism." "As the Democratic candidate, I favor going in," said Cox, and he promised that the first duty of his administration would be to ratify the treaty within the framework of his reservations.

Turning to problems at home, Cox devoted most of his remarks to these questions. Believing governmental power could solve the economic ills of the country, he called for a more equitable distribution of the tax burden. Proposing lower income taxes for middle-class wage earners, he again, to satisfy industry, promoted a 1 to 1 1/2 percent gross sales tax "on going concerns" to replace the excess profits tax. Reduced taxes, he explained, would diminish costs and thus curb inflation. The tax cut for industry would simultaneously take corporate money out of the securities market and put it into real growth investments.

Labor was conceded the right to strike, but government should protect life, property, and "the public welfare" in conflicts between capital and labor. Critical of past abuses of the injunction by the courts in labor disputes, he proposed the establishment of machinery for orderly collective bargaining between representatives of labor and capital. "We need," Cox said,

> ... a definite and precise statement of policy as to what businessmen and workingmen may not do by way of combination and collective action ... . The rules of business should be made more certain so that on a stable basis men may move with confidence.

Reasserting the need for Americanization programs, Cox observed "It is the duty of the Federal government to stimulate the work of Americanization on the part of church, school, community agencies, state governments and industry itself." Once the foreign-born population understood American ideals, Cox assured his listeners, the excessive turnover of labor in industry would be stopped and a majority of immigrants, "out of devotion to American life," would give up revolutionary ideas. Education could also help veterans adjust to peacetime, Cox believed, and he suggested a Federal Vocational Board of Rehabilitation to retrain and find jobs for disabled veterans. He further proposed an attack on illiteracy through federally sponsored pilot projects which the states could use as models. An active federal role in education, he pointed out, would not threaten local control of schools, and he was willing "to explore" the use of federal funds to improve teacher salaries and alleviate the shortage of good teachers.

Concerned about the relationship between "town and country," and fearing that rural migration to the city would lead to a decline in food production with disastrous implications for the cities, Cox called for "scientific preparation" between government and the farmer. He promised a "national effort" to bring rural schools up to urban standards. To make farming as efficient as manufacturing, he suggested legislation to create farm cooperatives that would promote techniques similar to those used in manufacturing—for businesslike purchasing, labor recruitment and marketing. To guarantee harmony between government and agriculture, he promised to appoint a farmer as Secretary of Agriculture. These efforts in agriculture, he reasoned, would help decrease the cost of living for people in the cities, while municipal marketing facilities created with federal help would lower cost of food by streamlining the marketing process. Following the same reasoning, Cox would make "the law of supply and demand operate again" by promoting a federal cold storage law which would limit the time food could be stored.

In addition to trying to lower food costs, Cox planned to alleviate housing problems for the urban nation by promoting home ownership for thrifty, hard-working Americans. This, he believed, would eliminate much of the tension among the urban lower-middle and the middle-class by providing them with a stake in the system. As a step in this direction, he would promote tax machinery to uncover hidden wealth and thereby lighten the burden of people "whose property is in sight." "In short," he said, "remove the penalty imposed upon home building thrift and thousands of contented households under the shelter of their own roof will look upon government with affection . . . ."

Committed to economic planning, resource development, and the idea of system, Cox continued to see the need for an efficient transportation network and believed the railroad was the surest means to that end. In agreement with the Democratic platform, he would use the threat of government ownership to prod the railroad industry to serve the nation efficiently. Cox still considered the automobile as supplementary, but called for a continued federal-state highway building program. At the same time, he supported federal programs to develop the St. Lawrence Seaway in order to establish ocean ports for the highly developed Northeastern-Great Lakes industrial belt.

As a businessman turned politician, Cox considered systematic management techniques fundamental in government and politics. Calling attention to the effective use of the budget system by the states, he would adopt the same business methods in the federal government, to save "money by eliminating surpluses in labor." Of more importance, he went on, the budget system "provides the mechanism by which the government can recommend disbursement of funds after investigation of the need for services."

Politically, Cox's acceptance speech reflected his orderly outlook toward voting blocs. To tender women the vote and at the same time broaden the base of the Democratic Party he urged ratification of the women's suffrage amendment. He believed that the progressive nature of the democratic platform would appeal to women's "natural" humanitarianism. Rather than alienate the drys, he ignored the question of prohibition. In general terms, the speech was designed to meet the needs of a broad spectrum of interests throughout the society. He identified the key interest groups in an urban-industrial society and promised something to each of them. Summarizing his position, Cox depicted himself as a humanitarian and a progressive willing to promote constructive change. In contrast to his efficient progressivism, the Democratic candidate charged that the Republicans represented "bossism" and "government by party." Pledging to use his best judgment for "the people of the United States," Cox claimed he was continuing the fight against vested interests. This language and group approach was a manifestation of what future political theorists would characterize as the liberal-conservative model.[5]

Compared to the front porch approach of Harding, Cox campaigned strenuously. He promised to "take the campaign to the people" and "visit every doubtful state." Ultimately touring thirty-six states and traveling 22,000 miles, Cox delivered 394 scheduled speeches, and spoke innumerable times on street corners and from the backs of automobiles and train platforms. The pace was hectic. Near Marion, Ohio, Harding's home town, he received a speeding ticket. In Nevada, his railroad car was derailed. At various times while speaking to an estimated two million people, he suffered fatigue, laryngitis, and acute indigestion. Although generally effective on the stump, his campaign style suffered serious limitations. When exposed to heckling and jeering, Cox often succumbed and began answering his detractors, acts which lent credence to his already prevalent image as a ward politician chosen by the urban bosses. In addition, the pace worked against carefully planned position papers, consequently, most of Cox's speeches were improvised statements taken from his acceptance address.

The advance material given to the press simply high-lighted sensational aspects of the speeches and failed to develop detailed press coverage of his views. Senator Key Pittman, the chairman of the western campaign, complained that this aspect of the western tour gravely limited Cox's exposure.[6]

In the early part of the campaign, as he toured parts of the Midwest and the East, Cox stressed progressivism which he defined as working "to keep government responsive to changed conditions and . . . [making] out of these agencies of progress means to improve human welfare." Progressive laws, Cox repeated over and over again, represented the best way to combat revolution. "I believe," he said in a *New York Times* interview,

> . . . in the middle ground which is fair to capital and labor. Both should follow the Golden rule, and we should deal justice with an even hand. By following this policy we have preserved the law, protected property and person, and have not engendered bitterness between classes.

To establish his credentials, Cox consistently called attention to his record in Ohio. Placing particular emphasis upon industrial relations, he alluded to the humaneness of Ohio legislation and called for a national child labor law. Boasting that during his tenure as governor the militia had not been needed to keep industrial peace, he emphasized the need for collective bargaining. At the end of August, the American Federation of Labor announced support for Cox because of his "understanding of the needs of working people," his record in congress and in Ohio, and the Democratic platform that "makes a measure of progress not found in the Republican platform."[7]

Cox developed progressive rhetoric to arouse middle-class moral indignation. He consistently equated Senator Harding with bossism by characterizing him as the candidate of the "senatorial oligarchy" and "reactionary business interests" who sought to buy the presidency with a "huge slush fund." Taking a cue from wartime fund raisers, the Republicans had adapted the technique of regional quotas to fill campaign coffers. Well aware of the procedure and lacking funds, Cox tried to turn the disadvantage into an asset by describing it as "a deliberate plot that has been carried into every county in America . . . to buy the presidency . . . ." In a major address at Pittsburgh, Pennsylvania, billed as a speech where Cox would deliver "the goods that would convict every mother's son of them," Cox read from Republican Party quota lists. The fund, he charged, represented a "business plot" by those who "wanted the bayonet at the factory door, profiteering at the gates of the farm, the burden of government on shoulders other than their own, and the Federal Reserve system as an annex of big business."[8]

The slush fund charges dominated the news during the last week in August and drew attention in numerous quarters. Harding and the Republican Party denied them, many independents looked at them as mudslinging, and a Senate committee began investigations. Although the charges hampered Republican fundraising, influential Democratic contributors also became hesitant. Before long, the old conflict of interest charges from Cox's gubernatorial campaigns were resurrected. By September 2, as Cox began his western tour, the Democrats had raised only $60,000. Feeling this negative impact, Cox consequently deemphasized the slush fund charges.[9]

The slogan launching the western tour had a clear populistic ring. "The people are sovereign and I'm going to their front porch," Cox announced. He told the National Board of Farm Organizations that he would appoint "dirt farmers" to responsible government positions so that the farmer's interests would be served by governmental agencies. To midwestern farmers and workers he continued to charge that reactionary big business dominated the Republican Party. On labor Day at Minneapolis, cognizant of the Farmer-Labor coalition in Minnesota, Cox stressed the similarity of interests uniting farmers and workers as producers. Government, the candidate said, "must be concerned with the people as a whole" and he called for good roads, modern rural schools, labor's right to organize and bargain collectively, national child labor laws, and a national Americanization program.[10]

Throughout the western tour, Cox stressed local and regional issues popular in the areas he passed through. In arid eastern Washington, he spoke of the need for land reclamation. In Seattle, which had experienced a general strike and considerable labor violence, Cox emphasized law enforcement while reaffirming the need for labor to organize and bargain collectively. In Oregon were dry sentiment was strong, he pledged to enforce the law of the land and pointed out that Ohio had ended Sunday sales. In Utah, where Senator Borah had just stumped the state against the League of Nations, Cox noted that the American Bar Association had found nothing unconstitutional about the Treaty and explained that the United States would have a veto over any League action.

In rapidly urbanizing California, which voted Democratic in 1916, Cox labored long and diligently. Appealing to California boosterim by praising Hiram Johnson's progressivism, he pointed out that the Republicans had passed over Johnson for Harding. In San Francisco, Cox approved of Asiatic exclusion and pledged:

> . . . if California does not desire her lands to come into the possession of orientals, [sic] she may expect in consonance with established Democratic principle the genuine cooperation of the national government on working out a plan whereby she excludes the oriental [sic] settlers.

In Oakland, he proposed to end inflation by legislation to halt profiteering. He again suggested a cold storage law and a form of price controls requiring the producers to stamp prices on goods involved in interstate transit. In the agricultural southern part of the state, he emphasized the League, forms of taxation, and promised a protective tariff on citrus fruits.[11]

By the end of September, the campaign lagged badly and many Democratic leaders perceived the battle lost. Finances were so poor that some Cox managers were ready to close campaign headquarters. According to Mrs. Funk, a McAdoo stalwart, Cox asked Ed Moore to take direct charge of the New York office. Moore refused. The Wilsonians believed Cox erred by not emphasizing the League, and many doubted that he had a real understanding of the international organization. Some internationalists feared the Ohioan would abandon his commitment to Article X of the League charter. To alleviate these fears, Cox wrote Baker that

> You need have no concern about any abandonment of our position on Article X. My thought is now and always has been that we need only have people understand what this means.[12]

Especially Joseph Tumulty, among the Wilsonians, continued to press Cox to accentuate the League issue. As the campaign train moved eastward across the Great Plains, Cox began to mention the League more frequently. After a speech in Paducah, Kentucky, where he was introduced by Congressman Alben Barkley who had supported McAdoo, Cox wired Tumulty that the League's simplicity "has taken hold of my very soul." David Houston, Wilson's Secretary of Agriculture, cynically observed that Cox turned to the League because his campaign did so poorly without it.[13]

Early in October, the Democratic nominee began to stump the East. Aware of ethnic animosity towards the Wilson administration and the shortcomings of his own record with ethnic groups, he began to make distinctions between reactionary Irish, German, Italian, and Eastern Europeans who supported Harding and opposed the League and the "true Americans" in these groups who supported world order and progress. In a widely publicized letter, Cox charged that

> ... an attempt has been made by our opponents to distract from the issue of the League by setting up racial groups, each with a selfish purpose. To each of these groups something has been promised ... to my mind the most serious of all things is the attempt to arouse racial hatred.

In the face of this danger, he challenged the ethnic groups to demonstrate their loyalty by voting for him and the League.[14]

A strong effort was made to win the traditionally Democratic Irish vote. First Cox and then national headquarters asked Wilson to issue a pro-Irish statement about the potential of the League of Nations to facilitate Irish independence. Twice Wilson refused. Cox argued that Irish independence represented a world issue. In New York, he promised to bring the questions before the League under the provisions of Article XI of the charter, once the United States became a member. Soon after this statement, Michael Francis Doyle, the attorney for Roger Casement and Eamon De Valera, strongly urged Irish-Americans to vote for Cox. Doyle believed that the Democratic candidate's

> ... promise to advocate the cause of the Irish people before the League of Nations and to appeal to the conscience of the world for the recognition of their rights is the most advanced step for Ireland taken by any statesman in the world .... [15]

The German-American press was especially vitriolic towards Cox and the Democrats. Cox's message of April 1919 to the Ohio legislature on the issue of German propaganda in

German Catholic schools was repeatedly quoted and Wilson was depicted as the pro-British "Despot of the White House." In Ohio a widely circulated broadside urged German-Americans to vote against anyone who referred to them as "Huns" during the war. Cox's identification with the League of Nations led to his being characterized as an Anglophile and the Cincinnati *Freie Press* cynically called him "Sir James of Trailsend," a reference to his estate and lifestyle in suburban Dayton. His strong support of public education led to criticism that the divorcè was anti-Catholic because he opposed parochial education. Democrats lamely countered the German-American critique by claiming Cox was being misrepresented and pointed out that he supported German admission to the League of Nations along with that of the United States.[16]

The campaign also suffered because of Italian-American opposition to the Versailles Treaty. While the German-American press attacked him, for the most part the Italian-American press ignored the Cox candidacy. It focused instead on the denial of Italian territorial claims at the Paris Peace Conference. In local politics Italian-Americans were, more often then not, Republicans. Their antipathy towards the League and Cox's general criticisim of immigrant culture worked against him in the Italian community.[17]

During the last week of the campaign, as he had eleven weeks earlier, Cox summarized his position on the League. The League of Nations was not one man's idea but the evolutionary product of civilization, and it was the surest way to keep world peace without denying national self-determination. It would foster business stability, economic growth, and a return to prosperity. In addition, it was the surest way to resolve the Irish question, a situation that had become a "world tragedy." Reasserting his willingness to accept reservations, Cox clarified his interpretation of Article X when he promised to

> . . . accept a reservation stating explicitly that the United States assumes no obligation to use military or naval forces to defend or assist any other member of the League, unless approved and authorized by Congress in each case.

Two days later, he declared that the League of Nations represented the paramount issue of the campaign.[18]

Although Cox accented the League during the last phase of the campaign, he did not tone down his brand of progressivism, for he saw it as intricately tied to the need for international order. He continued to call for efficiency measures such as the budget system and reduction of spending for armaments, which would be made possible if the United States entered the League. On several occasions, Samuel Gompers appeared with him to emphasize Cox's pro-labor positions on collective bargaining, support of national child labor legislation, and condemnation of abuses of the injunction. Still picturing Harding as the candidate of vested interests, Cox labeled "normalcy" as an euphemism for "reaction." Withstanding pressures from leading Democrats to come out "bone dry," the candidate instead promised to enforce the law of the land. Rather than battleships and armaments he favored using national resources for "schoolhouses, playgrounds, health, child hygiene and child happiness." "America first," Cox argued enigmatically, "is not selfishness. It means . . . honor, loyalty, progress, humanity, and peace. To shout 'America first' and then oppose making America first throughout the world is to turn our backs on progress and on the ideals which the framers of our great Constitution wove into the soul of America." "My Campaign," he said, "has been made from coast to coast upon the issues of peace and progress in America and peace and progress in the world."[19]

As the League received added emphasis the Wilsonians began to campaign for Cox. In October Wilson on several occasions spoke on behalf of the League, and Homer Cummings recorded that the President whole heartedly approved of the new developments in the campaign. McAdoo, Baker, Daniels, and other administration officials now went out preaching the League gospel. Still, doubts continued about the sincerity of Cox on the question. Several of McAdoo's leading backers for the presidency interpreted the increased emphasis on the issue as part of a strategy to keep control of the National Committee for 1924. There may have been some validity to the observation. Despite numerous optimistic statements from Cox's campaign entourage, the candidate and his immediate advisers sensed the futility of it all. Only at the end of the eastern tour, with the administration forces working on his behalf, did Cox privately express some optimism when he said, "Now it looks as though we have a possible chance."[20]

As the early returns came in, Cox's single ray of optimism vanished. The Democrats suffered their worst defeat since 1860. Analyzing the result as an expression of pent up resentment emanating from the war experience, Cox concluded that

> Those who voted for us did so from conviction. Those who were against us were moved by prejudice and selfishness—some from misunderstanding. . . . The war brought so many reactions that the landslide was inevitable.

In later years he recalled:

> . . . the Italians were against us because of Fiume, the Germans were against us because of the war, the Irish opposed the Democratic ticket because Wilson refused to bring the question of Irish freedom before the Peace Conference.

Revealing as they are, these assessments lacked insight into the larger process of the American party system.[21]

Despite Cox's energetic and tireless campaign, the Democrats were doomed to defeat in 1920. The country rejected the party in power as too unstable to solve the economic problems of postwar reconstruction. Inflation reduced real purchasing power to a pre-1914 levels. By the summer of 1920, "boom" had turned to "bust," prices fell rapidly, and unemployment soared to four million at the end of October. Steel plants operated at half their capacity and the building trades came to a virtual standstill. Farm income dropped more rapidly than costs, because the crop had been planted before the bottom fell out of the economy. The economic distress affected precisely those elements of the electorate that Cox had hoped to forge into a solid coalition.

The philosophic climate permeating the nation also worked against the party in power. The surge of nativism manifested a society seeking to stabilize itself after the war—a war presided over by Democrats. Rather than question the process of war and its impact upon American institutions, most Americans blamed those elements in the society seeking change. Labor unions, discontented farmers, culturally distinct immigrants, and reformers, bore the brunt of the blame for national ills as the red scare developed and dampened enthusiasm for change. The plea for normalcy represented a stroke of political genius. "By normalcy," Harding said, "I don't mean the old order, but a regular steady order of things. I mean normal procedure, the natural way, without excess. I don't believe the old order can or should come back, but we must have normal order or, as I have said, 'normalcy'."[22]

The Wilson coalition created in 1916, could not contain the postwar resentments, and the League of Nations as an issue lacked the power to sustain a Democratic preponderance. Harding received 16,181,289 popular votes to 8,141,750 for Cox, giving him 404 electoral votes to 127 for Cox. A large part of the workingman's vote which Cox hoped to capture went to Socialist Eugene Debs who received 902,310 votes. In an election marked by a low turnout of 54 percent, many voters failed to turn out and others returned to the traditional loyalties they had established in 1896. The West voted solidly Republican. The GOP also maintained solidarity in the East, regained the dominance lost in Ohio in 1916, and even made temporary inroads into the solid South by carrying Tennessee.

In spite of this defeat, in 1920 the Democrats had begun adjusting to political realities and moved in the direction of creating a new party. This new direction, fostered by Cox, had several components. The urban and southern based coalition which nominated Cox later came to dominate the Democratic Party. In addition, although Wilson had captured the support of organized labor, Cox continued Democratic efforts to keep the workingman's vote. He received the endorsement of the American Federation of Labor. Cox also used the language of the liberal-conservative model. This interest group orientation and rhetoric came to serve the Democrats well in the New Deal coalition. Lastly, the Cox campaign introduced electronic communications to the political process using an electronic amplification system, in order to be heard by large crowds. The returns were broadcast by radio, for the first time, to a limited number of listeners in Pittsburgh, Pennsylvania. The coalition building, rhetoric, and technology of the election of 1920 all represented a systematic effort to build a new Democratic Party that would emerge more clearly in the next decade. Cox, the candidate of the urban leaders and progressivism, served as a catalyst in that secular process. [23]

XII
COX AND THE NEW DEMOCRATIC PARTY

Discouraged by the wide margin of defeat suffered by the Democrats, Cox could not bring himself to concede. Three days after the election he issued his only statement. "In spirit," he said, "I am as proud as when the fight started . . . . It was a privilege to make the contest for the right in the face of overwhelming odds. There is a distinct difference between defeat and surrender." Cognizant of prophecies that the Democratic Party had been destroyed, Cox declared, "Talk of a new party is absurd."[1]

Almost immediately after the election, two distinct groups representing the northern and western wings of the party fenced for control. George Brennan wired Cox that he had made a great fight and "must now assume leadership of the party before 1922 rolls around." Similar sentiments were expressed by A. Mitchell Palmer, Oscar Underwood, Key Pittman, and others. In response, Cox soon made known plans to gain first hand information about the League of Nations and foreign policy problems by making a European tour. He intended to vindicate his pro-League campaign and keep the support of internationalists in the new north-south coalition. At the same time, proponents of William G. McAdoo launched a program to oust George White as party chairman, to reorganize the National Committee, and to elect Tom Chadbourne, a Wilsonian, as chairman. Aware the move would be challenged, Robert Woolley wrote that

> Opposition, of course, will come from the group which forced the nomination of Cox at San Francisco, I am informed though, that a number of National Committeemen whose delegations voted for Cox finally in 1920, are for a new deal in 22 and 24 [sic].[2]

Woolley spearheaded the movement to unseat White and toured the West whipping up support among party leaders. The prevalent attitude among western leaders was that the League of Nations should be deemphasized.[3]

As the sentiment mounted to remove White, Cox made his first national appearance since the election when he visited Washington, D.C., to confer with party leaders. In late January 1921, after five days of discussion with Joseph Guffey, Homer Cummings, Pat Harrison, Tom Love, Woodrow Wilson, and other Democrats, Cox announced that White would stay on as party chairman. In addition to Cox's involvement, timely contributions from Thomas Fortune Ryan and Bernard Baruch calmed concern about the $300,000 campaign deficit. Woodrow Wilson let it be known that he favored retaining White "for the time being." These maneuvers, however, simply postponed the inevitable. The anti-White forces soon demanded a reorganization meeting of the full National Committee. White, who controlled the executive committee, bought time with a resolution requesting that the full committee respond by mail as to whether they wanted to reorganize. White was forced to call a National Committee meeting for September 21, 1921. The anti-White bloc secured enough proxies to unseat him, and White resigned on the eve of the meeting.[4]

Although the Cox faction lost its grip on the National Committee, the anti-White coalition failed to elect a pro-McAdoo chairman. Chadbourne lost primarily because of opposition from William Jennings Bryan and the urban leadership. Several alternate choices met a similar fate. In the end, Cordell Hull was chosen as a compromise. Hull's dry posture satisfied Bryan, the Wilsonians approved of him because of his loyalty to the New Freedom, and Cox, who had served with the Tennessean in congress, had considered him in 1920 as a good compromise for the job as chairman. In his new role, Hull eliminated the Democratic Party's indebtedness in a businesslike manner and produced a reasonable degree of harmony among the various blocs.[5]

After the initial confrontation over the chairmanship, Cox remained aloof to the political infighting. Adopting a statesmanlike posture, he confined his public statements and energy to promoting the League and United States involvement in the reconstruction of the world economy. By the fall of 1921, Joseph Tumulty found it "heartening" that Cox continued to promote internationalism in the face of the dwindling political prestige behind the issue. By mid-1922, Newton D. Baker and Cox agreed that it remained a national imperative for the Democrats to keep the League alive as a political issue.[6]

Cox spent most of the summer of 1922 in Europe consulting with political leaders and observing economic conditions. Well covered by the press, the trip helped keep international problems before the nation. While abroad, Cox reaffirmed his belief that the United States must not pursue a foreign policy based only upon self-interest. Convinced that the economic stagnation of the world grew out of the balance of payments situation, he took it upon himself to confer with the heads of state in Germany, France, and England to try to resolve the reparations issue. All three governments, Cox found, wanted war debts scaled down, but domestic political considerations limited their actions. To overcome the political dilemma, Cox proposed that the United States take its seat on the Reparations Commission and mediate a scaling down of the debts in the interest of world prosperity. Cabling a detailed plan to the Department of State, Cox publicized the idea in the *New York Times*. The Harding Administration immediately issued a noncommittal response. In a dispatch to the *New York Times*, the President explained that the time was not right for American participation in European economic reconstruction.

Returning to the United States, Cox noted the continued economic stagnation and explained, "Our international policy is closely interlocked with domestic problems." He again called for United States membership in the League to bring order to the world economy. Cox was not alone in his belief that American prosperity was linked to the international economy. Secretary of Commerce Herbert Hoover, numerous corporate leaders, and the leadership of the American Federation of Labor also stood firmly committed to the idea of American overseas economic expansion in the 1920's. In general, these concerns were rooted in the belief that the industrial system of urban America would fail without expansion into foreign markets. Cox differed only in that he believed that United States membership in the League of Nations was the most efficient way available to promote American prosperity.[7]

Cox helped keep the League of Nations alive as a political topic and by late 1922, a coalition of Democratic politicians organized to make it a key issue in 1924. John H. Clarke resigned from the United States Supreme Court to devote all his energies to the cause. In January 1923, Clarke delivered a major address in New York City stressing the need for nonpartisan acceptance of the League. Cox used his journalistic and political influence to give Clarke's activities extensive press coverage, particularly in the South where the greatest number of newspapers were Democratic with strong internationalist sentiment. At the same time, Cox considered renouncing any political ambitions for 1924. He reasoned that unless he did so, his advocacy of the League cause would appear opportunistic. Clarke saw this as a noble gesture but pointed out that as the 1920 standard-bearer, he had great influence within the Democratic Party. Woodrow Wilson renewed his interest in Cox's pro-League posture and asked Baker how Cox felt about the Corfu crisis and the handling of it by the League. Cox regretted that the international organization could not respond more vigorously in the conflict between Greece and Italy for control of the island. A short time later, Wilson wrote Cox that he admired

> ... steadfast advocacy of the League of Nations. It constitutes the great and only issue worth fighting for and I know of no one who has been more true to the faith than you have.

Thus as the presidential election year approached, a powerful movement had developed to promote the League issue and Cox had become the leading spokesman.[8]

Newton D. Baker planned the strategy for a strong League commitment in the Democratic Party platform. Early in 1923, the Bok Peace Prize competition caught the imagination of much of the nation and Baker hoped it would sufficiently change the political climate to turn the convention to the League as a central issue. To facilitate matters, he proposed that the Ohio delegation support Cox and that someone from Ohio, preferably Cox, get on the resolutions committee and issue, if necessary, an unequivocating minority report that would force the convention to deal squarely with the question. Baker believed that in light of an imminent deadlock between Alfred E. Smith of New York and McAdoo, the League of Nations issue could turn the convention to Cox. Informing both Baker and Clarke that his main concern was a solid front for the League with the Ohio delegation as a rallying point, Cox assured them he did not want the nomination. He preferred to have Baker make the formal fight and perhaps be nominated. He would accept the nomination only as "an ultimate last extreme" to make the League a major issue.[9]

In addition to the Ohio group, Woodrow Wilson continued to promote the international organization. The former President, with the advice of numerous associates, prepared a party platform for 1924. The document was a strong statement in favor of the United States entrance into the world organization. Wilson also preferred to have Baker make the convention plea and shortly before his death, sent Baker the platform and concluded:

> ... when I know that you have won your deserved place on the Committee on Resolutions my mind will be more at rest, and I hope that the committee will have the good sense to heed your advice.[10]

Baker ultimately defended the League of Nations plank at the convention.

By mid-February, Cox consented to enter his name in the Ohio primary but emphasized that he would not seek delegates outside the State. He entered the primary to guarantee an anti-McAdoo slate of electors because McAdoo had turned against the League. Although the McAdoo group challenged him vigorously, Ohio voters elected a pro-Cox delegation.

The McAdoo forces continued to deemphasize the League as an issue. Early in 1924, in preparation for a visit from McAdoo, Woodrow Wilson had asked his wife not to leave him alone with the presidential aspirant. Fearing his son-in-law wanted an endorsement, Wilson at the time considered a public declaration against McAdoo. When McAdoo explained his League of Nations position, the reason for the coolness became apparent. The Californian now hoped to wage the campaign solely on domestic issues and straddled the League question by proposing a national referendum in the first congressional election after 1924. The McAdoo organization later adopted that position at the convention.[11]

Ironically, while McAdoo, the leading Wilsonian of 1920, moved away from the League of Nations, Al Smith, the leading urban personality in 1924, moved toward the idea. In 1920, when Tammany supported Cox, Smith paid little more than lip service to the League, but by 1924, Smith had moved toward middle ground. Ethnic Irish sentiment appeared to be changing after Ireland had entered the League. Franklin Delano Roosevelt, Smith's campaign manager, assured the internationalists that Smith understood world problems and would be "liberal" in his foreign policy. Discussing the issues on the eve of the convention, Smith wrote that the United States "must assume responsibility in foreign affairs. We must help build machinery for peace." He promised to examine international agencies to secure the peace of the world. In the same issue of the *New York Times*, Cox wrote similarly of the need for American leadership in foreign affairs.[12]

Another presidential aspirant was John W. Davis. More than a dark horse, Davis was a Wilsonian with Wall Street affiliations. He had served as Solicitor General under Wilson, and as a postwar ambassador to England. William Allen White observed that Davis was "courageous and convinced in his belief that the League of Nations must become eventually the great agency of world peace." In 1924, he was a lawyer for J. P. Morgan and Company and, as early as 1923, party leaders were talking Davis. By January of 1924, Kansas National Committeeman Ed Galtra pointed out that Davis was frequently mentioned as a compromise in the event of a deadlock. In March, however, the leading internationalists were disappointed that so little enthusiasm had developed for Davis.[13]

The Democratic convention opened in New York's Madison Square Garden amidst prophecies of deadlock. George Brennan predicted the meeting would be long and drawn out and most party leaders saw an impasse between McAdoo and Smith. Josephus Daniels suggested that on the 255th ballot they could put both men in a room, equip them with a full array of firearms, and order only one man to come out alive. But the deadlock between Smith and McAdoo symbolized larger problems than just personality. On the second day of the convention, the order of business was changed because the Resolutions Committee could decide neither on a League of Nations plank nor on a resolution having to do with religious liberty. What followed was two and a half days of monotonous nominating speeches and prepared demonstrations while the Committee tried to work out solutions. Finally, on the fifth day the delegates had to decide both the League and religious liberty questions because the Resolutions Committee could not work out a compromise.[14]

Senators Alfred Lucking of Michigan and Key Pittman of Nevada defended the majority report on the League, a replica of the referendum idea McAdoo had earlier proposed. The two senators pleaded for adoption of the majority plan in the name of political expediency. Baker, in a fervent address, defended the minority report calling for American entrance into the League. He compared the majority position with the vacillations of Henry Cabot Lodge, who praised the League and the World Court but who continuously worked to stay out of the world community. Concluding with rhetoric reminiscent of Woodrow Wilson, he asked the delegates to "Save mankind" and "Do America's duty." Despite Baker's plea, political expediency won as the majority report carried by a two to one margin. The convention divided more evenly on the religious liberty question which specifically dealt with whether the platform should openly denounce the Ku Klux Klan. The Committee on Resolutions, dominated by pro-McAdoo people who generally disapproved of the bigotry of the Klan, wanted to avoid open warfare with the clandestine organization and the cultural tensions it represented. The Smith contingency, on the other hand, sought to identify Mcadoo with intolerance by amending the majority report to read:

> We pledge the Democratic party to oppose any effort on the part of the Ku Klux Klan or any organization to interfere with the religious liberty or political freedom of any citizen . . . .

William Jennings Bryan defended the majority report and argued that a specific denunciation of the Klan would divide the party. Bryan was right. When the delegates were polled the majority won, but just one vote separated the two sides.[15]

What is often forgotten, however, was that the Democrats divided not two ways but three. The confrontation over the Klan brought into focus the polarization between the Smith and McAdoo forces, but the League of Nations advocates represented a third force which transcended personalities, cultural issues, and sectional lines. At the center of the international phalanx stood James M. Cox and the Ohio delegation. As long as the convention remained in its suicidal deadlock, the internationalists would wield the balance of power and in the end decide who would be the candidate.[16]

As the impasse persisted, there were numerous efforts to resolve it. On the eighth day, William Jennings Bryan again addressed the convention. In the midst of jeers and objections, the erstwhile populist now turned Florida banker and real estate man, suggested a host of candidates acceptable to him. Conspicuous by their absence were Smith and Davis. Bryan opposed Smith because of his "wetness" and the rift over the Klan plank further alienated him from the Tammany candidate. Davis, despite Bryan's brazenly capitalist activities in the Florida land bubble, was opposed as a tool of Wall Street and as an easterner unable to carry a state west of the Alleghenies. Another indication of Bryan's sentiment toward Davis might be the failure of the former Secretary of State to support Cox and the League in 1920. Bryan's appeal failed. The roll calls droned on. On July 4, the tenth day of the convention, a determined effort developed to work out a compromise. Indiana Senator Samuel M. Ralston and Cox both withdrew their names from consideration. That evening, Breckenridge Long, a McAdoo manager, convinced his candidate to offer Smith the vice-presidential nomination, but Smith refused. Daniel C. Roper suggested that McAdoo give the nomination to Smith providing that Smith support McAdoo in 1928. Roper reported that both McAdoo and his wife rejected the idea because it would give Tammany control of the party, a control it would never willingly relinquish.[17]

Two days later, in response to requests from party leaders, Cox went to New York to help end the deadlock. Replying to inquiries, he announced that he had no interest in the nomination. During an early morning caucus among Cox, George Brennan, and Al Smith, the New York governor admitted he could not be nominated. The leaders of the urban coalition then decided to turn to Davis. Cox approached Davis, but before the coalition underwrote the nomination, Cox extracted a promise from the Wall Street lawyer to support entrance into the League of Nations. Several obstacles, however, delayed the move to Davis. The New York delegation divided, and Tom Taggart revived the Ralston candidacy. Cox countered these developments with token support to Carter Glass as a possible alternative. Working behind the scenes, Taggart diligently gathered support for the senator from Indiana. Appealing to southern delegations and the McAdoo faction, he gathered 600 of the 732 votes needed for the nomination. At this point, Ralston withdrew for the second time. Claude Bowers, a journalist and Ralston supporter, later recalled that Ralston had withdrawn because of poor health. Cox, however, asserted that the Smith forces could not accept a man who wore the Klan stigma, and the internationalists would not accept the "Hoosier" politician. After the collapse of the Ralston boom the tide gradually turned to Davis. On the 103rd ballot, the pro-League Wall Street lawyer received the nomination by acclamation.[18]

The internationalist delegates lacked the power to make the League of Nations a dominant issue, but their influence and the determination of the urban leadership to keep the old Wilsonian establishment from regaining control of the party machinery resulted in a tenuous alliance. Adding to this, two and a half stifling July weeks in New York City fostered frustration, fatigue, and financial burdens that played havoc with the loyalties of more than one delegate. This atmosphere permitted Cox to use his good offices to end the deadlock and tender the fragmented prize to Davis who later recalled that "the nomination wasn't worth purchase by anybody." For his role in resolving the discord within the party, Cox received the praise of Democratic leaders and the press. Charles Michelson wrote in the *New York World*, then the leading Democratic newspaper, that "No small percentage of the credit for restoring party harmony . . . and the nomination of John W. Davis goes to James M. Cox . . . ."[19]

In 1924, the Democrats and the League of Nations fared little better than in 1920. Yet in spite of the defeat, 1924 stands as victory for the urban wing of the Democratic Party. The internationalists and the urban leadership selected the candidate and the rural-western Democrats acquiesced in the decision. Davis, seeking the continued support of the urban leaders, sent word to McAdoo that he remained "most anxious" to appoint a national chairman acceptable to Smith. Clement L. Shaver of West Virginia, a nonentity in the Democratic power structure, met the requirement. After the election, Smith and a number of eastern business interests succeeded in retaining Shaver as chairman until 1928. Some other indications of the urban transformation of the party were the selection of Frank Hague of Jersey City as party vice-chairman and New York financier, James W. Gerard, as party treasurer.

Ironically, Cox blamed the Democratic defeat of 1924 on the failure of local leadership to make the League a central issue. He believed "ward leaders and courthouse politicians," because of their provincialism and concern with "local patronage," refused to promote the more cosmopolitan international questions. Doubtless, the landslide victory of Harding in 1920 and the La Follette campaign fostered this sentiment, yet the grass roots apathy towards the League may actually have diminished Democratic strength in 1924. Harding had recognized the continued internationalist sentiment and prior to his death had actively promoted the World Court to gain internationalist support. Concurrently, Irish independence and entrance into the League as well as the Dawes plan, which removed some of the Versailles "diktat", drew these two important ethnic groups toward internationalism. In addition, the demise of the "red scare" and renewed prosperity cleared the political air. The election could have served as a barometer of voter sentiment toward the League of Nations, but instead it was marked by lack of interest and low voter turnout. Had internationalism been given a fair hearing perhaps the urban trend within the Democratic Party might have emerged even more clearly in 1924.[20]

The difference between the Democratic presidential and congressional vote was found in the La Follette candidacy. The Progressive Party candidate did well in the cities. In ten major cities between Boston and Chicago, he earned 23.6 percent of the vote and drew support from Democratic congressional voters. Similarly, on the sectional level, La Follette depressed the Democratic presidential vote, especially in the Northeast and Midwest. In 1928 these voters, particularly in the industrial areas, voted for Al Smith. Nevertheless, the

Democrats did make urban gains in 1924. Because of the three-way presidential race, the congressional results indicate true Democratic strength. Here the Democrats earned 42 percent of the vote as compared to their 29 percent presidential vote. In a presidential year the Republicans, while winning the White House, gained only 21 seats in the closely divided House of Representatives. Another indication of Democratic gains over 1920 can be seen in county strength. Davis won 183 more counties than Cox, while Coolidge carried 377 counties less than Harding.[21]

The lesson learned from the La Follette candidacy was that the Democrats needed a new party image. Cox remained convinced that the Democrats would have to portray themselves as liberals opposed to the Republican moneyed interests. The millionaire publisher emphasized the need for the Democrats to capture the loyalties of ethnic groups and the working class. Cox first urged Claude Bowers, in 1924, to write his *Jefferson and Hamilton*—which portrayed Jefferson as the man of the people and Hamilton as the servant of the wealthy. Similarly, he pressed Arthur Krock, then a columnist with the *New York World*, to write an article describing the similarities between European socialists and American liberals. "A French socialist," Cox wrote, "in America would be a liberal progressive."[22]

Cox believed the candidacy of Governor Smith of New York would move the Democrats in the desired direction. Smith had been the first choice of the Cox-led Ohio delegation in 1924. When Smith emerged as one of the few Democrats to be reelected Governor in 1924, Cox favored him for the Democratic nomination more than ever. In 1925 after Tammany won the New York City mayorality contest, Cox wrote an influential journalist:

> The New York election made a good deal of an impression throughout the country. Tammany is being more highly regarded . . . from the obvious predominate belief that New York City is the best governed one in the world, and that Tammany knows how to run it.
>
> Al Smith is coming in for his share of fair public judgment. I know what we thought about the probability of religious warfare if he were nominated, but I'm beginning to ask myself whether he could not be sold to the country as a self made American whose experiences parallel the average man who came out of his experience with fine poise and understanding of government. This contrast to Coolidge in human emotions might bring a landslide and submerge the religious issue.
>
> In confidence Smith would come closer to a national victory than anyone else.[23]

The Democratic congressional gains of 1926 further strengthened the idea of a Smith candidacy. By the spring of 1927, Cox reported that Democrats who visited him in Miami during the winter stood, by and large, for Smith. Cox continued to urge dissociation from Wall Street in order to capitalize on the common man image. In Houston, in June 1928, Al Smith was tendered the Democratic nomination on the 1st ballot. In the heart of Dixie the delegates cheerfully sang "The Sidewalks of New York" reflecting, finally, northern urban dominance in the Democratic Party.[24]

XIII
PUBLISHER AND ELDER STATESMAN

During the 1920's politics became an avocation for James Cox and he turned his main energies to expanding his newspaper chain, the *News League*. In the winter of 1923, he vacationed in booming Miami, Florida. Impressed by the beauty, climate, and surging growth of the state, and encouraged by Carl Fisher, the developer of Miami Beach, Cox decided to extend his journalistic empire into the deep South. Convinced that Miami would grow into a prominent metropolitan area, he enthusiastically wrote Arthur Krock that "It looks like another Los Angeles." "I saw," he added,

> the chance to become a part of a city which promises to assume large growth in a few years. It is a port of some importance and when it grows, it will be a stopping off point for the South American trade.[1]

The *Miami Metropolis* became part of the Cox chain of newspapers on April 8, 1923. Assuming ownership, Cox notified the editorial department that the paper was

> ... an investment. Publication of newspapers is my business. Miami, one of the magic places of the world, is beyond doubt destined to be a large city. I have been impressed with its progress, its civic pride and the enthusiasm with which it is doing its share in the development of the new empire of Florida. It is our wish to become part of the fascinating task.
>
> The *Metropolis* will uphold the principles of Jeffersonian Democracy and devote itself to the public interest. Any city growing as Miami is needs a vigilant press. The public interest must always be paramount. The function of a newspaper carries a grave responsibility. It is the agency of information and the utmost care should be taken to publish the truth. Its news columns should give all sides of an issue of general concern, regardless of the convictions which the paper has. A journal without conviction is of little use to a community. Influence of public opinion should be sought in the fairest manner. Either misrepresentation or suppression of essential facts profanes the tradition of a great profession. Every useful interest should be treated fairly, but it must be remembered that individual and corporate designs sometimes trespass upon the rights of the public. These interests are organized and they employ their own representatives while the people without organizations must look to an honest and courageous press for protection. *And yet the press should go no further than measures of restraint against chartered interests. They are essential to the growth of the city.* [italics added].[2]

On the following day the *Miami Herald*, observing the change in ownership, discerned that "the passing of this paper from a purely Southern man . . . to a purely Northern man as Mr. Cox is, will be noted as a distinctive change in Southern journalism." Cox decided to ignore the chilly reception and chose a "dignified" entrance in the South. Nevertheless, the observation of the *Herald* proved prophetic.[3]

As part of the new Miami, Cox wanted the *Metropolis* to become "a cooperative agency willing at all times to be helpful to everything that advances the good of the community." The first advice tendered to the editor reflected this booster orientation. Give good publicity to Carl Fisher, Cox wrote, "He is a tremendous asset to Miami. The almighty gave you your climate—Carl Fisher has given you most of your publicity. The Miami Beach crowd will never attempt to impose upon you . . . ."[4]

The *Metropolis*, now renamed the *Miami Daily News*, had been inadequately housed in a small building on Flagler Street. Adhering to the theory that a newspaper should exude prosperity, Cox decided to build the paper a new home. He anticipated the sprawling nature of the city, and chose a site on Biscayne Boulevard which paralleled the bay. In the midst of the Miami land bubble and the national skyscraper craze, Cox built the 279 foot News Tower, the first skyscraper in Miami. The Tower represented more than a million dollar investment, "to keep up with the growth of the town." A good investment, Cox said, because the "business is here for the asking."

Having changed the name and location of the paper, Cox set about the task of creating a metropolitan daily. Prior to moving into the Tower, a basic reorganization of the *News* was begun. "Nothing that you can do will so popularize the paper," Cox instructed his editor, as an efficient classified advertising section. The ad section, he explained, provides a means of communication for new residents who have not yet acquired newspaper loyalties. In addition to building circulation, he pointed out, advertising drawn from the booming real estate business represents a prime source of revenue. To insure success for the new operation in its modern facilities, Cox transferred from his other papers, or recruited first class proof readers, pressmen, and writers. He was determined to have the *News* present the image of an efficient, well managed paper.[5]

By November of 1924 Cox had been in Miami for a year and a half. Despite the growth of the city, profits failed to meet his expectations. Although circulation had increased 50 percent, the competing *Herald* grew faster. Because advertising revenues at the *News* trailed the *Herald* Cox again emphasized the need for an aggressive advertising force. To improve suburban circulation he told the business manager to establish sub-stations to handle the *News* in those areas without independent newstands. Create the image of dependability, Cox prodded, by getting each edition on the streets at the scheduled time. He demanded "a new birth of thought." Dissatisfied with the paper's appearance, he characterized the masthead as "sloppy" and considered the general layout of the paper "unattractive." Instructing the management to unionize the press and stereotype departments in order to guarantee competent workers, he shrewdly urged:

> have the . . . unions call on you—that would be better than you calling on them. It will be their task to convert you to their view, and this would enable you to talk very frankly about the size of crews and compensation.

To insure a metropolitan character Cox insisted that "the towns in any way contiguous to Miami should be covered fully." He recommended thorough coverage of the capital and leading cities in the state by newsletter in order to generate a statewide impact for the Sunday issue. Areas not connected to Miami by railroad should be covered by a "pre-date" edition made attractive with strong national and statewide sections, as well as with first-rate features such as theatrical and women's sections. The features, Cox said, would tie rural areas to Miami and build circulation. With Cox's brand of journalism, community service, and systematic business techniques, the *News* in the 1920's became the leading newspaper in the city.[6]

During a decade when Miami grew by 275 percent, the *News* won the reading loyalties of the city's new residents. The paper became the most potent political journal in southern Florida. Cox's son-in-law, Daniel J. Mahoney, became publisher. One scholar has argued that Mahoney approached the status of a political boss in sprawling Dade County during the 1930's. With the power of the press, control over a considerable number of jobs, and a willingness to spend large sums of money for his candidates, Mahoney throughout the 1930's and early 1940's regularly delivered the votes in the low and middle-rent residential sections of northern and western Miami. With an influx of new residents after World War II, the *News* lost much of its influence when if failed to attract new readers. The *Miami Herald*, by then a property of the Knight chain, regained journalistic dominance. In 1966 the *News* closed its plant and consolidated its operations with the rival *Herald*, but remained a Cox property.[7]

During the growth years, Cox was a persistent Miami booster. To a Columbus, Ohio banker he described the city as a "cosmopolitan community." "As I dictate to you," he explained from his office overlooking Biscayne Bay,

> I see large vessels in the harbor going to and from Nassau, Havana, New York, Jacksonville, Savannah, Charleston and Boston . . . .
>
> I have taken the pains to go through the warehouses, and examine the great diversity in commodities. The contact of land transportation with sea, is bringing a great deal of traffic. The docks and warehouses, which were doubled in capacity last year, are very inadequate now. It is not unusual for boats to remain outside the harbor until other boats clear.
>
> The net profits of our paper the first three months are 12% greater than they were the entire twelve months of 1924. Incidentally, we did not have a single month last year where we did not show a satisfactory profit . . . .
>
> It has all been interesting, because it is a new country. The place is filled with ambitious young men who are here to shape their destinies. You cannot find a pessimist anymore, because those who come here either for employment or health have found the joy of success and improvement of physical condition.[8]

What Cox described in Miami represented the emergence of the new urban-industrial South. Florida in 1920, with 36.7 percent of its population living in urban areas, was the most highly urbanized state in the region. Greater Miami, with an estimated population of 110,000 people in 1925, was the leading metropolitan area in the state. In 1930, the urban population of Florida had risen 51.7 percent.[9]

Late in the summer of 1926, a severe hurricane ripped southern Florida. The publicity given the destruction wrought by the storm broke the boom psychology and curtailed much of the migration into the area. Before long, a number of leading Florida investors, including Cox, began pooling their thoughts and influence. They formed a greater Florida organization to promote industrial development. Cox observed to James Gilman, the president of The Bank of Biscayne Bay,

> I quite agree with you that the ballyhoo stuff should end. There are

three types who should be shot at sunrise—first, the fellow who talks about the hurricane; second, the individual who persists in thinking about a building lot forty miles from nowhere; and third, the fellow who thrusts himself into a discussion of the industrial situation much upon the theory that "fools rush in where angels fear to tread."[10]

As part of an unofficial Miami chamber of commerce, Cox acquainted Ed Hurley, a Chicago industrialist and a director of the United States Chamber of Commerce, with the potential an industrial survey of Florida might offer to growing companies as a future investment site. He observed that "the Florida people" lacked both the capital and industrial outlook necessary to develop the state. As a model for the survey, the former governor of industrialized Ohio suggested that the study determine

> . . . what manufactured products could be turned out, having in mind escaping the long freight haul from the north; What raw materials there are in Florida . . . which could become factors in industry; and third what are the outstanding needs in the Caribbean empire, namely, the West Indies, Central and South America, etc., which could be filled by manufacturing plants at this accessible shipping point?

Whatever headway that might have grown out of Cox's Florida boosting was soon cut short. In a few years, with the country thrown into the depression of the thirties, industrial expansion greatly declined.[11]

Shortly after entering southern journalism, Cox purchased another northern newspaper, the Canton, Ohio, *Daily News*. Canton was a satellite city of Cleveland; publishing in the steel and roller bearing producing center represented a departure from his pattern of buying properties in metropolitan centers. Cleveland newspapers dominated the metropolitan area. The *Canton Repository* predominated locally. Cox urged the staff of the *Canton Daily News* to develop a unique image for the paper. "Arouse interests in different groups of readers . . . which your competition is overlooking," he encouraged. To win the circulation and the advertising race, he told his staff to plan "like an artist does his picture."[12]

As in the case of Miami, Cox offered detailed instructions. Again he encouraged service to the community, ranging from boosting new business ventures to appealing to the "sensuous interests of steel workers in sports," to finding "things of interest in Canton" for more local editorials. Since the *Repository* was a Republican paper, Cox insisted that the *News* give full coverage to Democratic activities. This, he said, was not only good politics, but would also win Democratic readers. Cox again built a new plant with a modern press and equipment in order to put out a first-rate paper.[13]

With a limited geographic area for journalistic expansion, Canton did not prove a fertile field for metropolitan journalism. (On population growth in the area see TABLE I) The *Canton Daily News* experienced financial difficulty. In the winter of 1926, *News* editor Don R. Mellet launched a crusade against gangland wars and organized crime in the city. Within a few months the Chief of Police was suspended and several people were convicted. In response, Mellett was murdered. At the funeral bier of the slain editor, Cox pledged to carry out relentlessly what Mellet had begun and he established a substantial reward for information leading to the arrest of the killers. He then appointed Charles Morris his executive secretary as the new editor. Cox and Morris pressed the anti-crime campaign until arrests were made. For these efforts, the *Canton Daily News* was awarded a Pulitzer Prize for 1928. The sensational aspects of the crusade stimulated readership. When the situation cooled, however, circulation figures fell to their previous unsatisfactory level. As the economy grew sluggish and it "became apparent that the city could not properly support two newspapers," Cox sold the Canton property to the Brush-Moore Company on July 3, 1930 for a "handsome offer."[14]

A short time before selling the Canton paper late in 1928 Cox expanded his holdings in south-central Ohio. From the Charles Knight chain he purchased the *Springfield Sun*. Situated between Dayton and Columbus, Springfield also had a limited geographic area to rely upon for readers and could not support two competing newspapers. Knight turned the area over to Cox. Before purchasing the paper, Cox tested community sentiment in a meeting with leading merchants to determine if they would support two papers operated by the same publisher. Rather than allow the morning paper to go out of existence and make the city prosperous territory for Dayton and Columbus advertisers, Springfield businessmen enthusiastically lent their support. At the meeting, Cox and the leading merchants in the city reached an agreement to lower advertising rates if the merchant advertised in both the morning *Sun* and afternoon *News*. Cox cut costs by consolidating both operations in one plant and Springfield merchants gained efficient advertising.

In 1949, Cox industries acquired complete control of journalism in the Dayton-Springfield territory when they purchased the *Dayton Journal* and the *Dayton Herald* from Louis Rock. Soon Dayton, like Springfield, became a two newspaper city when the acquisitions were consolidated into the morning *Journal-Herald*.[15]

The depression had slowed expansion of the Cox empire and it was not until December 1939, that the sixty-nine year old publisher acquired the *Atlanta Journal*. This addition to the Cox chain represented "the rounding out of a dream." After studying the paper for a year, Cox wrote to an influential advertising executive,

> I wouldn't know of another property in America I would want outside of this one. Georgia is a great empire with an inescapable progress of agricultural development ahead of it. That appeals strongly to me. The town is progressing more than any city in the South . . . .[16]

Atlanta was a metropolitan center with potential for regional newspaper dominance. (On population growth see TABLE I) In one day, Cox gained control of the afternoon field in the Georgia capitol by also purchasing and promptly discontinuing *The Georgian*, the other afternoon paper in the city. In 1950, Cox Industries bought the *Atlanta Constitution* and thereby acquired control of the entire market. But the move into Atlanta represented a larger strategy for Cox. The *Journal* became the master link in a north-south communications chain that "gave us three climates and the air from the Great Lakes on the north to Latin America on the south."[17]

Cox predicted that Atlanta would become the geographic terminus for northern and southern economic interaction, and the leading city in the Southeast. In *Journey Through My Years* he lauded the city's location and resources:

> Movements from Detroit, Chicago, Cincinnati, the Northwest and St. Louis to Florida southeastward through the Georgia capital, and that from New York, Philadelphia, Washington, Baltimore and Richmond . . . flows southwestward through Atlanta. Eight railway systems provide fifteen main lines. It is the third largest telegraph center in the south; it ranks fifth or sixth in airmail volume. Fifteen hundred manufacturing concerns maintain distribution offices in Atlanta.[18]

A year and a half after entering the Atlanta field the *Journal* joined with Ellis Arnall to fight Eugene Talmadge for control of the Georgia statehouse. Believing the crusade against Talmadge would be good for business, Cox also felt it was politically necessary and he threw the weight of the paper behind the effort. A few years later, he explained the role his newspaper played.

> The *Journal* bore an excellent reputation. People believed it. It had always dealt with them in good faith, and this made it a tremendously useful instrument in the governmental reforms that the public interest gravely required.

The former Ohio progressive privately reported to a leading columnist:

> I promised him [Arnall] our support with the understanding that a platform would be drawn up embodying the things which were much needed in the governmental affairs of Georgia.[19]

The *Journal* was only one of the anti-Talmadge forces operating in the 1942 Georgia reform movement. A known quantity in Georgia politics, Arnall had been an integral part of the Talmadge machine as State Attorney General prior to breaking with the organization. Campaigning on an efficiency platform akin to the state reforms in the northern states three decades earlier, Arnall called for educational reform and reorganization of the State Board of Regents, budget reform, a state civil service program, electoral changes, constitutional revision, prison and parole reforms, and numerous other changes. By running well in the cities and county seats, Arnall beat Talmadge.

One student of the Georgia reform movement has asserted that the urban press was not a major influence in the anti-Talmadge fight. However, Cox and the *Journal* joined the reform cause early and stayed to the end. Indeed, other forces did work to Arnall's advantage. Roy Harris, campaign manager for Arnall, had been floor leader of the House of Representatives during the 1935 legislative session. Urban labor consistently opposed Talmadge. Similarly, large parts of the academic community hoped to break the machine. In 1936 Philip Weltner had resigned his position as Chancellor of the University of Georgia to mount an oust-Talmadge movement which failed. In addition, a large group of good government people had long sought reform. By election time, even the traditionally pro-Talmadge *Atlanta Constitution* joined the voices in opposition to the machine. Collectively, they succeeded. However, without the early support of the leading newspaper in the State, the *Journal*, it seems doubtful that Arnall would have been able to sustain the reform offensive.[20]

Once Arnall became governor, Cox was satisfied that he "never deviated from the platform." A successful part of this early reform movement in Georgia, the Cox newspapers continued as a powerful force in the creation of a new South. In 1950, Cox Industries purchased the morning *Atlanta Constitution* and employed Ralph McGill as publisher. For two decades, McGill represented a voice of englightenment in southern politics and civil rights. Although personally not involved in the civil rights movement, the ageing Cox was glad to have directed his newspapers to the cause of political reform. At the age of seventy-five, Cox reflected, "We all want to contribute something to our time and it just so happens that I can be more useful in the newspaper business.[21]

Although active in national politics during the 1920's, Cox privately doubted that the Democrats could win the presidency as long as prosperity continued. After the Davis defeat he wrote, "I am just a little afraid . . . that the executive branch of the government will not be turned over to us until the country needs an undertaker." In 1928, after futilely campaigning for Smith in the South, he agreed with Joseph P. Tumulty that, "Rum, Romanism, and prosperity were too much for Smith to overcome." When the depression set in, Cox was finally convinced that a Democrat could win. In 1932, he emerged as a "dark horse" possibility.[22]

On numerous occasions during the twenties, Cox had been mentioned as a possible candidate for high elected office. Each time he rejected the possibility. In 1930, Newton D. Baker, with his eye upon the presidency, urged Cox to run for United States Senate. Baker noted that a "coherent and effective Party organization" would "sustain" a Democratic president. Cox responded that "I would be the unhappiest man in the world were I to wake up and find myself either Governor or Senator or President." Addressing the Democratic National Committee in March 1931, he again emphasized the need for a strong North-South coalition within the party. Nonetheless, the New York press now saw the former candidate as a likely compromise if the Democratic convention again deadlocked. Cox himself sounded very much like a candidate in the early part of 1932, when, on several occasions, he spoke of the need for fiscal responsibility, a balanced budget, and cooperation between labor and business to support state supervised unemployment insurance programs. This need for "rainy day" income, he believed, was as fundamental as the Magna Charta and the Emancipation Proclamation. He stressed the importance of a middle-ground between reactionaries and revolutionaries. Still, these acts were a service to the Democratic Party and the business leaders who dominated it, rather than a return to office seeking. He decided to support the candidacy of Newton D. Baker.[23]

As the Baker campaign developed, Cox became part of the effort. In December of 1931, Baker agreed with Cox that a North-South coalition was essential to victory and raised the possibility of Harry Byrd of Virginia as a running mate to balance the ticket and to assure southern loyalty. Cox approved, pointing out that he had suggested Byrd to Smith in 1928, but the candidate was already committed to Senator Joseph Robinson of Arkansas. Cognizant that the solid South had cracked in 1928, Cox explained to Baker that Bryd's southern establishment roots would strengthen the weakened party in the South.[24]

When the 1932 Democratic convention opened, Cox was part of a movement designed to deadlock the meeting and nominate Baker as a compromise choice. Cox actively participated in the stop Roosevelt effort. First, he joined Al Smith, John W. Davis, and others in condemning the abortive Roosevelt effort to eliminate the two-thirds rule. He then approved of Ohio's casting 52 votes for favorite son George White with the understanding that they would turn to Baker at the right moment. For three ballots the anti-Roosevelt forces kept the prize from the governor of New York. Supporting a motion to adjourn, the Baker forces soon discovered they had made a crucial error. Cox reported that Mississippi had decided to leave Roosevelt on the next ballot. He told Baker that Alabama and Arkansas would have followed and broken Roosevelt's southern support. The recess gave the Roosevelt forces the opportunity to bring John Nance Garner into their camp. The McAdoo-led California delegation followed. On the fourth ballot, Roosevelt won the nomination. Besides the tactical mistakes at the convention, Cox believed that the failure to mobilize the large business interests, who "were interested in a guaranteed Democratic policy of intellectual honesty and courage," also contributed to Baker's defeat.[25]

Disappointed, Cox probably for the first time in his life questioned whether he should support the Democratic nominee. To Baker he wrote that

> ... if Roosevelt is elected he may play politics the first four years with our international questions. Hoover, on the other hand, having the vindication of reelection, would probably do nothing of the sort. After all, it is not a question of what should be done as a matter of equity with the international debt, but what we will have to do in measurement of the practicalities of the situation.

In spite of his disdain for Roosevelt's seeming demagoguery, Cox could not leave the Democratic Party. He delivered several addresses in the candidate's behalf, including a nationwide radio speech which stressed government efficiency and international interdependence. The Cox newspapers also gave their support.[26]

Cox, however, refused to become a member of the administration. He rejected offers of appointments as Ambassador to Germany and Chairman of the Federal Reserve Board. He preferred journalism and winters in Florida. Befitting an elder statesman, he offered to serve in special capacities from time to time. The opportunity soon came when Roosevelt asked him to serve as a delegate to the London Economic Conference.

During the hectic first one hundred days, Roosevelt had to complete plans for the already scheduled World Monetary and Economic Conference to be held in London in 1933. The delegation was not chosen until mid-May and consisted of a strange mixture of economic thought. Delegation Chairman and Secretary of State Cordell Hull, Vice-Chairman Cox, and Tennessee Congressman Samuel McReynolds were sound money internationalists. Senators Key Pittman and James Couzens were high tariff men and silver proponents. Ralph Morrison, a Texas businessman, whose views were unknown, rounded out the delegation. On the advisory staff James Warburg and Herbert Feis were gold standard enthusiasts while William C. Bullitt favored easy money. Of the pre-planning for the conference Cox observed, "The rush of events made better plans and understanding difficult."[27]

Prior to leaving for London, Cox was briefed by Raymond Moley and Walter Lippmann. According to Moley, Cox explained that he knew little about international monetary exchange and asked for some reading on the subject. Moley suggested John Maynard Keynes',*A Treatise on Money*, and sent the delegation Vice-Chairman a copy for reading during the Atlantic crossing. Moley doubted Cox had ever read the book. Leaving later than the other delegates, Cox made the voyage with Warburg, George Harrison, the governor of the New York Federal Reserve District, and Oliver Sprague of Harvard University. All three were sound money men. At London Cox emerged sympathetic to the objectives of Hull on tariff matters and to Warburg on monetary questions.[28]

Much impressed by his surroundings and the attention the American delegation received, Cox recounted this aspect of the conference with great detail. Unfortunately, he shed little light on his activities as Chairman of the Monetary Committee. The chairmanship of the committee had been agreed upon by Great Britain and the United States before the Conference. However, when the Conference convened, George Bonnet, the French Foreign Minister was also nominated. Tensions were high. In the course of events Bonnet remarked, "In view of the United States favoring inflation of currency, we feel that we can scarcely favor an American as Chairman of the Monetary Conference." With disdain Cox promptly replied, "The United States can scarcely favor as Chairman of the Monetary Conference a national of the greatest defaulting nation in the world." Eventually, France gave in and Cox took his seat as chairman. His duties were political rather than economic. Cox depicted them "as keeping the Monetary Commission and its committees and subcommittees in motion and in hand as well."[29]

Politically Cox was loyal to the President. This was reflected most clearly in two incidents. When the President decided not to ask Congress for Hull's long sought after reciprocal trade agreements legislation, Hull was ready to resign. Cox wired Roosevelt and urged him to assure Hull of his support. F. D. R. promptly cabled Hull, "I am squarely behind you" and urged the Secretary to continue work on individual reciprocal agreements. He promised a special session of the Senate to approve them. Hull later recalled "there was no hope for me here. The President was behind me in words, but I needed actions, too, if I was to have any success in London." Nevertheless, Hull did not resign.[30]

Cox's greatest service to Roosevelt at the Conference was as Chairman of the Monetary Committee. Hull noted that Cox exercised "splendid tact and skill in dealing with the numerous ticklish monetary questions that came up." When Roosevelt decided that the rising value of the dollar at home ruled out monetary stabilization, Cox recalled that "the whole machinery of the conference was put out of gear." British Prime Minister Ramsey MacDonald charged that Roosevelt had reneged on the topics to be dealt with at the Conference. At the daily executive session the prevailing belief was that Roosevelt wanted to sabotage the entire meeting. The delegates turned to Cox for an explanation. Defending Roosevelt, Cox emphasized the dilemma at home. He explained that the President hoped to raise prices with a cheap dollar and wanted "to slow down" events in London until domestic situations would permit stabilization. The week ended and the Conference did not disband. Cox wired Roosevelt, "If you love us at all, don't give us another week like this one." Two weeks later, reflecting upon these events, Cox wrote that the President erred in not personally explaining domestic problems to the Conference and not promising to return to stabilization later.[31]

In spite of disenchantment over the London Conference, Cox remained loyal to the New Deal. At a Dayton, Ohio Jefferson Day dinner, his first public pronouncement after returning from London, Cox applauded the confidence Roosevelt generated by "the mere fact of action." He challenged old line Democrats and leading businessmen who charged that business was being taken over by government. To the contrary, the New Deal, he implied, was saving capitalism:

> Did not the banks and railroads come forward to be saved? Has supplication come from government to enter business or has business as a whole turned to Washington for relief?

The work of F. D. R. has been directed at recovery, he went on, and he characterized it as "pump priming."[32]

However, as the second New Deal unfolded Cox began to question Roosevelt's program. In the summer of 1935 he wrote

> I want this administration to do well. By that I mean, to promote the general welfare and thus receive credit for constructive service in these stressful times. I believe you will agree with me that one who has been honored by our party with the presidential nomination should not articulate opposition to anything less than treason or semi-treason.

Nevertheless, Cox privately let his concern about several matters be known. In conversations with the President about the various work relief projects he questioned the financing and urged that the money be "put to sensible use." It was the Wagner Act, however, that troubled Cox most. With the measure pending before Congress he told Roosevelt of the need for "business not to be straight-jacketed." But Cox's opposition to Roosevelt was not strong enough to drive him to answer the call to arms of the American Liberty League.[33]

With the perspective of time Cox generally approved of the New Deal. In 1946 he wrote:

> The New Deal was but the legislative form of necessary measures to remedy the greatest economic and social convulsons since Andrew Jackson's time . . . . The days were dark and ominous. The closing of the banks, to mention but one aspect of the crisis, made imperative the establishment of a sound base of operations upon which banking could be resumed. The ensuing measures were not products of any man's theorizing but of practical necessity.[34]

An internationalist, Cox was deeply interested in the events leading up to World War II. The Munich Conference convinced him more than ever that the reparations situation still contributed to world problems. Had the European economy been stabilized after World War I, Cox on numerous occasions wrote, "we would have had no Hitler." In the debate that developed on the question of preparedness Cox and his newspapers supported the repeal of the arms embargo, increased armaments spending, the destroyer-bases deal, Lend-Lease, and in general, aid to the British. In September 1941, he wrote the President that "it will be written of you in time to come that in the face of the appeasers shortsighted selfishness and cowardness, you refused to enter into armistice with the devil." In 1944, with the nation in the throes of war, Cox at the age of seventy-four once again rallied to F. D. R. and the Democratic Party. In a nationwide radio broadcast on behalf of Roosevelt's bid for a fourth term, the elder statesman expressed his faith in the American people and spoke of the need for continued cooperation in the war in order to create a lasting peace.[35]

XIV
EPILOGUE

During World War II Cox had turned his attention and energy to a new venture. He decided to reflect upon his experience and wrote *Journey Through My Years*. Not an autobiography in the classic sense, Cox sought to "report here on what I saw and upon the men I knew in the course of the pilgrimage." Sure of the life he led, he wrote in the "hope that in such a review of the past may be found some clue to the enigma of the future . . . ." In the ideal sense autobiography should help the writer discover his life, but Cox instead reaffirmed himself. Similarly, autobiography can be a valuable corrective to historiography. *Journey*, although revealing, suffered shortcomings on this count as well.[1]

By design Cox avoided large parts of his personal life and career. This was especially true of the politics of the twenties and thirties. In the process of deleting events and attitudes Cox hoped to add dimension to his own historical image. Rather than reveal his opposition to Franklin Delano Roosevelt, Cox tried to connect his own past with the New Deal. To his readers Cox emerged as a New Deal liberal which he characterized as the pragmatic hero of the common man. Another shortcoming of the book, common to memoirs by older men, was that it took on the characteristics of an apology. Writing to reassure posterity of the idea of progress and the need for order Cox referred to the future. He optimistically and rationally concluded that

> Human nature may not change, but intelligence can and does increase. It is clear now that with the new destructiveness of war, nations must conform to the demands of decency and humanity or perish at each others throats. Upon it all issues hinge.
>
> Despite past and present discouragements, I still have faith in the ultimate good and progress of mankind. Whether that ultimate good comes immediately enough to serve our own times is a question to be determined by prompt and intelligent action now.[2]

Throughout his life, James M. Cox took the ideals of democracy for granted. Consequently, he failed to see the ironies implicit in his actions. The anxieties of his youth drove Cox to gain success and recognition. The example of John Q. Baker provided him with a model upon which to build a career. Turning to the city, he observed the search for order and came to recognize the interaction of groups. He learned that individuals and groups with power could use that power to achieve their objectives. As secretary to Paul J. Sorg, Cox came to know that effectively responding to the interests of specialized groups would be repaid with support.

In journalism Cox soon saw the value of efficient administration and technology as a means to build a powerful newspaper. Before long the *Dayton Daily News* had become the leading afternoon daily in the area, and a strong influence in setting community standards. By boosting the interests of the powerful, Cox became an integral part of the Dayton power structure. Seeing geographic areas as systems and the sum of their parts, Cox came to know that groups in the system were vertically organized. Each group with power had an elite who, when conflict arose, could be relied upon to share power through the help of mediators. The mediator, Cox believed, should decide what was in the common good based upon expertise, efficiency, and a systematic understanding of the society. Through the *News* and personally Cox assumed the role of mediator. He attained both wealth and prestige and before long turned his energy to politics.

In politics, Cox transferred the standards of business efficiency and power brokerage to government. To get elected he skillfully appealed to distinct interest groups in the community. Once in congress he championed the objectives of Dayton industry and business while espousing the need for business efficiency in government. Using congress as a stepping stone to become governor of Ohio, Cox continued to promote system in government as a way to secure the objectives of those groups with power. Mediating the conflicting interests, he directed the activities of the state to maintain the existing power structure. In the process, the nexus of decision making shifted to correspond to what one scholar referred to as the "cosmopolitan considerations, technical expertness, and the objectives of those involved in the wider networks of modern society."[3]

During World War I Cox continued to advocate system and efficiency to achieve the goals of the nation at war. Possessed with the fears accompanying war, he helped create control mechanisms designed to produce maximum military participation in an urban society. In the aftermath of war he capitalized politically on the xenophobia as well as real problems of the country by offering systematic solutions to the nation's ills. His postwar activities catapulted him into presidential politics.

On the national level Cox became part of a coalition designed to redirect the Democratic Party. By appealing to diverse groups and gaining control of the party machinery, he helped forge a coalition consisting mainly of Democrats from the urban-industrial North, the South, and leading internationalists. They sought to advance systematic labor-business relations, employ business techniques in government, establish harmony between agriculture and the consumer, and create an open-door international order. In 1928 this coalition, behind the candidacy of Alfred E. Smith of New York, succeeded in winning a majority of the votes in the large industrial cities of the North for the Democratic Party. In 1932 with the world in the throes of depression Franklin D. Roosevelt was elected President.

After Cox's defeat in 1920, he again turned his energy to journalism. Using the tested formula of efficient technology and administration, Cox gained control of afternoon journalism in metropolitan Miami, Florida, and complete control of newspaper zones in Dayton and Springfield, Ohio, as well as in Atlanta, Georgia. In politics, even though Cox reached his peak long before the cataclysmic events of the 1930's and 1940's, the New Deal coalition was a partial monument to his efforts.

James Middleton Cox died on July 15, 1957, of heart failure at Trailsend, his home for more than forty years. Cox left most of his estate, valued at $10 million, to his son James, his daughters Anne and Barbara, and his wife of thirty-eight years Margaretta Blair Cox. He also provided a small annual income for a second son John W. Cox who had long been institutionalized for reasons of health. James, Jr., was given outright control of the Atlanta newspapers while the controlling stocks of the Dayton, Miami, and Springfield newspapers were put into a trust fund at the Winters National Bank and Trust Company of Dayton. His wife, son James, son-in-law Daniel J. Mahoney, and Ralph Sadler of The Dayton News Company were appointed trustees. The former governor directed the trustees to run the papers "in accord with the principles of Thomas Jefferson" and he urged "devotion to the best interests of those communities wherein my papers are located." Since "the working people" bought and read the papers, Cox asked his trustees and children "to recognize this debt." Remain "champions of the rights of the weak" he pleaded but he also counseled "never be pressed to an encroachment on the just rights of anyone."[5]

The ideas of efficiency and system permeated the personal as well as the public life of James Cox. At the age of seventy-five and "still functioning . . . with a fair measure of efficiency," he wrote:

> To me, health is a matter of maintaining a rhythmic way of living. Except for rhythm and the balance which rhythm keeps, the world would collapse.

"Our great war effort," he went on,

> manifested as never before, the power of rhythm. We have here had the correlated labors of millions of people both on and away from the battle fronts. It may prove to have been worth the cost of the war to discover in this, the most stupendous human effort in all history, the possibility of human cooperation.[4]

James M. Cox reflected his times. In 1929 sociologist Karl Mannheim wrote of western society that "The chief characteristic of modern culture is the tendency to include as much as possible in the realm of the rational and to bring it under administrative control—and, on the other hand, to reduce the 'irrational' element to the vanishing point." But the liberal urban middle-class emphasis upon system and efficiency possessed limitations. In the process of fashioning a liberal democratic society this ideology of efficiency sanctioned a new irrational sphere embodied in the domination by various elites. Commenting about liberal-democratic bourgeois thought, Mannehim observed that "As regards ends, this theory teaches that there is one right set of ends of political conduct which, in so far as it has not already been found, may be arrived at by discussion." Taken to its logical extension this thinking could lead to the sentiment Cox expressed in a moment of failure:

> Sometimes I feel that we would be better off in an emergency with a dictator. In [Woodrow] Wilson we had all the virtues of a dictatorship, and lost nothing in Democratic principles.[6]

TABLE A
Urban and Rural Population,
3rd Ohio Congressional District: 1910

	CITY	SUBURBS	RURAL
Metropolitan Dayton	116,577	28,544	
Metropolitan Hamilton-Middletown	48,431	8,441	
Rural and Villages			55,875
Totals	165,008	36,985	55,875

Source: U. S. Department of Labor and Commerce, Bureau of the Census, *Thirteenth Census of the United States: 1910, Abstract with Supplement for Ohio*, 575-588

TABLE B
Agriculture, 3rd Ohio Congressional District: 1910

Area	Number Of Famrs	Avg. Size, Acres	Value	Native White Owner	Tenant	Foreign Born Owner	Tenant
Ohio	272,045	88.6	6,994	176,507	73,598	14,298	2,981
Butler	2,606	107.0	9,071	1,337	1,008	151	50
Montgomery	4,994	53.7	7,682	2,625	2,064	214	43
Preble	3,309	80.3	7,772	1,693	1,454	78	19

Source: U.S. Department of Commerce and Labor, Bureau of the the Census, *Thirteenth Census of the United States: 1910 Abstract with Supplement for Ohio*, 641-685.

TABLE C
Urban — Rural Vote, 3rd Ohio Congressional District: 1908

	Dayton	Urban Hamilton	Middletown	Butler	Rural Preble	Montgomery
Cox	18,799	4,356	1,346	3,561	3,162	5,137
Harding & Frizell	12,979	3,553	1,802	2,783	3,672	5,631

TABLE D
Election Totals

Cox — D	32,524	Cox's plurality — 13,218
Frizell — R	12,593	Cox's percent of vote 49.8
Harding — I	19,306	
Caldwell — S	2,943	

Source: *Dayton Daily News*, November 4, 1908, p. 4; *Hamilton Evening Journal*, November 4, 1908, p. 6; Ohio, Secretary of State, *Annual Reports: 1908*, p. 194.

TABLE E
Supporters and Opponents of Reform,
House of Representatives — 61st Congress

	Dem.	Rep.	Urban	Rural	1st Term
Supporters of Reform	169	56	58	167	54
Opponents	5	160	61	104	28

Total Membership: 391   Democrats: 172   Republicans: 219

Source: Jerome M. Clubb, "Congressional Opponents of Reform" (unpublished Ph.D. dissertation, University of Washington, 1963), pp. 194-226.

TABLE F
Supporters and Opponents of Reform:
House of Representatives — 62nd Congress

	Dem.	Rep.	Urban	Rural
Supporters of Reform	206	138	110	234
Opponents of Reform	0	24	6	18
Total Membership 391	Dem.	228	Rep.	162

Source: Jerome M. Clubb, "Congressional Opponents," pp. 290-291.

TABLE G
Taxonomy of Reforms of 1st Cox Administration

Ohio
Efficiency*
Reforms

STATE WIDE	INTEREST GROUP
Educational Reform	Flood Control
Film Censorship	Prison Reform
Good Roads	Women and Children
Liquor Licensing	Race
Reference Bureau	Labor
Budget System	Public Utilities
Tax Reform	"Blue Sky Law"
Civil Service System	Lobbies
Judicial Reorganization	Agricultural Commission
Home Rule	Industrial Commission
Recall of Elected Officials	
Initiative and Referendum	
Direct Primary	

*The Cox reforms can be conveniently grouped into statewide and interest group categories. Each reform, of course, had backing and opposition from distinct socio-economic and cultural groups within the state. Cox played the role of mediator as far as possible, and responded from the perspective of an urban middle-class businessman seeking to promote efficiency in government. The taxonomy derives from the models advanced by Robert H. Dahl, *Who Governs?* (New Haven: Yale University Press, 1961) and Floyd Hunter, *The Atlanta Community* (Chapel Hill: University of North Carolina Press, 1953).

TABLE H
GUBERNATORIAL ELECTIONS: 1903-1916

Election	Party	Results	Turnout	Type Pres. or Off Year
1903	Democrat	361,748	866,316	Off Year
	Republican	475,500		
1905	Democrat	473,264		
	Republican	430,617	961,505	Off Year
	Socialist	17,795		
1908	Democrat	552,569		
	Republican	533,197	1,123,198	Presidential
	Socialist	28,573		
1910	Democrat	477,077		
	Republican	376,700	924,463	Off Year
	Socialist	61,656		
1912	Democrat	439,323		
	Republican	272,500	1,028,016	Presidential
	Progressive	217,903		
	Socialist	90,144		
1914	Democrat	493,323		
	Republican	523,074	1,129,016	Off Year
	Progressive	60,904		
	Socialist	51,441		
1916	Democrat	568,218		
	Republican	561,602	1,174,165	Presidential
	Progressive	7,347		
	Socialist	36,908		

Source: Ohio, Secretary of State, *Annual Reports*. The off year election of 1914 attracted a large number of votes. High voter turnouts usually occur in presidential races or off year elections when the voters are aroused. In the latter case, usually the party in power fails to satisfy the voters on matters that closely affect them. The table indicates that over the years the Democratic Party predominated in Ohio and the Republican victory of 1914 grew out of short term forces, i.e. discontent over the implementation of the reforms called for in 1912. See Angus Campbell, et al., *Elections and Political Order* (New York: John Wiley and Sons, Inc., 1966), p. 62, and the *American Voter*, pp. 89-115.

TABLE I
POPULATION CHANGE AND PERCENT INCREASE, 1920 TO 1950, IN COX NEWSPAPER ZONES

	1920	1930		1940		1950	
Miami	42,753	142,739	234.4	267,739	87.3	495,084	84.9
Canton	177,218	221,218	25.1	234,887	5.9		
Atlanta	325,688	440,906	35.4	581,100	17.5	671,797	29.7

Source: Donald J. Bogue, Population Growth in Standard Metropolitan Areas: 1900-1950 (Washington, D.C.: United States Government Printing Office, 1953) pp. 61-66.

NOTES
I
EARLY LIFE

1. Four works stressing variations of this theme are: John Patrick Diggins *The Lost Soul of American Politics*, (New York: Basic Books, Inc., 1984); Louis Hartz, *The Liberal Tradition in America* (New York: Harcourt, Brace & World, Inc., 1955); Samuel P. Hays, *The Response to Industialism*, (Chicago: University of Chicago Press, 1957); Robert H. Wiebe, *The Search for Order*, 1877-1920 (New York: Hill and Wang, 1967). Diggins revives the thesis that liberalism has dominated the American political culture and he cites a fundamental tension within that culture between individualism and pluralism (pp. 4-6).

2. Wiebe, *Search*, p. xiv.

3. Hereford Dugan to James M. Cox, September 22, 1947, Wright State University, Library, Personal Papers of James M. Cox (hereafter cited as Cox Personal Papers).

4. Henry Howe, *Historical Collections of Ohio*, (Cincinnati: Derby, Bradley and Co., 1847), pp. 72-79; Warren Jenkins, *Ohio Gazette and Travellers Guide*, (Columbus: Issac N. Whitney, 1837), pp. 95, 216, 299. See also Harry N. Scheiber, *Ohio Canal Era: A Case Study of Government and the Economy* (Athens, Ohio: Ohio University Press, 1969), p. 205, for a statement on the effect of the Miami Canal on these service centers and the canal's impact upon the growth of Cincinnati.

5. James M. Cox, *Journey Through My Years* (New York: Simon and Schuster, 1946), pp. 6-8; Henry Miller Cox, *The Cox Family in America* (Somerville, N. J.: Unionist Gazette Association, 1912), pp. 196-197, 200. The second Gilbert Cox sold the family homestead and James M. Cox purchased it years later as a country estate and farm.

6. *History and Biographical Cyclopaedia of Butler County Ohio, 1882* (Cincinnati, Ohio: Western Biographical Publishing Co., 1882), p. 612; Bert S. Bartlow, *et al.*, *Centennial History of Butler County Ohio* (Middletown, Ohio: B. F. Bowen and Co., 1905), pp. 348-349.

7. *United States Bureau of the Census Tracts*, Butler County, Ohio, 1880; Cox, *Journey*, pp. 3-19.

8. Cox, *Journey*, p. 8.

9. Roger Babson, *Cox, the Man* (New York: Bretanos, 1920), p. 2; Cox *Journey*, p. 12; Harvey C. Minnich, ed., *Old Favorites From the McGuffey Readers* (New York: American Book Co., 1936), *passim*. For the values and impact of the McGuffey books see Louis Atherton, *Main Street on the Middle Border* (Chicago: Quadrangle Books, 1966), pp. 65-108.

10. Cox, *Journey*, pp. 12-13; William H. Venable, *Venable's History of the United States* (Cincinnati, Ohio, 1880), *passim*. Alfred Golberg, "School Histories of the Middle Period" in Eric Goldman, ed., *Historiography and Urbanization: Essays in American History in Honor of William Stull Holt* (Port Washington, N. Y.: Kennibeat Press, Inc., 1943), fails to mention Venable the book.

11. Venable, *History*, p. 261.

12. Cox, *Journey*, p. 14; Henry Ford, *History of Cincinnati, Ohio* (Cleveland: Williams and Co., 1880), p. 291: William Coyle, *Ohio Authors and Their Books 1796-1950* (Cleveland: World Publishing Co., 1958), pp. 657-658; Zane L. Miller, *Boss Cox's Cincinnati* (New York: Oxford University Press, 1968), pp. 74, 76; Frank Luther Mott, *American Journalism* (New York: The Macmillan Co., 1950), pp. 459-460.

13. Hartz, *The Liberal Tradition in America*, pp. 224-227. Hartz notes the relationship between these feelings and the Horatio Alger idea of opportunity in America.

14. Cox, *Journey*, p. 14. Typical accounts of rural life in Ohio during these years can be drawn from William Cooper Howells, *Recollections of Life in Ohio* (Cincinnati: Robert Clarke Co., 1895).

15. Henry Howe, *Historical Collections of Ohio*, (2 vols.; Columbus, Ohio: Henry Howe and Son, 1890), I, pp. 349-351; George C. Crout, *Middletown U.S.A.: All American City* (Middletown, Ohio, 1960), p. 96; John C. Hoover, *et al.*, eds., *Memoirs of the Miami Valley* (3 vols.; Chicago: Robert O. Law Co., 1919), II, pp. 481-482.

16. James J. Burns, *Educational History of Ohio* (Columbus: Historical Publishing Co., 1905), pp. 120-121; Philip D. Jordan, *Ohio Comes of Age: 1873-1900* (Columbus: Ohio State Archaeological and Historical Society, 1943), pp. 391-392; Cox, *Journey*, p. 15.

17. *Ibid*.

18. Babson, *Cox*, p. 18; Cox, *Journey*, p. 15; Henry Simms, *Middletown in Black and White* (Middletown, Ohio, 1906), p. 136.

19. Babson, *Cox*, p. 10; Cox, *Journey*, pp. 12-15; *Dayton Daily News*, September 24, 1898, p. 4; February 13, 1907, p. 4.

20. Cox, *Journey*, p. 15-16; Hoover, *et al.*, *Memoirs*, II, pp. 481-482; Osman C. Hooper, *History of Ohio Journalism: 1793-1933* (Columbus: Spaler and Glenn, 1933), pp. 132-134.

21. Charles and Mary Beard, *The Rise of American Civilization* (2 vols.; New York: The Macmillan Company, 1930), II, pp. 460-463; Arthur M. Schlesinger, *The Rise of the City*; 1878-1889 (New York: The Macmillan Company, 1933, pp. 186-201; Babson, *Cox*, p. 15. For the transformation of the *New York Herald* of James Gordon Bennett see Mott, *American Journalism*, pp. 41-421.

22. Cox, *Journey*, p. 15; for Cox's reporting in Middletwon see the *Daily Signal* from June 1891 through March 1892.

23. *Cincinnati Enquirer*, March 3, 1892, p. 6; Cox, *Journey*, p. 16.

24. Babson, *Cox*, pp. 18-19; Harry Brown, *et al.*, eds., *Southern Ohio and Its Builders* (n.p.: The Southern Ohio Biographical Association, 1927), p. 40.

25. Cox, *Journey*, pp. 16-17. Cox said that Joseph Pulitzer and Frank Cobb of the *New York World* and James Faulkner of the *Cincinnati Enquirer* influenced him most.

26. Zane L. Miller, "Boss Cox's Cincinnati: A Study in Urbanization and Politics, 1880-1914," *Journal of American History*, LIV (March, 1968), p. 823.

27. Zane L. Miller, "Boss Cox and the Municipal Reformers: Cincinnati Progressives, 1880-1914" (3 vols., unpublished Ph. D. dissertation, University of Chicago, 1966), pp. 186-261. This chapter, "City in Crisis," describes the volatile situation in Cincinnati during the years from 1884 through 1894.

28. Sherry O. Hessler, "'The Great Disturbing Cause' and the Decline of the Queen City," *Historical and Philosophical Society of Ohio Bulletin*, XX (July, 1962), pp. 169-185; Charles Henry Ambler, *Transporation in the Ohio Valley* . (Glendale, California: Arthur H. Clarke Co., 1932), pp. 184-192; George Rogers Taylor, *The Transportaion Revolution 1815-1860* (New York: Rinehart and Company, 1951), p. 298, points out that in 1860 Cincinnati lacked rail connections to the emerging national economy.

29. Hoover, *et al.*, *Memoirs*, II, pp. 565-570.

30. For example see the *Cincinnati Enquirer*, April 10, p. 1; April 19, 1894, p. 1.

31. *Cincinnati Enquirer*, May 3, 1894, p. 1; Jacob H. Hollander, *The Cincinnati Southern Railway: A Study in Municipal Activity* (Baltimore: Johns Hopkins Press, 1894), pp. 50-53; Cox, *Journey*, p. 18. On the Cincinnati Southern see also E. M. Coulter, *The Cincinnati Southern Railroad and the Struggle for Commerce 1865-1872* (Chicago: University of Chicago Press, 1922); Nelson S. B. Gras and Henrietta M. Larson, "Cincinnati Southern Railway: Struggle Between Rival Cities for Metropolitan Dominance, 1860-1929" in N. S. B. Gras and Henrietta M. Larson, eds., *Case Book in American Business History* (New York: F. S. Crofts Co., 1939), pp. 373-384.

32. Cox, *Journey*, p. 18; Augustus W. Drury, *History of the City of Dayton and Montgomery County* (2 vols.; Chicago-Dayton: S. J. Clarke Publishing Co., 1909), II, p. 323. Mrs. Cox lost the child at birth during Cox's first stay in Washington.

33. Cox, *Journey*, pp. 23-25; *Cincinnati Enquirer*, May 4, 1894, p. 5; Babson, *Cox*, pp. 17-18.

34. Constance McLaughlin Green, *Washington*, Vol. II, *Capitol City, 1879-1950* (Princeton, N. J.: Princeton University Press, 1963), pp. ix, 9-60; Cox, *Journey*, p. 25.

35. Cox, *Journey*, pp. 31-32.

36. *Ibid.*, pp. 26-34.

37. Simms, *Middletown*, p. 136; Cox, *Journey*, p. 32.

38. Cox, *Journey*, pp. 33-35; for the impact of these years on the Progressives intellectually see Richard Hofstadter, *The Progressive Historians* (New York: Vintage Books, 1970), pp. 41-43.

II
COX: THE NEW CITY AND THE NEW JOURNALISM

1. Drury, *History of Dayton*, I, pp. 401-405; Cox, *Journey*, p. 38; Charlotte Reeve Conover, *The Story of Dayton* (Dayton: The Otterbein Press, 1917), p. 138.

2. Cox, *Journey*, pp. 38-39; *Dayton Daily News*, October 12, 1901, p. 4; April 9, 1906, p. 4.

3. *Dayton Daily News*, January 2, 1899, p. 4; *Dayton Daily News*, September 12, 1898, p. 2. For a modern day version of this functional approach to the development of cities see Leo Schnore, *The Urban Scene* (New York: The Free Press, 1965),p. 107.

4. George E. Stevens, "From Penny Paper to *Post and Times-Star*: Mr. Scripps First Link," *The Cincinnati Historical Society Bulletin*, XXVII (Fall, 1969), p. 212; *Dayton Daily News*, December 22, 1898, p. 4. December 27, 1898, p. 4; January 2, 1899, p. 4. Dayton was an intricate part of the first interurban railroad boom which ended about 1903. Of the seventeen lines built in Ohio, seven ran into Dayton. See George W. Hilton and John F. Due, *The Electric Interurban Railways in America* (Stanford: Stanford University Press, 1964), pp. 13-20.

5. *Dayton Daily News*, June 21, 1900, p. 4; September 23, 1900, p. 4; October 12, 1901, p. 4; April 9, 1906, p. 4; Cox, *Journey*, p. 43; John W. Oliver, *History of American Technology* (New York: The Ronald Press, 1956) describes the development of presses. Horace Greeley is quoted in Robert E. Park, Ernest W. Burgess, and Roderick D. McKenzie, *The City* (Chicago: University of Chicago Press, 1967), p. 84. See the first few months of the *News* for the gradual expansion of suburban columns.

6. Conover, *The Story of Dayton*, pp. 209-210; Ada Cook, "The Growth of Industry in Dayton" (unpublished M.A. Thesis, Miami University, 1940), pp. 23-24; Drury, *History of Dayton*, I, pp. 608-658; Harvey W. Crew, comp., *History of Dayton, Ohio* (Dayton: United Brethren Publishing Co., 1899), pp. 380-472. For the development of railroads into Dayton see U.S., Department of Interior, Bureau of Census, *Tenth Census of the United States, 1880: Social Statistics of Cities*, XIX, p. 397; for detailed discussions of Dayton's industrial development see Carl M. Becker, "Mill, Shop, and Factory: The Industrial Life of Dayton, Ohio, 1830-1900" (unpublished Ph.D. dissertation, University of Cincinnati, 1971) and Charles H. Paul, "Industrial History of Dayton", in Charlotte Reeve Conover, ed., *Dayton and Montgomery County* (4 vols.; New York: Lewis Historical Publishing Company, 1932), pp. 475-520.

7. Conover, *Dayton and Montgomery County*, II, 481; Drury, *History of Dayton*, I, 638-653. Joseph W. Sharts, *Biography of Dayton: An Economic Interpretation of Local History* (Dayton: The Miami Valley Socialist, 1922), pp. 61-62. On the assembly line process and how Patterson's concept of a factory as an organism preceded Taylorization see Siegfrid Giedion, *Mechanization Takes Command* (New York: W. W. Norton and Co., 1969), pp. 95-100, and Samuel Crowther, *John H. Patterson: Pioneer in Industrial Welfare* (Garden City, New York: Doubleday, Page and Company, 1923), *passim*.

8. Drury, *History of Dayton*, I, 234-242, 574-576; Dayton City Plan Board, "The City of Dayton Growth of Annexation May," April, 1969; U.S., Department of Commerce and Labor, Bureau of the Census, *Thirteenth Census of the United States, 1910: Abstract of the Census, Supplement for Ohio*, 568.

9. Drury, *History of Dayton*, I, 504-536; *Tenth Census 1880: Social Statistics of Cities*, XIX, 397-407; Ohio, Bureau of Labor Statistics, *Twenty-Fourth Annual Report, 1900*, pp. 3, 15-18.

10. *Thirteenth Census, 1910: Supplement for Ohio*, 701. Dayton received the nickname Gem City because of its "beautiful location and prosperity"; see Crew, *History of Dayton*, p. 2.

11. Drury, *History of Dayton*, I, p.177.

12. Cox, *Journey*, p. 36.

13. *Dayton Journal*, August 15, 1898, p. 2. These techniques were the basic innovations that characterized the journalism of the 1880's. See Frank Luther Mott, *American Journalism*, pp. 411-415 and Arthur M. Schlesinger, *The Rise of the City*, pp. 187-195.

14. Cox, *Journey*, pp. 39-42.

15. Cox, *Journey*, pp. 42-49; Hilton and Due, *The Electric Interurban Railways*, pp. 23-29; *Dayton Daily News*, September 10, 1902, p. 1; September 25, 1902, p. 1; September 26, 1902, p. 1; September 30, 1902, p. 4. Some other crusades involved attacks on Republican bossism, the "Clean Up Dayton Program," a defense of Dayton from John H. Patterson's eccentricities, an attack on the Barney and Smith Car Company's contract labor system, garbage collection, police reform, and numerous others. In 1899, after the first crusade against Dr. Joseph Lowes, Republican "boss" of Dayton, Cox faced his first lawsuit. Lowes challenged Cox to prove charges of corruption. Unable or unwilling to do so, Cox resolved the matter outside the courts. When the case came to trial Cox paid a token settlement of $1. *Dayton Daily News*, December 15, 1899. p. 4.

16. Cox, *Journey*, pp. 36-53; *Dayton Daily News*, December 10, 1900, p. 4; May 10, 1907, p. 1; December 30, 1901, p. 4; the April 9, 1906 "Greater Dayton Edition" is an example of town boosterism to promote circulation.

17. Drury, *History of Dayton*, I, 405; Cox, *Journey*, p. 38; Walt Whitman coined the phrase "kept editor," see Park, *et al.*, *The City*, p. 90; *Dayton Daily News*; November 17, 1900, p. 4; the *News* of May 25, 1904, p. 1 and *Dayton Journal*, May 27, 1904, p. 1 both reveal Cox's open conflict with Dowling. *Dayton Daily News*, March 20, 1905, p. 4 is the citation for the "new era" quotation. Cox announced the independence of the *News* on February 7, 1906, p. 4; and the statement on society is found in the *News* of Frebruary 13, 1907, p. 4.

18. Cox, *Journey*, pp. 38, 52; *Dayton Daily News*, April 9, 1906, p. 4; December 3, 1900, p. 7; December 20, 1900, p. 4; April 15, 1904, p.4; April 3, 1907, p. 1.

19. In general these ideas and crusades are scattered throughout the *News* from 1898 to 1908 when Cox turned to politics. Specifically, the *Dayton Daily News*, January 14, 1902, p. 4, contains the "greatest good" quotation, and February 4 and 5, 1900, p. 4 are the statements on the fire. The other recommendations can be found in the following places, September 2, 1898, p. 4; September 13, 1898, p. 4; October 17, 1898, p. 4; December 14, 1898, p. 1; March 3, 1898, p. 4; April 19, 1900, pp. 1, 4; April 28, 1900, p. 4; May 3, 1900, p. 4; August 29, 1900, pp. 1,4; May 2, 1901, p. 4; August 15, 1901, p. 4; January 15, 1902, p. 4; July 5, 1902, p. 4; January 2, 1904, pp. 1, 4; March 28, 1905, p. 2; March 14, 1906, p. 2; February 16, 1907, pp. 1, 4; March 1, 1907, p. 4.

20. *Dayton Daily News*, May 22, 1900, p. 4; April 13, 1901, p. 4.

21. *Dayton Daily News*, March 28, 1905, p. 2; May 29, 1907, p. 6.

22. *Dayton Daily News*, December 25, 1903, p. 4; January 2, 1904, p. 4.

23. *Dayton Daily News*, April 2, 1907, p. 4. Cox had called for the creation of a Chamber of Commerce in Dayton since 1898; see *Dayton Daily News*, October 6, 1898, p. 2.

24. *Thirteenth Census, 1910: Ohio Supplement*, 635. Almost half of the 13,847 foreign-born population of Dayton in 1910 were German. Hungarians were about 25 percent. The Germans had come early and the Hungarians were brought by Barney and Smith early in the preceding decade as contract laborers.

25. *Dayton Daily News*, April 4, 1906, p. 4; August 5, 1903, p. 2; August 11, 1903, p. 4; June 26, 1905, p. 4.

26. Frank Quillin, "The Color Line in Ohio: A History of Race Prejudice in a Typical Northern State" (unpublished Ph. D. dissertation, University of Michigan, 1913), pp. 134-140. See Louis Filler, "Truth and Consequence: Some Notes on Changing Times and the Muckrakers," *The Antioch Review*, XXVIII (Spring, 1968), 27-41 for a statement to the effect that the new journalism appealed to the new residents coming into the city. For detailed accounts of labor union and hiring discrimination see the *Cleveland Gazette* during these years, but see especially

the issue of January 20, 1906, p. 2. On residential patterns, Quillin's observations have been confirmed through the bi-weekly social notes column of the *Gazette*. The local columnist usually noted the address of blacks and the location of events. The locations are generally in the west side. On the paucity of black economic opportunities and the tiny size of the city's black middle-class see the *Gazette* of March 14, 1902, p. 2; January 17, 1903, p. 1; January 24, 1903, p. 1; March 7, 1903, p. 1; August 1, 1902, p. 1.

27. *Dayton Daily News*, November 16, 1898, p. 2; November 10, 1898, p. 4; May 30, 1899, p. 4; June 24, 1899, p. 4; March 9, 1904, p. 4; January 9, 1907, p. 2; February 28, 1906, p. 4; March 2, 1906, p. 4. See also Charles Crowe, "Racial Massacre in Atlanta," *Journal of Negro History*, LIV (April, 1969), pp. 150-173 for an analysis of the relationship between efficiency and racism in the South.

28. *Dayton Daily News*, October 14, 1898, p. 4; July 15, 1899, p. 4; July 31, 1900, p. 4.

29. *Dayton Daily News*, May 4, 1901, p. 4 contains the statement on N.C.R.; July 11, 1902, p. 4 discusses the place of labor; September 5, 1902, p. 4; October 5, 1901, p. 4; Cox's reply to the socialist is found in the *News* of March 14, 1906, p. 4.

30. Cox, *Journey*, pp. 52-53.

31. Mott, *American Journalism*, p. 436; *Dayton Daily News*, January 2, 1901; September 24, 1898, p. 4; May 2, 1899, p. 4; September 28, 1901, p. 4; Blake McKelvey, *The Emergence of Metropolitan America: 1915-1966*, (New Brunswick, New Jersey: Rutgers University Press, 1968), pp. 72-73. Cox's conception of the unity of the community was graphically pointed out in his dispute with John Patterson. For this see, Cox, *Journey*, pp. 46-49.

32. Richard Hofstadter, *The Age of Reform* (New York: Alfred A. Knopf Inc. 1955), pp. 186-197; Herbert Shapiro, ed., *The Muckrakers and American Society* (Boston: D. C. Heath and Company 1968), p.v.; *Dayton Daily News*, June 24, 1899, p. 4; January 14, 1902, p. 4; Cox, *Journey*, p. 49.

33. *Dayton Daily News*, March 3, 1908, p. 4; September 9, 1898, p. 4; March 26, 1907, p. 4.

III
A BUSINESSMAN TURNS TO POLITICS

1. Drury, *History of Dayton*, I, 512-514, *Cincinnati Commerical Tribune*, November 1, 1908, p. 7; *Dayton Daily News*, November 5, 1906, p. 10; Thomas E. Powell, *The Democratic Party in Ohio* (2 vols.; Columbus: Ohio Publishing Company, 1913), I, p. 456; *Dayton Daily News*, April 12, 1908, p. 1 stated the *News* circulation at 35,000 copies daily.

2. *Thirteenth Census, 1910: Abstract for Ohio*, 575-588.

3. Cox, *Journey*, p. 48; *Thirteenth Census, 1910: Abstract for Ohio*, 701-703; 735-739.

4. *Thirteenth Census, 1910: Abstract for Ohio*, 641-685.

5. Cox, *Journey*, p. 60; see Chapter I for the relationship between Cox, Sorg, and the veterans.

6. *Cincinnati Enquirer*, September 12, 1908, p. 9; September 18, 1908, p. 3; *Dayton Daily News*, September 17, 1908, pp. 1, 11.

7. *Dayton Daily News*, September 19, 1908, p. 4.

8. *Dayton Daily News*, September 25, 1908, p. 1; September 28, 1908, p. 1.

9. Cox, *Journey*, pp. 57-60; *Dayton Daily News*, September 29, 1908, p. 1; September 30, 1908, p. 1; October 15, 1908, p. 2; October 20, 1908, p. 6.

10. *Dayton Daily News*, October 10, 1908, p. 2; October 23, 1908, p. 1; *Journey*, p. 58. See the *News* in general from September 25 through October 31, 1908.

11. *Dayton Daily News*, October 1, 1908, p. 1; October 9, 1908, p. 13; October 10, 1908, p. 7; October 8, 1908, p. 6; October 27, 1908, p. 4; October 30, 1908, p. 1.

12. Edgar Eugene Robinson, *The Presidential Vote, 1896-1932* (Stanford: Stanford University Press, 1934), pp. 13-14.

13. *Dayton Daily News*, November 4, 1908, p. 4; *Hamilton Evening Journal* November 4, 1908, p. 6; Ohio, Secretary of State, *Annual Reports: 1908* (Columbus, Ohio), p. 194. Working class wards are defined on the basis of the Socialist vote in the wards. If a ward had a large Socialist turnout it was assumed to be working class. In support of this assumption see Lee Benson, "Research Problems in American Political Historiography" in Mirra Komarovsky, ed., *Common Frontiers of the Social Sciences* (Glencoe, Illinois: The Free Press, 1957), pp. 159-171. The technique has added credibility in view of the extensive socialist activity in Ohio during the first decade of the 20th century.

14. Judson Harmon won the governship by also running well in the cities. Cortez A. M. Ewing, *Congressional Elections: 1896-1944* (Norman, Oklahoma: University of Oklahoma Press, 1947), pp. 27, 4-42; Charles G. Sellers, "The Equilibrium Cycle in Two Party Politics," *Political Science Quarterly*, XXIX (Spring, 1967), pp. 17-19.

15. Jerome M. Clubb, "Congressional Opponents of Reform" (unpublished Ph.D. dissertation, University of Washington, 1963), pp. 194-226.

16. Cox, *Journey*, p. 116; *World's Work*, September, 1920, p. 427.

17. Cox, *Journey*, pp. 116-117.

18. U.S. Congress, House, 61st Cong., 2nd sess., May 2, May 16, 1910, *Congressional Record*, XLV, 6177-6183, 6994-7006; Cox, *Journey*, pp. 60-61.

19. Drury, *History of Dayton*, I, 587; Cox, *Journey*, pp. 65-66.

20. U.S., Congress, House, 61st Cong., 2nd sess., May 2, May 16, 1910, *Congressional Record*, XLV, 6177-6183, 6994-7006.

21. U.S., Congress, House, 61st Cong., 2nd sess., January 15, January 20, Februrary 7, May 21, 1910, *Congressional Record*, XLV, 664, 857, 1565, 6715, 7776.

22. Cox, *Journey*, pp. 30, 64; James M. Cox to *New York Times*, December 14, 1910, Cox Personal Papers.

23. Cox, *Journey*, pp. 64-65; Richard Lowitt, *George Norris:The Making of a Progressive* (Syracuse, New York; Syracuse University Press, 1963), pp. 139-183; Kenneth W. Hechler, *Insurgency: Personalities and Policies of the Taft Era* (New York: Columbia University Press, 1940), passim.

24. Cox, *Journey*, p. 117; Lowitt, *The Making of a Progressive*, pp. 186-187.

25. Clubb, "Congressional Opponents," pp. 167-170, 177-180; U.S., Congress, House, 61st Cong., 2nd sess., June 7, June 24, 1910, *Congressional Record*, XLV, 7585-7586, 7764-7768, 9026-9027; Philip A. Grant, Jr., "Congressional Campaigns of James M. Cox, 1908 and 1910," *Ohio History*, LXXXI (Winter, 1972), 11-13; Cox, *Journey*, p. 117. See also Claude E. Barfield, "'Our Share of the Booty': The Democratic Party, Cannonism, and The Payne Aldrich Tariff," *Journal of American History*, LVII (September, 1970), pp. 308-327.

26. *Dayton Daily News*, November 9, 1910, p. 14, *Hamilton Evening Journal*, November 9, 1910, p. 10; *Eaton Herald*, November 9, 1910, p. 1. The survey research data of the Inter-University Consortium for Political Research at the University of Michigan suggests that working class voters fail to vote in large numbers in bi-elections. See Angus Campbell, *et al.*, *American Voter* (New York: John Wiley and Sons, Inc., 1960), pp. 89-115.

27. Clubb, "Congressional Opponents," pp. 290-291.

28. U.S., Congress, House, 62nd Cong., 2nd sess., January 19, January 27, 1912, Congressional Record, XLVIII, 1105-1109, 1322-1323.

29. *Ibid.*, August 11, 1911, 3855-3856.

30. *Ibid.*, May 2, 1911, 5752A; *Ibid., Appendix* ,April ll, April 30, 1912, 111-112, 254-255.

31. *Ibid.*, April 20, 1912, 5065-5066. The amendment was intended to replace a $987,400 allocation to experiment with mail transportation via pneumatic tubes.

32. For an important statement on the significance of efficiency in the progressive movement see Samuel Haber, *Efficiency and Uplift: Scientific Management in the Progressive Era 1890-1920* (Chicago: University of Chicago Press, 1964). For the legislative taxonomy see James D. Barber, *The Lawmakers: Recruitment and Adaption to Legislative Life* (New Haven: Yale University Press, 1965) p. 216 and *passim*. For similar conclusions that

progressive congressmen voted in the interests of their district see Barfield, " 'Our Share of the Booty'."

33. The Harmon Manuscripts from October, 1911 through the Spring of 1912, *passim.* indicate Cox's role in Judson Harmon's bid for the Democratic nominations; Cox, *Journey,* pp. 122-124.

IV
A CAMPAIGN FOR THE "COMMON GOOD"

1. Lloyd Luther Sponholtz, "Progressivism in Microcosm: An Analysis of the Political Forces At Work in the Ohio Constitutional Convention of 1912" (unpublished Ph.D. dissertation, University of Pittsburgh, 1969), pp. 1-36, 269-275. Hoyt Landon Warner, *Progressivism in Ohio: 1897-1917* (Columbus: Ohio State University Press for the Ohio Historical Society, 1964), pp. 312-353 is the best chronological account of the convention. Daniel Roy Beaver, *Herbert S. Bigelow, Buckeye Crusader* (Cincinnati: Peoples Church, 1957), Chapter IV, "A Minister Makes a Constitution," is the best account of the role played by the central figure of the convention.

2. S. Gail Lowrie to Hoyt Landon Warner, September 28, 1949 in Warner, *Progressivism,* p. 391.

3. Newton D. Baker to James M. Cox, (hereafter cited Cox), August 8, 1911; Newton D. Baker to Cox, March 30, 1912, Cox Personal Papers; *Cincinnati Enquirer,* February 13, 1912, p. 4.

4. Newton D. Baker to Thomas Johnson, June 24, 1910, Cleveland City Hall, Library, Newton D. Baker Papers (hereafter cited Baker Papers, C.C.H.); Warner, *Progressivism,* p. 265; Cox to Judson Harmon, April n.d., 1912, Harmon Papers; Cox, *Journey,* p. 117.

5. *Cincinnati Enquirer,* April 28, 1912, p. 13; Although Warner argues that Baker had reservations about Cox because the bulk of his support came from the Harmon faction, by April these had disappeared when the two men collaborated on a platform for the state convention. The text of Cox's announcement is found in the *Dayton Daily News,* May 16, 1912, p. 4.

6. *Cincinnati Enquirer,* May 31, 1912, p. 2; June 2, 1912, p. 2. For the fight between the Wilsonians and Harmon at the 1912 Democratic National Convention see Clarence H. Cramer, *Newton D. Baker, A Biography* (Cleveland: World Press, 1961), pp. 64-70.

7. C. C. Weybrecht to Judson Harmon, June 5, 1912, Harmon Papers; Carl Wittke, ed., *The History of the State of Ohio,* Vol. VI; *Ohio in the Twentieth Century* compiled by Harlow Lindley (Columbus: Ohio State Archaelogical and Historical Society, 1942), pp. 17-18; *Dayton Daily News,* June 7, 1912, p. 14; A. D. Follett to Judson Harmon, June 22, 1912, Harmon Papers.

8. Cox, *Journey,* p. 127.

9. Newton D. Baker to Cox, July 5, 1912, Baker Papers, C. C. H.; *Dayton Daily News,* November 6, 1912, p. 6; In addition to the speaking campaign Cox permitted the use of his franking privilege to distribute favorable information on the proposed amendments.

10. Cox to George Burba, July 8, 1912, Cox Personal Papers; Warner, *Progressivism,* pp. 371-373.

11. *Dayton Daily News,* September 5, 1912, p. 6; Charles B. Galbreath, "The Vote on the Ohio Constitution," *Independent,* December 19, 1912, pp. 1407-1410; Robert Cushman, "Voting Organic Laws," *Political Science Quarterly,* XXVIII (June, 1913), 220; Warner, *Progressivism,* pp. 371-373; Sponholtz, "Progressivism in Microcosm," p. 4; Herbert S. Bigelow to Cox, September 6, 1912, Cox Personal Papers.

12. Cox, *Journey,* pp. 126-129, 170; Warner, *Progressivism,* pp. 369, 376; Clement Brumbaugh to Cox, December 15, 1912, Cox Personal Papers; *Dayton Daily News,* November 6, 1912, p.6.

13. *Dayton Daily News,* November 12, 1912, p. 4. A Spearman rho correlation of the county percent urban against the combined Democratic-Socialist vote correlates at .903. Put another way, urbanization helps to explain approximately 80 percent of Cox's vote. For the significance of voter turnout see Campbell, *et al., The American Voter,* pp. 89-115.

14. James M. Cox, "Governor Judson Harmon," *Independent,* November 2, 1911, p. 956; Newton D. Baker to Herbert Bigelow, November 20, 1912, Baker Papers, C.C.H.; Warner, *Progressivism,* pp. 387-388; Newton D. Baker to Cox, November 18, 1912, Ohio Historical Society, Executive Papers of Governor James M. Cox

(hereafter cited Cox Executive Papers). John D. Buenker, "Cleveland's New Stock Lawmakers and Progressive Reform," *Ohio History*, LXXVIII (Spring 1969), 116-137, argues that the urban-based state representatives in the Ohio House and Senate reflected liberal self-interest in steering the various reforms through the legislature and that the new stock legislators were an essential part of the coalition enacting Ohio's progressive reforms.

15. Cox to Newton D. Baker, November 15, 1912; Newton D. Baker to Cox, November 18, 1912, William L. Finley to Cox, November 18, 1912, Cox Executive Papers. On the Wisconsin idea and efficiency see also Stuart Morris, "The Wisconsin Idea and Business Progressivism," *Journal of American Studies*, IV (July 1970), pp. 39-60.

16. Inaugural Address of Honorable James M. Cox, January 13, 1913 in James K. Mercer, *Ohio Legislative History*, II,(Columbus: n.p., 1917), pp. 27-29.

17. James M. Cox, 1st Message to the General Assembly, January 14, 1913 in Mercer, *Ohio Legislative History*, p. 30, Lysel E. Meyer, "Radical Response to Capitalism in Ohio Before 1913," *Ohio History*, LXXIX (Summer-Autumn, 1970), pp. 205-208, argues that much of the progressive reform movement in Ohio was geared to destroy socialism because it threatened the two party system.

18. Cox, 1st Message, p. 32. For full development of the consolidation of authority at the top see Samuel P. Hays, "Political Parties and the Community - Society Continuum," in William N. Chambers and Walter Dean Burnham, eds., *The American Party Systems, Stages of Political Development* (New York: Oxford University Press, 1967). pp. 152-181.

V
"ECONOMY, SYSTEM, AND EFFICIENCY": PLURALISM IN OHIO

1. Warner, *Progressivism*, p. 389.

2. Cox, *Journey*, p. 163; Warner, *Progressivism*, p. 390; Cox to John T. McCarthy, March 5, 1913, Cox Personal Papers.

3. Cox, 1st Address, p. 30; Warner, *Progressivism*, p. 389; S. Gail Lowrie to Fred Geier, June 28, 1913, Cox Executive Papers.

4. Cox, *Journey*, p. 161; Eugene H. Roseboom and Francis P. Weisenburger, *A History of Ohio* (Columbus: Ohio State Archaelogoical and Historical Society, 1958), p. 330.

5. Warren S. Hayden to Erastus Buckley, February 12, 1913; Erastus Buckley to Warren S. Hayden, February 17, 1913, Cox Executive Papers; Warner, *Progressivism*, pp. 400-401.

6. Cox, 1st Address, pp. 34-36; Erastus Buckley to Warren S. Hayden, February 17, 1913, Cox Executive Papers; *Dayton Daily News*, April 18, 1913, p. 1.

7. Newton D. Baker to Cox, February 14, 1914, Baker Papers, C.C.H.; Ohio Const. Art. 18, secs. 4, 12. *Dayton Daily News*, April 16, 1913, p. 1; *National Municipal Review*, January 15, 1914, pp. 73-74; Robert Graham, "James M. Cox and the Reform Movement in Ohio" (unpublished M. A. thesis, Ohio State University, 1931), p. 39; *Dayton Daily News*, February 16, 1914, p. 4; Lindley, *Ohio in the Twentieth Century*, p. 20.

8. Cox, *Journey*, pp. 142-145; Cox, 1st Address, pp. 51-52; Warner, *Progressivism*, p. 426; Herbert R. Mengert, "The Ohio Workmen's Compensation Law," *Ohio State Archaeiological and Historical Quarterly*, XXIX (1920), 18. Patrick D. Reagan, "The Ideology of Social Harmony and Efficiency: Workmen's Compensation in Ohio, 1904-1919," *Ohio History*, XC (1981), 324-329. In 1914 Ohio stood as the third largest state in the number of wage earners. See U.S., Department of Commerce, Bureau of the Census, *The Growth of Manufacturers*, 1899-1923, Census Monographs VIII, (Washington: U.S. Government Printing Office, 1928), p. 84. Consolidating labor-management relations took on added urgency for Cox as a result of the failure of arbitration during the then recent strike at the B.F. Goodrich tire plant in Akron. For an account of the strike see Daniel Nelson, "Hurrah! We're Out! The Auto Age Comes to the Rubber City," *Timeline*, 2 (April/May, 1985), pp. 2-15.

9. Cox, 1st Address, pp. 50-51. Contrast this position with Cox's earlier willingness to reward capital with adequate profits for the risks involved.

10. Mengert, "Ohio Workmen's Compensation," 18-19; Warner *Progressivism*, pp. 401-402; Newton D. Baker to Cox, September 9, 1913, Baker Papers, C.C.H.; Cox to Daniel R. Hanna, February 8, 1913; September 15, 1913, Cox Executive Papers. Green later became President of the American Federation of Labor.

11. Robert E. Cushman, "Voting Organic Laws: Action of the Ohio Electorate in the Revision of the State Constitution in 1912," *Political Science Quarterly*, XXVIII (June 1913), pp. 207-229; Cox, 1st Address, pp. 37, 56.

12. Warner, *Progressivism*, pp. 402-403; *Dayton Daily News*, April 11, 1913, p. 4.

13. *Cincinnati Times-Star*, April 9, 1913, p. 4; Cox, *Journey*, pp. 219-220.

14. Warner, *Progressivism*, p. 426; Mengert, "Ohio Workmen's Compensation," 18; Cox, *Journey*, p. 142.

15. Cox, 1st Address, pp. 51-54; Warner, *Progressivism*, p. 427. Cox to James W. Faulkner, January 4, 1913, Cox Executive Papers, outlines Cox's program for ties between the Commission and the University, as well as his efforts to marshal support among farmers and the existing farm bureaucracy. For a detailed account of the Agricultural Commission legislation and its political nuances see James H. Lee, "The Ohio Agricultural Commission, 1913-1915," *Ohio History*, LXXIX (Summer-Autumn 1970), pp. 219-230.

16. Roseboom and Weisenburger, *A History of Ohio*, pp. 450-451; Graham, "James M. Cox," p. 31; Cox, 1st Address, pp. 42-43. Wayne B. Wheeler to Cox, March 3, 1913, Cox Executive Papers.

17. Warner, *Progressivism*, pp. 428, 437; Wayne B. Wheeler to Cox, March 3, 1913, Cox Executive Papers; Cox to Frank Woods, September 29, 1914, Cox Personal Papers. The question of ownership was an important compromise as the brewers owned 80 percent of the saloons in the state.

18. Cox to George White, August 19, 1913; George White to James M. Cox, August 22, 1913; Cox to George Burba, November 13, 1913, Cox Executive Papers; Cox, *Journey*, p. 157.

19. Cox, *Journey*, p. 158; Samuel P. Hays, "The Politics of Reform in Municipal Governement in the Progressive Era," *Pacific Northwest Quarterly*, LV (October 1964), 164; Warner, *Progressivism*, p. 428.

20. Cushman, "Voting Organic Laws," pp. 216-217.

21. John O'Dwyer to Byron Clendenning, June 11, 1914, Cox Executive Papers.

22. National Association for the Advancement of Colored People to Chairman of the Committee in Charge of the Anti-Inter-Marriage bill, March 8, 1913; S. E. Huffman to Cox, February 15, 1913, Cox Executive Papers; *Cleveland Gazette*, April 3, 1913, p. 3; Mercer, *Ohio Legislative History*, II, p. 220.

23. Warner, *Progressivism*, pp. 404-407.

24. Cox, 1st Address, p. 56; M. A. Neff to Cox, February 3, 1913, Cox Executive Papers; Ohio, General Assembly, House, 80th Gen. Assem., February 10, 1913, *Ohio House Journal*, CIII, p. 475.

25. Cox, *Journey*, pp. 144-149; Cox, 1st Address, pp. 40-41; Warner, *Progressivism*, pp. 407-408.

VI
COMBATING "RIOT AND REVOLUTION:"
STRUCTURAL REFORM

1. Sponholtz, "Progressivism in Microcosm," *passim*; Cox, *Journey*, p. 135, Meyer, "Radical Responses," pp. 206-208.

2. Cox, 1st Address, pp. 31, 36; Warner, *Progressivism*, pp. 320-323; 392-393.

3. Newton D. Baker to Cox, September 4, 1913, Baker Papers, C.C.H.; Cox to Daniel R. Hanna, September 13, 1913; Cox to Carl Friebolin, August 11, 1913, Cox Executive Papers; Warner, *Progressivism*, pp. 393-394; Regan, "The Ideology of Social Harmony," p. 326; Cox, *Journey*, p. 143.

4. Warner, *Progressivism*, pp. 324-3256; 394-395; Sponholtz, "Progressivism in Microcosm," p. 23.

5. Cox, 1st Address, pp. 33-35.

6. Hoyt Landon Warner, *The Life of Mr. Justice Clarke* (Cleveland: World Press, 1959), p. 54; Warner, *Progressivism*, pp. 424-425; Cox to John H. Clarke, April 26, 1913; Newton D. Baker to Cox, April 26, 1913, Cox Executive Papers; Cox, *Journey*, pp. 161-162.

7. Cox, 1st Address, p. 28.

8. Cox, 1st Address, pp. 29, 34. The limitation on bond indebtedness and restrictions on the sale of publicly owned utility bonds further indicated this unwillingness to give the cities new revenues. It should also be noted that the National Municipal League generally favored the strong mayor plan at this time.

9. Cox, *Journey*, p. 160.

10. Warner, *Progressivism*, pp. 428-430.

11. Harley Leist Lutz, *The State Tax Commission*, Harvard Economic Studies, Vol. VIII (Cambridge: Harvard University Press, 1918), p. 503; Brief discussing the Warnes Law, n.a., n.d., Cox Executive Papers; "Commencement Address: Ohio State University," June 11, 1913, Cox Personal Papers; Address: Methodist-Episcopal Church Columbus, Ohio, October 20, 1913, Cox Personal Papers.

12. Cox to Collin C. Meekison, June 11, 1913; Cox to Jesse H. Webb, July 2, 1914; Cox to *New York World*, February 13, 1914, Cox Executive Papers; Warner, *Progressivism*, p. 430. The tax was computed on the basis of the Smith 1 Percent Law then in effect.

13. Milton Warnes to Cox, May 18, 1914, Cox Executive Papers.

14. Carl Friebolin to Cox, July 2, 1914; Cox to John Q. Baker; Cox to William F. Maag, August 8, 1914, Cox Executive Papers; Cox to Newton D. Baker, February 16, 1914, Baker Papers, C.C.H.; Warner, *Progressivism*, pp. 430, 438.

15. Cox, *Journey*, p. 161; Cox, 1st Address, p. 45; Sponholtz, "Progressivism in Microcosm," pp. 3, 18-19; Cox to Ohio Tax League, September 9, 1913; Cox to William A. Greenlund, June 9, 1913; Cox to Frank Hursh, June 12, 1913; Cox to George White, June 26, 1913, Cox Executive Papers; Oliver C. Lockhart, "Recent Developments in Taxation in Ohio," *Quarterly Journal of Economics*, XXIX (May, 1915), pp. 485-486; Warner, *Progressivism*, pp. 397-416.

16. Cox, 1st Address, p. 32; Cox, *Journey*, p. 163. The idea came from S. Gale Lowrie, an expatriate from the Wisconsin program and Cox's first director of the Legislative Reference Bureau, see Warner, *Progressivism*, p. 425; William O. Heffernan, "State Budget Making in Ohio," *Annals of the American Academy of Political Science*, LXII (November 1915), pp. 98-99.

17. Civic League of Cleveland to Cox, December 5, 1912, Cox Executive Papers; Warner, *Progressivism*, pp. 423, 436.

18. Cox, 1st Address, p. 46; Warner, *Progressivism*, pp. 405-408.

19. Oliver J. Thatcher, "Educational Reforms That Set a Whole State in Turmoil," *Survey*, January 24, 1914, pp. 494-495; James M. Cox, Press Release, November 24, 1913, Cox Executive Papers; Cox, *Journey*, p. 147. Horace L. Brittain to Cox, September 25, 1913; Cox to Horace L. Brittain, September 26, 1913; Cox to J. William Collier, Janurary 14, 1914, Cox Executive Papers.

20. Warner, *Progressivism*, pp. 408-409; James M. Cox, Message to the General Assembly, January 19, 1914 in *Inaugural Address and Messages and Proclamations of Hon. James M. Cox, 1913-1914-1915* (Columbus: n.p., 1915), pp. 50-53.

21. Cox, 1st Address, pp. 36-37; Charles Galbreath, "Vote on the Constitution," p. 1409; Warner, *Progressivism*, pp. 342, 409, 434; Cox, *Journey*, pp. 147-148; *Dayton Daily News*, March 12, 1913, p. 1; James M. Cox, "Improved Public Highways," *Annals of the American Academy of Political andSocial Sciences*, L (November 1913), pp. 35-36.

22. Cox to Don Young, April 17, 1914; Cox to William H. Herner, April 24, 1914; Cox to Newton D. Baker, May 7, 1914; Fred Rike to Cox, November 25, 1914; Cox to Fred Rike, November 28, 1914, Cox Executive Papers. While urban business interests looked upon the good roads idea favorably many property owners looked negatively upon the use of the property tax to build the road system. See Robert Black to Cox, September 10, 1913, Cox Executive Papers.

23. James M. Cox, "Ohio After the Flood," *Review of Reviews*, June, 1913, pp. 699-704; Cox, *Journey*, pp. 165-173; Cox to John H. Patterson, March 2, 1913 in Arthur E. Morgan, *The Miami Conservancy District* (New York: McGraw Hill, 1951), pp. 51-52; Mercer, *Ohio Legislative History*, II, 405; Speech of John Patterson, April 16, 1913, Cox Personal Papers; Ohio, General Assembly, House, 80th Gen. Assem., April 18, 1913, *Ohio House Journal*, CIII, p. 1191.

24. Morgan, *The Miami Conservancy*, pp. 133-201; Roseboom and Weisenburger, *A History of Ohio*, pp. 331-333; Ohio, General Assembly, House, 80th Gen. Assem., February 6, 1914, *Ohio House Journal*, CIV, pp. 16-17; Edward A. Deeds to Cox, February 7, 1914, Cox Personal Papers. It should be noted that this regional planning development antedates the 1916 New York Port Authority, generally viewed as the first metropolitan specialized planning agency.

25. Cox, *Journey*, pp. 136, 178. For a stimulating discussion of the idea of the progressive as "public man," see Robert H. Wiebe, *The Search For Order* (New York: Hill and Wang, 1967), Chapter VI, "Revolution in Values," pp. 133-163.

VII
DEFEAT AND VINDICATION

1. Cox, *Journey*, pp. 179-183; Cox to George White, September 29, 1913, Cox Executive Papers; *Cincinnati Enquirer*, June 10, 1914, p. 10; Ohio State University, Library, Republican Campaign Material: 1914, p. 9. The direct primary system also served as a control mechanism which severely limited choice in regular elections. See Walter Dean Burnham, *Critical Elections and the Mainsprings of American Politics*, (New York: W. W. Norton & Company, Inc., 1970) pp. 74-76.

2. *Dayton Daily News*, August 7, 1914, p. 2; August 4, 1914, p. 2; August 8, 1914, p. 1; August 12, 1914, p. 10; Warner, *Progressivism*, p. 471; *Cincinnati Enquirer*, August 13, 1914, p. 1. The commission to study city finances was designed to avoid an open rift with Newton D. Baker at the convention. Baker favored county home rule on taxes but remained silent on the question at the convention which opened four days after Cox appointed the commission on municipal finances.

3. Warner, *Progressivism*, pp. 472, 474, 492; Graham, "James M. Cox and Reform," p. 80; *Dayton Daily News*, August 25, 1914, pp. 1, 7. The quote from Cox's acceptance speech can be found in the *Dayton Daily News*, August 26, 1914, p. 1.

4. George E. Mowry, *Theodore Roosevelt and the Progressive Movement* (New York: Hill and Wang, 1963), pp. 313-314.

5. Warner, *Progressivism*, p. 474; *Dayton Journal*, October 3, 1914, p. 1; *Dayton Daily News*, October 4, 1914, p. 1; Graham, "James M. Cox and Reform," pp. 79-81.

6. *Dayton Daily News*, October 5, 1914, p. 9; October 6, 1914, p. 3; October 15, 1914, p. 3; October 25, 1914, p. 1; October 26, 1914, p. 1; October 8, 1914, p. 1; October 27, 1914, p. 1; Cox, *Journey*, p. 185.

7. Andrew Sinclair, *The Available Man; The Life Behind the Masks of Warren Gamaliel Harding* (New York: Macmillan, 1965), pp. 53-55; W. O. Wallace to Cox, October 27, 1914; George Burba to W. O. Wallace, October 28, 1914; Cox Executive Papers. Cox later said he encouraged Hogan to stump with him, but the campaign was not marked by many joint appearances. More than likely Hogan probably wanted to avoid the unpopularity of the "Cox laws." On Hogan see Charles M. Hogan, *Timothy S. Hogan: Ohio's Crusading Attorney General* (Cincinnati: n.p., 1972). Cox, *Journey*, pp. 178-179; George Burba to O. Harrington, August 25, 1914, Cox Executive Papers. See also numerous letters in the Governor's file of September and October 1914. For the Senate campaign see Francis Russell, *The Shadow of Blooming Grove: Warren G. Harding in His Times* (New York: McGraw-Hill Book Company, 1968), pp. 250-253.

8. James M. Cox, "Why the Administration Should be Continued," *Dayton Daily News*, Novemeber 2, 1914, p. 1.

9. Cox, *Journey*, pp. 185-186; Cox to George Burba, March 11, 1914; William A. Greenlund to Cox, March 12, 1914, Cox Executive Papers; Cox, *Journey*, p. 185. There are also in the Governor's papers letters to support from such groups as the Ohio Medical Association, Ohio Good Roads Federation, Ohio Federation of German Societies; Ohio Engineering Society; Ohio Teachers Association, Ohio Federation of Labor and numerous locals.

10. Address of Frank Willis, September 26, 1914, Ohio Historical Society, Library, Republican Campaign Material: 1914; Cox, "Why the Administration," *Dayton Daily News*, November 2, 1914; p. 1.

11. Cox to William Jennings Bryan, November 24, 1914, Cox Personal Papers; *Dayton Daily News*, November 24, 1914, p. 1; Cox, *Journey*, p. 185.

12. Message of James M. Cox to the General Assembly, December 31, 1914 in *Messages and Proclamations of James M. Cox*, pp. 85-98.

13. *Dayton City Directory* (Cincinnati: Williams Directory Co., 1915), p. 175; Cox, *Journey*, p. 191; Allen Nevins, "Not Capulets, Not Montagues," *American Historical Review*, LXV (Janurary 1960), 257; Roger Babson, *Cox, The Man* (New York: Brentanos, 1920), pp. 37-38.

14. Lindley, *Ohio in the Twentieth Century*, pp. 29-31; Roseboom and Weisenburger, *A History of Ohio*, pp. 333-334.

15. William L. Finley to Cox, July 12, 1915; Cox to William L. Finley, July 15, 1915; William Green to Cox, November 6, 1915; Hugh Nichols to Cox, November 11, 1915; Dwight Matchette to Cox, November 6, 1915; Herbert R. Mengert to Cox, November 5, 1915; Cox to Thomas McNamara, November 5, 1915, Cox Personal Papers.

16. Cox to Harry R. Wolfe, November 5, 1915; William A. Marker to Cox, December 15, 1915; Cox to Judge John J. Koch and the other members of the Van Wert County Democratic Central Committee, December 8, 1915; William Green to Cox, January 14, 1916; Cox to William Green, January 21, 1916; Cox to Joseph H. Newton, January 25, 1916; Cox to James Bretton, January 23, 1916; Cox to Herbert Wheaton, March 6, 1916, Cox Personal Papers.

17. Cox to R. L. Clements, December 22, 1915; Cox to Dr. William Gregory, January 10, 1916, Cox Personal Papers; *Dayton Daily News*, March 16, 1916, p. 1.

18. Cox to Cal Stroup, April 10, 1916; Cox to Woodrow Wilson, March 1, 1916; Woodrow Wilson to Cox, May 11, 1916; Newton D. Baker to Cox, October 14, 1915; Newton D. Baker to Cox, Februray 23, 1916, Cox Personal Papers; Daniel Roy Beaver, *Newton D. Baker and the American War Effort* (Lincoln: University of Nebraska Press, 1966), p. 83; Cox to R. L. Clements, December 22, 1915, Cox Personal Papers.

19. Matthew B. Hammond to Cox, March 12, 1916; Cox to Matthew B. Hammond, March 17, 1916; Matthew B. Hammond to Cox, April 26, 1916.

20. Cox to C. C. Lyons, n.d., Cox Personal Papers.

21. *Dayton Daily News*, June 12, 1914, pp. 6-8; Warner, *Progressivism*, pp. 479-480.

22. *Dayton Daily News*, June 22, 1916, p. 1; Warner, *Progressivism*, pp. 479-480.

23. *Datyon Daily News*, July 8, 1916, pp. 1-2; August 8, 1916, p. 13.

24. *Dayton Daily News*, June 1, 1916, p. 6; July 10, 1916, pp. 1-4; July 15, 1916, p. 6; July 19, 1916, p. 6.

25. *Dayton Daily News*, July 17, 1916, pp. 1, 4; August 2, 1916, p. 6.

26. *Dayton Daily News*, August 14, 1916, pp. 6-7.

27. Warner, *Progressivism*, pp. 481-482; for the efficiency theme see especially *Dayton Daily News*, November 2, 1916 and in general the *News* from June through October 1916; *Dayton Daily News*, Novemeber 3, 1916, p. 1; Cox, *Journey*, pp. 192-193. On the importance of the peace issue see Cox's statement in the *Dayton Daily News* of November 12, 1916, sec. 2, pp. 1, 4.

28. Warner, *Progressivism*, p. 481. Warner advances the argument that Cox's gains were in the rural counties which voted against him in 1914. This seems correct, however a test of Cox's vote against urbanization yields a

Spearman rho correlation of .92. This indicates that the urban vote again accounted for more than 80 percent of Cox's vote. The rural voters went back to traditional habits but new voters in the cities voted for Cox and accounted for his gains over 1914.

29. Ohio, Secretary of State, *Annual Report: 1917*, pp. 225-238; Warner, *Progressivism*, p. 481; *Dayton Daily News*, November 12, 1916, sec. 2, pp. 1, 4. For a reinterpretation of V. O. Key's theory of critical elections see John R. Shover, "Was 1928 a Critical Election in California?", *Pacific Northwest Quarterly*, LVIII (October 1967), pp. 196-204. Shover argued that in 1916 the cities of California voted Democratic but that post-war problems moved them back to Republican ranks in 1920. From 1922 onward the trend was back to the Democratic Party in urban areas. This pattern is born out in Ohio gubernatorial elections. See also V. O. Key, "A Theory of Critical Elections," *Journal of Politics*, XVII (February 1955), pp. 3-18.

VIII
WAR GOVERNOR

1. Beaver, *Baker and the War Effort*, Chap. IV, "Crisis and Regeneration," pp. 79-109; Bernard M. Baruch, *Baruch ,II: The Public Years* (New Youk: Holt, Rinehard and Winston, 1960), pp. 44-52; Newton D. Baker to Woodrow Wilson, July 24, 1918, Library of Congress, Manuscripts Division, Woodrow Wilson Papers. For an analagous situation of the President subordinating the role of the states to the federal government during wartime see William B. Hessestine, *Lincoln and the War Governors* (New York: Alfred A. Knopf, 1945). For an account of the division in the nation see Gilbert C. Fite and Horace C. Peterson, *Opponents of War, 1917-1918* (Madison: University of Wisconsin Press, 1957). For a study of another state council see William J. Breen, "Mobilization and Cooperative Federalism: The Connecticut State Council of defense, 1917-1919," *The Historian* (November 1979), pp. 58-84. In his book, *Uncle Sam at Home: Civilian Mobilization, Wartime Federalism, and the Council of National Defense, 1917-1919* (Westport, Conn.: Greenwood Press, 1984), Breen writes about the Ohio effort from the perspective of the National Council and does not consider the point of view from inside the Ohio Branch.

2. Mercer, *Ohio Legislative History* II, pp. 265-279; Lindley, *Ohio in the Twentieth Century* ,pp. 32-33, Roseboom and Weisenburger, *A History of Ohio*, pp. 336-337.

3. William F. Willoughby, *Government Organization in Wartime and After* (New York: D. Appleton and Company, 1919), pp. 10-18; Beaver, *Baker and the War Effort* p. 30.

4. Beaver, *Baker and the War Effort*, pp. 71-72; James M. Cox, "Ohio's War Work," *Forum*, August, 1918, p. 156.

5. Ohio, *A History of the Activities of the Ohio Branch, Council of National Defense* (Columbus, 1919), pp. 7-17, 31-33; *Dayton Daily News*, March 21, 1918, p. 2.

6. See the business addresses of the Council and Committee members in the *History of the Ohio Branch*, pp. 7-17.

7. Press Release, September 8, 1918, Ohio Historical Society, Ohio Branch, Council of National Defense Papers; *History of the Ohio Branch*, p. 191; Cox to Mayors of Ohio Cities, October 20, 1917; Cox to James Reed, December 17, 1917, Ohio Branch Papers. The first area of war activity Cox lost control over was the National Guard. See Beaver, *Baker and the War Effort* p. 83.

8. Cox, *Journey*, pp. 197-198.

9. Frederic C. Croxton to Danial J. Ryan, June 14, 1917; Ohio Branch, Council of National Defense, Minutes of the Meeting of June 19, 11917, Ohio Branch Papers.

10. Cox, "Ohio's War Work," p. 198; *History of the Ohio Branch*, p. 70; "Ohio's Labor Plans, "folder marked June, 1917, Ohio Branch Papers.

11. *History of the Ohio Branch*, pp. 71, 72, 112-114; William Leiserson, "Outline of a National System of Employment Bureaus for Mobilizing Labor," n.d., p. 3, Ohio Branch Papers; William Leiserson, "The Shortage of Labor and the Waste of Labor," *Survey*, March 30, 1918, p. 39.

12. Beaver, *Baker and the War Effort*, pp. 159-160; *History of the Ohio Branch*, pp. 82-89. Another problem which emerged was the need to provide labor for specific war industries. Ohio was willing to export only its "fair share" on the spring of 1918. Cox was also concerned about the state bearing the cost of the program.

13. "Ohio's Labor Plans," Ohio Branch Papers; *History of the Ohio Branch*, pp. 72-73, 77-79.

14. *History of the Ohio Branch*, pp. 118-119, 125-129; Press Release, February 12, 1918, Ohio Branch Papers.

15. *History of the Ohio Branch*, pp. 120-123.

16. Press Release, August 17, 1917, Ohio Branch Papers; Max Thelan, "Federal Control of Railroads in War Time," *The Annals of the American Academy of Political Science*, LXXVI (March, 1918),pp. 16-19. The interurban lines had been in the small load freight business for urban wholesalers into outlying metropolitan areas for a long time. Often the cars returned empty. The lines were suffering because the war adversely affected passenger business and the automobile was increasingly coming into vogue. This type of freight service helped extend the life of the interurbans. See Hilton and Due, *The Electric Interurban Railways*, pp. 119-148.

17. Fredrick L. Paxson, *American Democracy and the World at War*, Vol. II: *America at War, 1917-1918* (Boston: Houghton Mifflin, 1939), p. 213; Thelen, "Federal Control of Railroads," pp. 14-24; Press Release, November 7, 1917, Ohio Branch Papers; *History of the Ohio Branch*, pp. 152-155; Cox, *Journey*, p. 156.

18. *History of the Ohio Branch*, pp. 155-156; Press Release, March 6, 1918, Ohio Branch Papers.

19. Ohio Branch, Council of National Defense, First Annnual Report, p. 33; *History of the Ohio Branch*, pp. 197-199; Melvin Copeland to J. R. Morrill, September 12, 1917, Ohio Branch Papers. On the relationship between the state councils and the Committee on Public information see Breen, *Uncle Sam at Home*, pp. 34-35.

20. *History of the Ohio Branch*, pp. 156-157; Clark Chamberlain to Carl Parry, November 27, 1917; W. E. Mosher to Carl Parry, November 24, 1917; Karl Geiser to Carl Parry, December 5, 1917, Ohio Branch Papers.

21. The Diary of Josephus Daniels, April 4, 1918, Library of Congress, Manuscripts Division, Josephus Daniels Papers; *History of the Ohio Branch*, pp. 131-135; Walter Gilford to the Ohio Branch, Council of National Defense, June 28, 1918, Ohio Branch Papers. For an overview of propaganda techniques during the War see Harold D. Lasswell, *Propaganda Techniques in the World War* (New York: Alfred A. Knopf, 1927).

22. *Dayton Daily News*, March 14, 1917, p. 4; Cox, *Journey*, p. 196.

23. 1st Annual Report, p. 25; *History of the Ohio Branch*, pp. 148-151.

24. Press Release, August 17, 1917, Ohio Branch Papers, Beaver, *Herbert S. Bigelow*, pp. 119-121; J. Edgar Hoover to Cox, December 20, 1917, Ohio Branch Papers. The most detailed account on Bigelow during World War I is Herbert Shapiro, "The Herbert Bigelow Case: A Test of Free Speech in Wartime," *Ohio History*, LXXXI (Spring, 1972), pp. 108-122.

25. Peterson and Fite, *Opponents of War*, p. 19; Emerson Hough, *The Web* (Chicago: The Reilly & Lee Co., 1919), pp. 257-276, 382-388.

26. "The Organization of County and Community Councils of National Defense," Folder marked June, 1918; Woodrow wilson to Cox (copy), March 13, 1918, Ohio Branch Papers.

27. Ohio Branch, Council of National Defense, Transcript of Proceedings of the Meeting of March 22, 1918, p. 3-6; Notes on the Meeting of State Heads of War Work, April 30, 1918; Proclamation of Governor James M. Cox, June 17, 1918, Ohio Branch Papers.

28. "The Organization of County and Community Councils of National Defense," pp. 1-8; *History of the Ohio Branch*, pp. 20-22.

29. Elbert J. Benton, "The Cleveland World War Machine," *Ohio Archaeological and Historical Quarterly*, XXXVIII (April, 1929), pp. 448-474; *History of the Ohio Branch*, p. 22.

30. Cox to The War Workers of Ohio, December 24, 1918, Ohio Branch Papers.

31. Stanislav Andreski, *Military Organization and Society* 2nd ed., (Berkeley: University of California Press, 1968), pp. 27, 33-34; Stanley Coben, "A Study in Nativism," *Political Science Quarterly* LXXXIX (March, 1964), pp. 53-54.

CHAPTER IX
EMERGENCE OF A PROGRESSIVE PRESIDENTIAL CANDIDATE

1. *Cincinnati Enquirer*, August 14, 1918, p. 1; August 30, 1918, pp. 1, 3; Cox, *Journey*, p. 211. Cox did find time in March to travel to Wisconsin and campaign for Joseph Davies in a special election for the United States Senate.

2. Cincinnati Enquirer, August 28, 1918, p. 1; *Dayton Daily News*, October 29, 1918, p. 6; *Cincinnati Enquirer*, July 4, 1918, p. 1; *Dayton Daily News*, October 29, 1918, p. 6; *Cincinnati Enquirer*, September 24, 1918, p. 3; October 12, 1918, p. 3; October 27, 1918, p. 2.

3. *Dayton Daily News*, October 24, 1918, p. 6; October 29, 1918, p. 6; *Cincinnati Enquirer*, October 15, 1918, p. 2; October 16, 1918, p. 8; September 6, 1918, p. 3; Cox, *Journey*, p. 211. A flu epidemic led to a ban on public meetings for two weeks late in October.

4. Ohio, Secretary of State, *Annual Reports: 1918*, pp. 210- 287; *Dayton Daily News*, November 6, 1918, p. 1.

5. Mercer, *Ohio Legislative History*, III, pp. 13-15;*Dayton Daily News*, April 24, 1919, p. 18; May 18, 1919, p. 1. The legislature, ultimately, refused to pass an income tax and created a graduated auto tax which actually cut license revenues. See the *Cincinnati Enquirer*, January 7, 1929, p. 1.

6. Mercer, *Ohio Legislative History*, III, pp. 16-18, pp. 154-155; *Dayton Daily News*, April 26, 1919, p. 1; June 19, 1919, p. 1.

7. Mercer, *Ohio Legislative History*, III, pp. 16-18, pp. 154-155; *Dayton Daily News*, June 19, 1919, p. 1.

8. Mercer, *Ohio Legislative History*, III, pp. 32-33.

9. *Ibid.*, pp. 18-20, pp. 143-145

10. *Dayton Daily News*, February 21, 1919, p. 1; Mercer, *Ohio Legislative History*, III, p. 26, pp. 71-84, 129, 135-136, 150. Because of the charges leveled by Cox in his message of February 21, 1919, the House voted not to print the message in the *House Journal*. Stanley Coben, "A Study in Nativism," pp. 52-75, describes the post-war mentality as a cultural phenomenon which societies undergo during periods of disequilibrium in order to revitalize the society and restore stability, generally without coming to grips with the real problems. For the reaction of the German Comminity in Ohio see Don H. Tolzmann, "The Survival of An Ethnic Community: The Cincinnati Germans, 1918 through 1932" (Unpublished Ph.D. Dissertation, University of Cincinnati, 1983).

11. Mercer, *Ohio Legislative History*, III, pp. 30-31; *Dayton Daily News*, February 27, 1919, p. 1.

12. David L. Sterling, "The 'Naive Liberal', the 'Devious Communist' and the Johnson Case," *Ohio History*, LXXXVIII (Spring, 1969), pp. 94-95, 149; Elbridge F. Dowell, *A History of Criminal Syndicalism Legislation in the United States* (Baltimore: John Hopkins Press, 1939), pp. 87-89; Robert K. Murray, *Red Scare: A Study in National Hysteria* (Minneapolis: University of Minnesota Press, 1955), pp. 232-233. Years later Cox stated that perhaps Ohio had acted too harshly in 1919.

13. Mercer, *Ohio Legislative History*, III, pp. 56-57; Lindley, *Ohio in the Twentieth Century*, p. 112; Philip Taft,*Organized Labor in American History* (New York: Harper and Row Publishers, 1964), pp. 355-362.

14. *Dayton Daily News*, October 25, 1919, p. 1; October 26, 1919, p. 1; October 27, 1919, p. 1; October 28, 1919, p. 1; October 30, 1919, p. 1.

15. Cox, *Journey*, p. 219.

16. Andrew Sinclair, *Era of Excess*, pp. 87-91; Joseph Gusfield, "Prohibition: The Impact" in John Braeman, *et al.*, eds., *Change and Continuity in Twentieth-Century America:The 1920's* (Columbus: Ohio State University Press, 1968), pp. 258-267; Peter Odegard, *Pressure Politics* (New York: Columbia University Press, 1928), pp. 166-174).

17. Cox, *Journey*, pp. 157-158; Gusfield, "Prohibition," pp. 258-267.

18. Mercer, *Ohio Legislative History*, III, p. 34.

19. *Ibid.*, p. 33; William E. Leuchtenburg, *The Perils of Prosperity, 1914-1932* (Chicago: University of Chicago Press, 1957), p. 185; *Dayton Daily News*, January 16, 1919, p. 6;Mercer, *Ohio Legislative History*, III, pp. 140-141.

20. *Dayton Daily News*, March 3, 1919, p. 3; January 28, 1919, p. 1; January 26, 1919, p. 1.

21. *Ibid.*, March 3, 1919, p. 3; *New York Times*, March 3, 1919, p. 3; March 1, 1919, p. 1.

22. *New York Times*, March 4, 1919, p. 4; March 5, 1919, p. 24; *Dayton Daily News*, March 7, 1919, pp. 24-25 contains the text of the speech.

23. *New York Times*, March 6, 1919, p. 1. These were also the basic proposals advanced by the National Municipal League.

24. *Dayton Daily News*, March 4, 1919, p. 2; July 26, 1919, p. 1; July 30, 1919, p. 1; August 1, 1919, p. 1; August 28, 1919, p. 1;*New York Times*, August 29, 1919, p. 1. On the post-war economy see Paul A. Samuelson and Everett E. Hagan, *After the War, 1918-1920* (Washington, D.C.: National Resources Planning Board, (1943).

25. Murray, *The First Red Scare*, pp. 162-163; *Dayton Daily News*, October 21, 1919, p. 1; December 5, 1919, p. 1; January 4, 1920, rev. sec., p. 3. The miners wanted a 60 percent wage increase.

26. *Dayton Daily News*, October 3, 1919, p. 6; October 15, 1919, p. 1; January 5, 1920, p. 1; January 6, 1920, p. 1; March 26, 1920, p. 1; March 27, 1920, p. 1; *New York Times*, March 28, 1920, p. 1.

27. "Budget System Reforms," n.d., Cox Personal Papers; *Dayton Daily News*, October 18, 1919, p. 1.

28. *Dayton Daily News*, September 21, 1898, p. 4; November 7, 1898, p. 4; October 9, 1903, p. 4; August 30, 1899, p. 4; May 11, 1900, p. 4; December 16, 1904, p. 4; Cox, *Journey*, pp. 62-63, 245; Chapter V above.

29. Cox to Earle Martin, October 14, 1918, Cox Personal Papers; *Dayton Daily News*, March 25, 1919, p. 8; July 10, 1919; p. 6; August 1, 1919, p. 6; September 28, 1919, p. 6.

30. *Washington Post*, January 8, 1920, p. 5; *Cincinnati Enquirer*, January 8, 1920, p. 2; *Nation*, January 17, 1920, p. 68; *Cincinnati Enquirer*, January 11, 1920, p. 9; *Dayton Daily News*, January 11, 1920, pp. 1, 9; January 16, 1920, p. 6. At the Jackson Day Dinner William J. Bryan and James W. Gerard called for ratification of the treaty with reservations hoping to defuse the League question before the presidential campaign.

31. Text of the Washington, D.C., Jackson Day Dinner Speech, *Dayton Daily News*, January 9, 1920, p. 14. Arthur M. Schlesinger, the historian who developed the liberal-conservative model as a means for defining the American party system, was affiliated with Cox as the historian of the Ohio Branch, Council of National Defense while teaching at Ohio State University. Franklin D. Roosevelt, speaking to the Democratic National Committee at Chicago in may 1919, also developed a liberal versus conservative theme. See Frank Freidel, *Franklin D. Roosevelt*, Vol. II: *The Ordeal* (Boston: Little, Brown, 1955), p. 53.

32. *Cincinnati Enquirer*, January 8, 1920, p. 2; *Dayton Daily News*, February 1, 1920, p. 1; February 9, 1920, p. 1; February 19, 1920, p. 1; February 27, 1920, p. 1.

33. *Cincinnati Enquirer*, March 25, 1920, pp. 1, 3; *Dayton Daily News*, March 25, 1920, p. 1.

X
WINNING THE NOMINATION

1. Wesley M. Bagby, *The Road to Normalcy: The Presidential Campaign and Election of 1920* (Baltimore: John Hopkins Press, 1962), pp. 129-122; David Burner, *The Poltitics of Provincialism: The Democratic Party in Transition, 1918-1932* (New York: Alfred A. Knopf, 1968), pp. 62-63. The interdisciplinary approach to political history has yielded numerous insights into understanding the political system of the United States. Among the most important has been the realization the the United States, over time, has had a series of party systems which have preserved the two party process. See William Nisbet Chambers and Walter Dean Burnham, eds., *The American Party Systems: Stages of Political Development* (New York: Oxford University Press, 1967). The key to this stability is found in the ability of the political party, as a dependent variable, to respond to the pressing currents

affecting the majority of the voting population. See V. O. Key, Jr., *Politics, Parties, and Pressure Groups*, 5th ed., (New York: Thomas Y. Crowell, 1964), pp. 222-227. In 1920 the real possibility of defeat, indicated by the loss of the Senate in the election of 1918, necessitated a redirection within the Democratic Party.

2. Stanley Coben, *A. Mitchell Palmer: Politician* (New York: Columbia University Press, 1963), pp. 246-250; Bagby, *The Road to Normalcy*, p. 71.

3. Bagby, *Road to Normalcy*, pp. 63-69; Baruch, *Public Years*, pp. 145, 173-174, William G. McAdoo to Frank B. Niles, February 27, 1920 Library of Congress, Manuscripts Division, William G. McAdoo Papers. McAdoo urged Niles, an upstate Democrat opposed to Cox, to support the Governor rather than alienate possible second choice chances.

4. Kurt Wimer, "Woodrow Wilson and a Third Nomination," *Pennsylvania History*, XXIX (April, 1962), pp. 202-203; Bagby, *Road to Normalcy*, pp. 66-69; Coben, *A. Mitchell Palmer*, pp. 252-253.

5. Josephus Daniels Diary, April 20, 1920; Wimer, "Wilson and a Third Nomination," pp. 204-208; Cox, *Journey*, pp. 225-226. Wimer points out that Cary Grayson, the President's physician, said Wilson was able to "administer the office capably" but was thinking only in terms of the remainder of his second term.

6. Bagby, *Road to Normalcy*, pp. 74-75; *New York Times*, May 9, 1920, p. 2; May 18, 1920, p. 3; May 19, 1920, p. 3.

7. *New York Times*, June 19, 1920, p. 2; June 20, 1920, p. 1.

8. Coben, *A. Mitchell Palmer*, pp. 249-250; Cox, *Journey* p. 226.

9. *New York Times*, May 23, 1920, VII, p. 1. This same issue of the Times also published the first preliminary census report indicating that the nation was more than 50 percent urban. The idea of Federal Reserve branch offices overseas was first advanced by then Secretary of the Treasury McAdoo.

10. *New York Times*, May 14, 1920, p. 2; May 4, 1920, p. 2; June 26, 1920, p. 1.

11. James M. Cox File, p. 3, Library of Congress, Manuscripts Division, National Women's Party Papers.

12. Bagby, *Road to Normalcy* p. 76.

13. *New York Times*, May 23, 1920, VII, p. 1; June 17, 1920, p. 3.

14. Democratic Party, *Official Report of the Proceedings of the Democratic National Convention: 1920* (Indianapolis, 1920), p. 197. On prohibition Wilson had actually written a resolution to liberalize the Volstead Act but Carter Glass, a dry, did not produce it at the Resolutions Committee meetings. See Bagby, *Road to Normalcy*, p. 105.

15. *Proceedings: 1920*, pp. 242-254, 256-260, 264-265.

16. *Ibid.*, pp. 180-200; Charles Morris to John P. Shillady, February 22, 1920, Library of Congress, Manuscripts Division, National Association for the Advancement of Colored People Papers; George Foster Peabody to Robert Woolley, July 22, 1920, Library of Congress, Manuscript Division, George Foster Peabody Papers. Morris promised to bring the question of black equality before the Resolutions Committee but the platform does not contain any statement on the issue. During the campaign George Foster Peabody at the behest of Robert R. Moton asked Cox to make a statement but Cox refused. Cox to George Foster Peabody, September 19, 1920, Peabody Papers.

17. *Proceedings: 1920*, pp. 267-275; Bagby, *Road to Normalcy*, p. 113. Illinois, Indiana, Maryland, Massachusetts, New Jersey, New York, Ohio and Rhode Island accounted for 250 of Cox's 468 1/2 votes on the 15th ballot.

18. Antoinette Funk to William G. McAdoo, July 6, 1920, McAdoo Papers; Bagby, *Road to Normalcy*, p. 114; Freidel, *The Ordeal*, p. 65; Franklin D. Roosevelt to John W. Davis, July 24, 1920, Hyde Park, Franklin D. Roosevelt Library, Franklin D. Roosevelt Papers; Bainbridge Colby to Woodrow Wilson, July 4, 1920, Library of Congress, Manuscripts Division, Homer Cummings File in the Ray Stannard Baker Collection of Woodrow Wilson Material; Wimer, "Wilson and a Third Nomination," p. 209.

19. *Proceedings: 1920*, pp. 400-420; Coben, *A. Mitchell Palmer*, p. 262; William T. Goodman, "The Presidential Campaign of 1920" (unpublished Ph.D. dissertation, Ohio State University, 1950), pp. 199-200. Augustus O. Stanley to Mrs. A. O. Stanley, May 17, 1920, Lexington, Kentucky, Unviersity of Kentucky Library, A. O. Stanley Papers, indicates that the Kentucky delegation was unified behind Cox's candidacy. During the convention

it was Alben Barkley who moved three Kentucky votes to McAdoo. See William G. McAdoo to Alben Barkley, August 24, 1920, Lexington, Kentucky, University of Kentucky Library, Alben Barkley Papers.

20. Wimer, "Wilson and a Third Nomination," p. 210; Press Release, July 4, 1920, Library of Congress, Manuscripts Division, Joseph P. Tumulty Papers; John Blum, *Joe Tumulty and the Wilson Era*, (Boston: Houghton Mifflin Co., 1951), p. 246. Wilson had expressed doubt about a Cox candidacy and referred to it as "a joke." See Carter Glass Diary, June 19, 1920 quoted in Wimer, "Wilson and a Third Nomination," p. 204.

21. Freidel, *The Ordeal*, pp. 66-67; Cox, *Journey*, p. 232; In *The Ordeal*, Chapter IV "Candidate for Vice-Predident," Freidel makes the persuasive argument that Roosevelt actively worked for the vice-presidential nomination but that in the final analysis Roosevelt "was a pawn in Murphy's larger game" to nominate Cox.

22. Oswald Garrison Villard, *Fighting Years: Memoirs of a Liberal Editor* (New York: Harcourt, Brace and Co., 1939), pp. 474-475.

XI
COX AND THE ELECTION OF 1920

1. James Devine to James M. Cox, October 3, 1945, Cox Personal Papers. These feelings permeated the party. See Roger Babson to William G. McAdoo, July 8, 1920, McAdoo Papers; George Foster Peabody to R. W. Hogue, July 7, 1920; William E. Dodd to George Foster Peabody, October 31, 1920, Peabody Papers.

2. *Dayton Daily News*, July 11, 1920, p. 1; July 19, 1920, p. 1; Cox, *Journey*, pp. 242-243. During his brief stay in Washington, Cox conferred with leading Democrats including Morris Shepard of Texas and Joseph Folk of Missouri, two leading drys, who offered to "take to the stump" for Cox. Other drys ultimately would refuse to support Cox unless he came out "bone dry"; this Cox refused to do.

3. Memorandum of July 26, 1926, Homer Cummings File, Ray Stannard Baker Papers; R. Justus Hanks, "The Democratic Party in 1920: The Breakdown of the Wilson Coalition" (unpublished Ph.D. dissertation, University of Chicago, 1960), pp. 302-306; Blum, *Joe Tumulty*, p. 248.

4. *Dayton Daily News*, July 23, 1920, p. 1; Robert Woolley to Cox, July 30, 1920, Library of Congress, Manuscripts Division, Robert Woolley Papers; John H. Clarke to Newton D. Baker, July 30, 1920, Library of Congress, Manuscripts Division, Newton D. Baker Papers; Joseph P. Tumulty to Homer Cummings, August 4, 1920, Tumulty Papers.

5. Cox, "Acceptance of the Democratic Party Nomination for President," *New York Times*, August 8, 1920, pp. 4-16. Cox used a portable electronic amplification system throughout the campaign. For a view into its significance see Burnham, *Critical Elections*, pp. 72-73.

6. Bagby, *Road to Normalcy*, pp. 128-129; Cox, *Journey*, p. 267; Key Pittman to Cox, November 1, 1920, Cox Personal Papers; John H. Clarke to Newton D. Baker, September 13, 1920, Baker Papers, L.C.

7. *New York Times*, July 11, 1920, VII, p. 2; *Dayton Daily News*, September 2, 1920, p. 3; August 25, 1920, p. 1; August 27, 1920, p. 14; Bagby, *Road to Normalcy*, pp. 132-133.

8. Louise Overacker and Victor J. West, *Money in Elections, 1920-1928* (New York: Macmillan Co., 1932) pp. 115-116; *Dayton Daily News*, September 2, 1920, p. 3; August 25, 1920, p. 1; August 27, 1920, p. 14; Bagby, *Road to Normalcy*, pp. 132-133.

9. *New York Times*, August 27, 1920, p. 10; August 28, 1920, p. 1; September 1, 1920, p. 1; September 4, 1920, p. 1; September 5, 1920, p. 1; Bagby, *Road to Normalcy*, pp. 133-134; *Dayton Daily News*, September 2, 1920, p. 3.

10. *Dayton Daily News*, September 3, 1920, p. 18; September 2, 1920, p. 1; September 5, 1920, pp. 1-2; September 7, 1920, pp. 1-2.

11. *Dayton Daily News*, September 8 through September 18, 1920.

12. Bagby, *Road to Normalcy*, p. 130; Antoinette Funk to William G. McAdoo, September 3, 1920, McAdoo Papers; Diary of Josephus Daniels, September 27, 1920; Walter Lippmann to Newton D. Baker, August 10, 1920; John H. Clarke to Newton D. Baker to cox, September 7, 1920; Cox to Newton D. Baker, September 19, 1920, Baker Papers, L. C.

13. Joseph P. Tumulty to Cox, September 16, 1920; Cox to Joseph P. Tumulty, September 26, 1920, Tumulty Papers; Memorandum of October 5, 1920, Cummings File, Ray Stannard Baker Papers; Diary of Josephus Daniels, September 21, 1920; Bagby, *Road to Normalcy*, pp. 143-144; David F. Houston, *Eight Years with Wilson's Cabinet* (New York: Garden City Publishing Co., 1926), II, p. 92.

14. *New York Times*, October 15, 1920, p. 1; October 18, 1920, p. 2; October 24, 1920, p. 1; Cox to Frank L. Stouton, Jr. in the *New York Times*, October 27, 1920, p. 2.

15. Cox to Joseph P. Tumulty, October 10, 1920; Wilbur Marsh to Joseph P. Tumulty, October 24, 1920; Woodrow Wilson to Joseph P. Tumulty, memorandum of October 24, 1920, Tumulty Papers; *New York Times*, October 3, 1920, p. 1; October 24, 1920, p. 1; 200,000 copies of this statement were distributed at New York Catholic Churches on Sunday, October 31, 1920; Michael Francis Doyle to Cox, October 29, 1920, Cox Personal Papers.

16. Tolzmann, "The Survival of an Ethnic Community," pp. 198-202; On German-Americans see Frederick Luebke, *Bonds of Loyalty: German-Americans and World War I* (DeKalb, Illinois: Northern Illinois University Press, 1974).

17. Humbert Nelli,*The Italians in Chicago, 1880-1930: A Study in Ethnic Mobility* (New York: Oxford University Press, 1970), pp. 118-119.

18. *New York Times*, October 24, 1920, p. 1; October 26, 1920, p. 1; President Wilson, disturbed by Cox's interpretation of Article X, spoke to a small group of pro-League Republicans and independents on October 26, and said that Article X "is the specific pledge . . . to resist exactly the things which Germany attempted no matter who attempts them in the future." *New York Times*, October 27, 1920, p. 1.

19. *Dayton Daily News*, October 26, 1920, p. 1; October 18, 1920, pp. 1, 14; October 15, 1920, p. 17. For a contemporary statement of the liberal-conservative model in American politics see Norman Hapgood, *The Advancing Hour* (New York: Boni & Liveright, 1920).

20. Blum, *Joe Tumulty*, pp. 250, 253-254; Bagby, *Road to Normalcy*, pp. 143, 146; Memorandum of October 4, 1920, Cummings File, Ray Stannard Baker Papers; William Boyd to William G. McAdoo, September 25, 1920; Antoinette Funk to William G. McAdoo, October 6, 1920, McAdoo Papers; George Foster Peabody to Robert Woolley, October 16, 1920, Peabody Papers, Houston, *Eight Years*, p. 92; Charles Michelson, *The Ghost Talks* (New York: G. T. Putnams Sons, 1944), pp. 226-227.

21. Cox to Anna C. Sproul, November 10, 1920; Cox to Norman Hapgood, Novembewr 6, 1920, Cox Personal Papers; *New York Times*, June 27, 1921, p. 28; Cox to L. R. Parker, September 5, 1928; Cox to Maynard Niskern, March 3, 1954, Cox Personal Papers.

22. Bagby, *Road to Normalcy*, pp. 156-157; Coben, "A Study in Nativism," pp. 52-75; Robert K. Murray, *The Harding Era, Warren G. Harding and His Administration* (Minneapolis: University of Minnesota, 1969), p. 70.

23. V. O. Key, "A Theory of Critical Elections," *Journal of Politics*, XVII (February 1955), pp. 3-18; John L. Shover, "Was 1928 a Critical Election in California,"; *Pacific Northwest Quarterly*, LVIII (October 1967), pp. 196-204. Both scholars were concerned with changing attitudes and loyalties of voters and new voters in a given area. The point of view taken here is that political parties respond to voting blocs and attitudes in order to win elections. On the significance of this reality for the party system see Burnham, *Critical Elections*, pp. 175-193.

XII
COX AND THE NEW DEMOCRATIC PARTY

1. Statement of James M. Cox, November 5, 1920, Cox Personal Papers. During the post-war red scare, a number of high powered politically active intellectuals were deeply concerned about the reactionary politics of the Democrats. They formed a group known as the "Organization of 48" and explored the idea of starting a new party for 1920. After Cox's defeat the idea persisted.

2. George Brennan to James M. Cox, November 3, 1920, Cox Personal Papers; Burner, *Politics of Provincialism*,

p. 145; Cox to Norman Hapgood, November 6, 1920, Cox Personal Papers; Robert Woolley to Carter Glass, November 13, 1920; Robert Woolley to Tom Love, November 13, 1920; December 14, 1920; Robert Woolley to Breckenridge Long, November 29, 1920, Woolley Papers.

3. Arthur F. Mullen to William G. McAdoo, November 6, 1920, McAdoo Papers; Robert Woolley to Tom Love, December 20, 1920, Woolley Papers.

4. *New York Times*, January 25, 1921, p. 17; January 27, 1921, p. 2; January 30, 1921, p. 18; Bernard M. Baruch to Cox, February 10, 1921, Cox Personal Papers; Burner, *Politics of Provincialism*, p. 145; Robert Woolley to Joseph P. Tumulty, February 12, 1921; Members of the National Committee to George White, February 17, 1921, Woolley Papers; James M. Cox to Bernard M. Baruch, March 18, 1921, Cox Personal Papers.

5. Robert Woolley to Tom Love, September 22, 1921, Woolley Papers; Burner, *Politics of Provincialism*, pp. 146-147; Cox to Cordell Hull, November 23, 1921, Library of Congress, Manuscripts Division, Cordell Hull Papers; Cox, *Journey*, p. 239; Hanks, "The Democratic Party in 1920," pp. 301-302.

6. Cox to Cordell Hull, November 23, 1921, Hull Papers; Joseph P. Tumulty to Cox, October 13, 1921; Newton D. Baker to Cox, June 15, 1922, Cox Personal Papers.

7. *New York Times*, August 26, 1922, p. 1; Cox, *Journey*, pp. 291-299; *New York Times*, August 26, 1922, pp. 1-2; September 10, 1922, p. 1; September 24, 1922, p. 1. For the administration's position on reparations and foreign loans see Joseph Brandes, *Herbert Hoover and Economic Diplomacy* (Pittsburgh: University of Pittsburgh Press, 1962), pp. 170-191. One diplomatic attache found Cox's volunteer diplomacy embarrassing to the Harding administration and characterized efforts to control him as "nervous work." Brandes, *Hoover and Economic Diplomacy*, p. 176. For a statement on the widespread recognition of an interrelated international economy see William Appleman Williams, *The Contours of American History* (Chicago: Quadrangle Books, 1966), pp. 425-438.

8. Cox to John H. Clarke, December 26, 1922, Cox Personal Papers; John H. Clarke to Cox, May 29, 1923; Cox to John H. Clarke, June 1, 1923; Cox to Newton D. Baker, October 3, 1923; Netwon D. Baker to Cox, October 4, 1923; Woodrow Wilson to Cox, November 16, 1923, Cox Personal Papers. This view of Cox as leader of the party out of power is different than the one generally advanced. See Paul T. David, *et al. The Politics of National Party Conventions* (Washington, D. C.: The Brookings Institution, 1960), pp. 76-78.

9. Magazine publisher Edward Bok in January 1924, offered a large monetary prize to the author of the best plan to establish world peace. John H. Clarke to Cox, January 16, 1924; Cox to John H. Clarke, January 17, 1924; Cox to Newton D. Baker, January 22, 1924, Cox Personal Papers.

10. Woodrow Wilson to Newton D. Baker, January 20, 1924, Library of Congress, Manuscripts Division, Woodrow Wilson Papers. Baker later sent copies of the correspondence to Cox and other League of Nations exponents.

11. Cox to James E. Campbell, February 18, 1924, Cox Personal Papers; Cox, *Journey*, p. 324; Arthur Walworth, *Woodrow Wilson*, Vol. II: *World Prophet*, 2nd ed., (New York: Longmans, Green and Co., 1969), p. 420; Breckenridge Long Diary, February 20, 1924, Library of Congress, Manuscripts Division, Breckenridge Long Papers.

12. Franklin D. Roosevelt, "Smith—Public Servant," *Outlook*, June 25, 1924, p. 310; *New York Times*, June 22, 1924, VIII, p. 1.

13. William Allen White, *Politics, The Citizens Business*, (New York: Macmillan Co., 1924), p. 121; Burner, *Politics of Provincialism*, p. 131; David Burner, "The Democratic Party in the Election of 1924," *Mid-America*, XLVI (April 1964), p. 104; Newton D. Baker to Cox, March 3, 1924, Cox Personal Papers. The story of the Davis candidacy is told in William H. Harbaugh, *Lawyer's Lawyer: The Life of John W. Davis* (New York: Oxford Unviersity Press, 1973).

14. *New York Times*, June 19, 1924, p. 1; Josephus Daniels to Franklin D. Roosevelt, Daniels Papers; Democratic Party, *Official Report of the Proceedings of the Democratic National Convention: 1924* (Indianapolis, 1924), pp. 91-92, 246-278; "Democratic National Convention," *Current History*, August, 1924, p. 730. The most thorough account of the 1924 Democratic Convention is Robert K. Murray, *The 103rd Ballot* (New York: Harper & Row Publishers, 1976). Murray pays scant attention to the role of the internationalists at the New York convention and hence does not place much emphasis on Cox's part in the selection of Davis.

15. *Proceedings: 1924*, pp. 246-278, 248-333; Burner, *The Politics of Provincialism*, pp. 117-118. The votes on

both minority resolutions were tests of strenght. A Spearman rho correlation between the vote on naming the Ku Klux Klan and McAdoo's first ballot strength is a high .63, indicating that the supporters of McAdoo were also opposed to openly condemning the Klan. McAdoo's real strength was probably greater since votes were held back for a more critical moment. The Smith people made the issue a must and demonstrated their ability to deadlock the convention. The League of Nations vote also indicated a bloc with the potential to deadlock the convention.

16. A ranked differential correlation between the pro-league vote and the anti-Klan vote correlates at .35 and the inter-relationship between the two variables explains about 12 percent of the vote. The correlation between the pro-league vote and the vote for Smith, Davis, and other League candidates after Cox withdrew is .41 and helps explain about 17 percent of the voting. These correlations indicate the relationship between the urban forces and the internationalists, suggesting that the internationalist Democrats were an important factor in the urbanization of the Democratic Party.

17. *Proceedings: 1924*, pp. 527-532; *New York Times*, July 2, 1924, p. 1; William Jennings Bryan to M. L. Beard, March 10, 1923, Ohio Historical Society, William Jennings Bryan Letter File. On Bryan in the 1920's, see Lawrence W. Levine, *Defender of the Faith, 1915-1925* (New York: Oxford University Press, 1965) and Paolo Coletta, *William Jennings Bryan*, Vol. III *Political Puritan, 1915-1925* (Lincoln: University of Nebraska Press, 1969). *Proceedings: 1924*, pp. 667-772; Breckenridge Long Diary, July 20, 1924; Daniel C. Roper, *Fifty Years of Public Life* (Durham, North Carolina: Duke University Press, 1941), p. 223.

18. Cox, *Journey*, p. 328; Cox to Harry P. Wolfe, July 15, 1924, Cox Personal Papers. The three states united in their support of the minority report on the League were Ohio, Virginia, and West Virginia, the home states of Cox, Glass and Davis. See *Proceedings: 1924*, pp. 277-278. Cox to Manley O. Hudson, July 25, 1924, Cox Personal Papers. Glass called the League "a major issue" before the New York City Democratic Club in April, 1923. See *New York Times*, April 13, 1923, p. 7. A. C. Sallee, "Tom Taggart: Evolution of a Sandwich Man" (unpublished biography, Indiana State Library), pp. 158-159; Claude Bowers, *My Life; The Memoirs of Claude Bowers* (New York: Simon and Schuster, 1962), p. 117; Cox to Tom Taggart, July 20, 1924; Cox to Harry P. Wolfe, July 15, 1924, Cox Personal Papers; *Proceedings: 1924*, pp. 888-968.

19. John W. Davis, "Oral History Memoirs," Columbia University, 1954, p. 149; Burner, *Politics of Provincialism*, p. 135. In addition to supporting the League, Davis supported "personal liberty," the code phrase for opposition to prohibition. See the *New York World*, July 18, 1924, p. 5; Harbaugh, *Lawyer's Lawyer*, pp. 236-250.

20. John W. Davis to William G. McAdoo, July 15, 1924; Thomas L. Chadbourne to William G. McAdoo, July 15, 1924, McAdoo Papers; *New York Times*, November 7, 1924, p. 3; Burner, *Politics of Provincialism*, pp. 147-157; Cox to Manley O. Hudson, December 12, 1924, Cox Personal Papers; Robert K. Murray,*The Harding Era*, pp. 371-375.

21. Burner, *The Politics of Provincialism*, pp. 137-141; Duncan MacRae, Jr. and James A. Meldrum, "Critical Elections in Illinois: 1888-1958," *American Political Science Review*, LIV (September, 1960), pp. 674-677.

22. Claude Bowers to Cox, May 21, 1925, Cox Personal Papers; Cox to Arthur Krock, May 14, 1924, Firestone Library, Princeton University, Princeton, New Jersey, Arthur Krock Papers. In 1922 Arthur M. Schlesinger published *New Viewpoints in American History* (New York: The Macmillan Company, 1922) with its description of the Republicans as conservatives and the Democrats as liberals. See especially Chapter XII "The Riddle of the Parties," pp. 266-288.

23. Cox to Arthur Krock, November 12, 1925, Krock Papers.

24. Cox to George Ewing, May 25, 1927; Cox to Alfred E. Smith, March 26, 1927; Cox to Lee Olwell, December 27, 1927; Cox to Belle Moskowitz, May 4, 1928, Cox Personal Papers.

XIII
PUBLISHER AND ELDER STATESMAN

1. Cox to Arthur Krock, April 20, 1923, Krock Papers.

2. Cox to Editorial Department, *Miami Metropolis*, April 18, 1923, Cox Personal Papers.

3. Daniel J. Mahoney to Cox, April 18, 1923; E. R. Parker to Daniel J. Mahoney, April 19, 1923, Cox Personal Papers.

4. Cox to R. A. Reeder, May 4, 1923, Cox Personal Papers.

5. Cox, *Journey*, pp. 312-313; Cox to R. A. Reeder, September 25, 1924, Cox Personal Papers; Charles N. Glabb and A. Theodore Brown, *A History of Urban America* (New York: The Macmillan Co., 1967), pp. 284-285.

6. Cox to R. A. Reeder, November 10, 1924; Cox to Daniel J. Mahoney, November 22, 1924, Cox Personal Papers.

7. Thomas J. Wood, "Dade County: Unbossed, Erratically Led," *Annals of the American Academy of Political and Social Science*, CCCLIII (May 1964), pp. 64-71; Homer Hoyt, *The Structure and Growth of Residential Neighborhoods in American Cities* (Washington, D. C.: Federal Housing Administration, 1939), p. 186. It was in the 1950's that a strong two party system emerged in Florida.

8. Cox to Harry P. Wolfe, April 10, 1925, Cox Personal Papers.

9. U. S., Department of Commerce, Bureau of the Census, *Abstract of the 15th Census of the United States: 1930*, p. 15. On the impact of urbanization and industrialization in the South politically, see Dewey W. Grantham, Jr., "The South and the Reconstruction of American Politics," *Journal of American History*, LIII, (September, 1966), pp. 227-246.

10. Cox to James H. Gilman, January 9, 1928, Cox Personal Papers.

11. Cox to Edward N. Hurley, December 29, 1927, Cox Personal Papers.

12. Cox to George S. Thurtle, September 12, 1924; October 1, 1924.

13. Cox to Charles Morris, September 21, 1926; October 2, 1926, Cox Personal Papers.

14. Cox, *Journey*, p. 323; Charles Morris to Cox, October 1, 1926; Cox to Charles Morris, September 21, 1926, Cox Personal Papers.

15. Cox, *Journey*, p. 53; Cox to L. S. Glavin, May 18, 1928; Cox to Edgar Morris, May 14, 1928; June 1, 1928, Cox Personal Papers.

16. Cox, *Journey*, p. 387; Cox to Albert Lasker, October 9, 1939, Cox Personal Papers.

17. Cox to Ralph Sadler, December 19, 1946, Cox Personal Papers. Cox also had radio stations in each city but it was James M. Cox, Jr., who conceived of the idea of entering the radio field and presided over the early development of Cox broadcasting operations.

18. Cox, *Journey*, p. 388.

19. *Ibid.*, pp. 394-395; Cox to George Biggers, July 7, 1942; Cox to Ralph Smith, March 20, 1945, Cox Personal Papers. Through Biggers, the editor of the *Atlantic Journal*, Cox recalled his Ohio experience to suggest specific reforms to Arnall.

20. V. O. Key, *Southern Politics* (New York: Alfred A. Knopf, 1949), pp. 124-126. Floyd Hunter, *Community Power Structure: A Study of Decision Makers* (Chapel Hill: Unviersity of North Carolina Press, 1953), pp. 159-161 suggests that the Arnall victory was simply a transfer of the political mechanisms of the state to another faction in the power structure. After the election the power structure reunited to avert threats to the established order.

21. Cox, *Journey*, pp. 396-402; Cox to Ralph Smith, March 20, 1945, Cox Personal Papers. For the place of newspapers in the Atlanta power structure see Hunter, *Community Power Structure*, pp. 60-113, 181-183, *passim*.

22. Cox to Claude Bowers, December 10, 1924; Cox to Joseph P. Tumulty, December 4, 1928, Cox Personal Papers; Arthur M. Schlesinger, *The Age of Roosevelt*, Vol. I: *The Crisis of the Old Order, 1919-1933* (Boston: Houghton Mifflin Co., 1957), p. 282.

23. Cox to Newton D. Baker, May 15, 1930, Baker Papers, L. C., Cox to Joseph P. Tumulty, March 6, 1931, Cox Personal Papers; James M. Cox, Address to the Jackson Day Banquet, Washington, D. C., January 8, 1932, Cox Personal Papers; *New York Times*, March 7, 1931, p. 16; *Wall Street Journal*, March 11, 1931, p. 8; Press Release, March 14, 1932; Joseph P. Tumulty to Cox, March 14, 1932; Harry P. Wolfe to Cox, March 14, 1932, Cox Personal Papers; Schlesinger, *The Crisis*, pp. 290-293. After the election in November, 1929 Cox wrote to Jouett Shouse of the Democratic National Committee and stressed the need to continue building the north-south Demo-

cratic coalition in spite of the seeming Republican dominance throughout the nation. See Cox to Jouett Shouse, November 8, 1929, Cox Personal Papers.

24. Newton D. Baker to Cox, December 11, 1931; Cox to Newton D. Baker, December 15, 1931, Baker Papers, L. C. 25. Cox to Jouett Shouse, June 24, 1932, Lexington, Kentucky, University of Kentucky Library, Jouett Shouse Papers; Cox to Newton D. Baker, July 15, 1932, Baker Papers, L. C.; Schlesinger, *The Crisis*, pp. 306-307. Elliot A. Rosen, "Baker on the Fifth Ballot? The Democratic Alternative: 1932," *Ohio History*, LXXV (Autumn, 1966), pp. 226-246 discusses the Baker effort in detail and Clarence H. Cramer in *Newton D. Baker, A Biography*, pp. 235-258 argues that Baker was a "reluctant candidate" put forth by this Cleveland associates.

26. Cox to Newton D. Baker, July 15, 1932; September 20, 1932, Cox Personal Papers.

27. Franklin Delano Roosevelt to Cox, March 31, 1933; Cox to Franklin Delano Roosevelt, April 4, 1933, Franklin Delano Roosevelt Papers. For a statement by Cox as to why he preferred journalism to active participation in politics see Cox to David Lawrence, December 12, 1929, Cox Personal Papers.

28. Cox, *Journey*, p. 356; Raymond Moley, *After Seven Years* (New York: Harper and Brothers, 1939), p. 225; *The First New Deal* (New York: Harcourt, Brace, & World, Inc., 1966), pp. 407-408, 429.

29. Warren Delano Robbins to Franklin D. Roosevelt, June 15, 1933, in Edgar Nixon, ed., *Franklin Delano Roosevelt and Foreign Affairs, February, 1933-January, 1934*, (Cambridge: Belknap Press of Harvard University, 1969), I, pp. 237-238; Cox, *Journey*, p. 358.

30. *Foreign Relations of the United States, 1933*,I, pp. 633-634; Cordell Hull, *The Memoirs of Cordell Hull* (2 vols.; New York: The Macmillan Co., 1948), I, pp. 252-253.

31. Hull,*Memoirs*, I, 258; Cox, *Journey*, pp. 365-367. In addition to the above sources on the World Monetary and Economic Conference interested students should also consult the following as starting points. League of Nations, *Journal of the Monetary and Economic Conference, London, 1933, June 10-July 28, 1933* (London 1933); Herbert Feis, *1933: Characters in Crisis* (Boston: Little, Brown and Company, 1966); Robert Ferrell, *American Diplomacy in the Great Depression* (New Haven: Yale University Press, 1957), and Fred L. Israel, *Nevada's Key Pittman* (Lincoln: University of Nebraska Press, 1963).

32. *Cincinnati Enquirer*, May 13, 1934, pp. 1, 3.

33. Schlesinger, *The Crisis*, pp. 482-483; Cox to Joseph P. Tumulty, June 22, 1935; Cox to Fred Rike, April 2, 1935; Cox to Albert Lasker, July 11, 1935, Cox Personal Papers; *Cincinnati Enquirer*, October 11, 1936, p. 6; On the American Liberty League see George Wolfskill, *The Revolt of the Conservatives* (Boston: Houghton Mifflin Company, 1962).

34. Cox, *Journey*, p. 339.

35. James M. Cox to Thomas R. Underwood, January 3, 1938, Lexington, Kentucky, University of Kentucky Library, Thomas R. Underwood Papers; Cox to Viscount Waldorf Astor, October 19, 1938; Cox to David Lawrence, August 20, 1940; Cox to Thomas D. Lamont, June 8, 1943; Cox to Albert Lasker, September 26, 1939; October 7, 1949; Cox to Franklin D. Roosevelt, September 5, 1940; September 4, 1941, Cox Personal Papers; Cox, *Journey*, p. 421; Franklin D. Roosevelt to Cox, November 21, 1944, Cox Personal Papers.

XIV
EPILOGUE

1. Cox, *Journey*, p. vii.

2. *Ibid.*, p. 447. On the nature of autobiography see Roy Pascal, *Design and Truth in Autobiography* (Cambridge: Harvard Unviersity Press, 1960), pp. 120-125, 179-195.

3. Samuel P. Hays, *Conservation and the Gospel of Efficiency* (College ed.; New York: Atheneum, 1969), p. ix.

4. Cox, *Journey*, p. 433.

5. *Last Will and Testament of James M. Cox*, Montgomery County Courthouse, Dayton, Ohio.

6. Karl Mannheim, *Ideology and Utopia* (Harvest Books ed.; New York: Harcourt, Brace & World, Inc., 1962), pp. 114, 122-123; Cox to Newton D. Baker, July 15, 1932, Cox Personal Papers.

ESSAY ON SOURCES

The 1960's and 1970's witnessed a renewed interest in politics of the 1920's and the Harding era in particular. A monograph on the election 1920, a detailed account of the Harding administration, and three biographies of Warren G. Harding have been published since 1962. Much of the impetus for this flurry of activity stemmed from the availability of the official and personal papers of President Harding. This interest in the Harding era also prompted James M. Cox, Jr. to open the Personal Papers of James M. Cox to historians. The Cox papers have been turned over to Wright State University in Dayton, Ohio. The Cox Personal Papers and the Executive Papers of James M. Cox are the key sources for this study. Cox left no manuscripts for the years prior to 1910, nor for numerous aspects of his long career afterwards. Fortunately, *Journey Through My Years* contains insights into some of the activities not found in the manuscripts. Additional manuscript sources provide some balance. The application of behavioral models and techniques give the study a broader perspective.

Cox's autobiographic reminiscences about his youth and an emphasis upon place provide most of the information for the early years. The *Dayton Daily News* is a primary source for analysis of Cox's early career as a publisher. His editorial writing provides readily available statements on numerous questions of the day. The *Congressional Record* contains Cox's public positions on most of the issues that arose while he was in congress. *Journey Through My Years* conveniently presents personal reflections on many of the personalities present in Washington during the 1908-1912 time period. The *Dayton Daily News* provides the best accounts of Cox's election campaigns. For the years Cox spent as governor of Ohio the sources are more plentiful. The Executive Papers of James M. Cox at the Ohio Historical Society are a voluminous record of Cox's first term as governor. However, the Newton D. Baker papers at the Cleveland City Hall library contain important insights into Ohio Democratic politics and many of the issues dealt with by the Ohio progressives. The personal papers of Cox for the years 1915 and 1916 contain detailed information on the defeated governor's activities to gain reelection in 1916. Especially important during this period is the correspondence between Cox and Newton D. Baker related to the presidential election of 1916. For the governorship during World War I the Papers of the Ohio Branch, Council of National Defense at the Ohio Historical Society are the most important source. These papers contain accounts of Cox's "war cabinet" meetings, correspondence on the relationship between the state and federal governments during World War I, as well as, information on the organizational activities of the state during wartime. The Ohio Branch papers, compiled by Arthur M. Schlesinger, provide a detailed record of Ohio's wartime activities at virtually every level.

When Cox wrote *Journey Through My Years* he tried to find material related to the presidential campaign. He discovered that after leaving office in 1921 his personal papers were not forwarded to Dayton. This search indicated that the presidential campaign material was left with the official governor's papers. Unfortunately, sometime during the 1920's a fire occurred at the Ohio Historical Society and destroyed much of the material related to Cox's second and third terms. But it has not been definitely established that the presidential campaign papers were among those destroyed.

With most of the 1920 campaign material missing, research on this period has been supplemented with other sources. Cox's personal papers contain some correspondence related to the campaign, as well as several position papers and copies of speeches. This part of the collection also contains a large amount of revealing post-election correspondence. The James G. Johnson papers and the James E. Campbell papers, at the Ohio Historical Society, contain a few letters on pre-campaign activities. The scant collection of George White papers, also at the Ohio Historical Society, is important on campaign organization. The papers of John H. Clarke at the Case-Western Reserve University library have some interesting letters on Cox's attitude toward the League of Nations issue and the zealousness of the internationalist element within the Democratic Party. The papers of Newton D. Baker at the Library of Congress serve a role similar to the Clarke collection and are far more detailed.

Numerous other manuscript collections at the Library of Congress provide additional supplements on the 1920 campaign. The Ray Stannard Baker collection of Woodrow Wilson material contains files of letters and memoranda dealing with Wilson's third term bid and the President's inaction during the campaign. But for the role of the administration during the 1920 campaign the papers of Joseph P. Tumulty are the best source. The papers of William G. McAdoo, Josephus Daniels, and Robert Woolley are essential for the efforts of McAdoo to secure the nomination and the activities of his supporters during the campaign. The Robert Woolley papers, in addition, are important on the efforts to pull the various segments of the party together during the presidential campaign. The papers of George Foster Peabody are excellent for the efforts to consolidate non-partisan support on the League of Nations question as well as to get Cox to take a firm stand in favor of black equality. On the race issue in 1920 the papers of the National Association for the Advancement of Colored People reveal Cox's inaction. The paper's of the National Women's Party provides a detailed account of Cox's position on women's suffrage. The political campaign collection at the University of Kentucky Library has some of the campaign literature developed by both parties for the election.

The Cox personal papers are the principal source on Cox as an elder statesman. However, the Woolley, McAdoo, Clarke, and Baker collections are important for the efforts to redirect the Democratic Party in the 1920's. Also, the Arthur Krock collection at the Firestone Library of Princeton University contains a number of important Cox letters pertaining to national politics. The Alfred E. Smith papers at the New York State Library in Albany are virtually useless for Democratic Party politics. The Franklin Delano Roosevelt papers at the Franklin Delano Roosevelt Presidential Library contain several important Cox-Roosevelt letters, but the Cox personal papers are far more important for the relationship between the two men.

On Cox's activities as a publishing magnate the Cox personal papers are voluminous. This collection of material is an important representative source for the development of metropolitan journalism and newspaper zones. They are also revealing on the role played by the newspaper in relation to community power structures.

To a large degree the sources, and lack of sources, have dictated the nature of this study. The absence of detailed manuscript collections for certain aspects of Cox's career necessitated an application of less traditional techniques. Consequently, in determining Cox's hierarchy of motives and his place in American history interdisciplinary approaches and models, both implicitly and explicitly, have been used. Quantitative techniques brought to light voting patterns which qualitative data subsequently supported. The model developed by Erik H. Erikson, "On the Nature of Psycho-Historical Evidence: In Search of Gandhi," *Daedalus*, XCVII (Summer 1968), 695-730, for studying an individual within the context of their developmental history, their present state and stage of life, the present state of the individual's community, and the history of the community proved helpful throughout the study. The conception of the city developed by Robert E. Park and Ernest W. Burgess, *The City* (Chicago: University of Chicago Press, 1925) provided insights into Cox's conception of metropolitan journalism. A blending of Robert Dahl's idea of pluralism, *Who Governs?* (New Have: Yale University Press, 1961) with Floyd Hunter's model on community power structures, *Community Power Structure* (Chapel Hill: University of North Carolina press, 1953) helps to explain many events where Cox's influence was present. The idea of party systems as conceived by William Nisbet Chambers and Walter Dean Burnham, *The American Party Systems* (New York: Oxford University Press, 1967) helped to promote a better understanding of Cox's impact upon the Democratic Party. The interdisciplinary approach can and should be used for biography, and by historians in general. Models from disciplines related to history have long been available to the historian. Unfortunately, for whatever reason, historians have been slow to adapt to the work of sister disciplines to their own labors. As traditional print sources for the historian diminish, the interdisciplinary approach to history will have to be relied upon and perhaps it will promote a more usable historical literature.

INDEX

Absentee voting, 73
Addams, Jane, 37
Agricultural Extention Service, 48, 77
Americanization, 74, 89-95
American Federation of Labor, 42, 48, 98, 112, 117, 120
American Protection League, 83-85
American Rolling Mills, 29
Amidon, Samuel, 106
Andrea, Percy, 48
Andrews, Eliza, 12
Ansberry, Timothy, 106
Anti-miscegnation bill, 50
Appleyard, A. E., 22
Army Appropriations Act of 1916, 73
Arnall, Ellis, 132
Asiatic exclusion, 113
Associated Press, 20, 22, 67
Atlanta, 131-132, 145
Atlanta Constitution, 132
Atlanta Journal, 131
Automobile license tax, 59

Baker, John Q., 13-16
Baker, Newton B., 63, 139
    Constitutional Convention, 40
    Council of National Defense, 73-74, 80-81
    Democratic Party Conventions, 39, 70-72
    Election of 1912, 39-42
    Election of 1914, 63
    Election of 1916, 68-69, 71
    Election of 1924, 121
    Election of 1932, 133-134
    home rule for cities, 54
    legislative reforms of 1913, 47, 54, 56, 59
    Secretary of War, 73, 77, 83, 99, 114
Barkley, Alben, 114
Barney and Smith Car Compay, 20
Baruch, Bernard, 101, 119
Bennett, James Gordon, 14
Bigelow, Herbert, 40, 83
Blair, Margaretta, 67, 138
Board of City Affairs, 21
Board of Police Commissioners, 21
Bok Peace Prize, 121

Bonnet, George, 134
Borah, William E., 113
Bowers, Claude, 123, 125
Boy's Working Reserve, 78
Brennan, George, 101-107, 119, 122-123
Brice, Calvin, 16
Brittain, Horace, 56-59
Brown, Robert B., 41
Brush-Moore Company, 131
Bryan, William Jennings, 30, 71, 104, 109, 119, 120, 123
Buckley, Erastus, 46
Burba, George, 30, 40, 70
Bush, Samuel, 74
Butler County, 11
Bureau of the Budget, 56, 96
Byrd, Harry, 133

Campbell, Edith, 59
Campbell, James E., 29, 70, 103
Cannon, Joseph, 32-35, 37
Canton, 76, 82, 130, 145
Canton Daily News, 130-131
Canton Canton Alloy Steel Co. strike, 92
Capples, M. J., 79
Censorship, 51
Chadbourne, Thomas L., 101, 109
Chamber of Commerce
    Cleveland, 45, 86, 89-90
    Dayton, 24
    Ohio, 47-48
    United States, 130
Children's Bureau, 37
Children's Code, 49-50
Cincinnati, 11, 13-17
Cincinnati Commercial Gazette, 13
Cincinnati Enquirer, 15-16, 74
Cincinnati Post, 19
Cincinnati Southern Railroad, 16
Cincinnati Times-Star, 19
Citizens Relief Commission, 61
Committee Civil Service reform, 57
Clarke, John H., 54, 110, 120
Cleveland, 24, 25-26, 60, 64, 84-85, 94
Coal, 75, 95
Cockran, Bourke, 104-105
Colby, Bainbridge, 106

Cold Storage Law, 45, 113
Commons, John R., 37, 49
Congress
  Campaign of 1908, 29
  Campaign of 1910, 33
  fifty-third, 17
  sixty-first, 33-35, 142
  sixty-second, 36-38, 143
  Third Ohio District, 29, 141-142
Conference of mayors, 91
Cooper, Kent, 67
Couzens, James, 134
Cox, Anne, 12
Cox, Eliza, 11
Cox, Gilbert, 12
Cox, James Middleton
  Agriculture, 48
  Americanization, 82, 83, 87, 90, 91, 92
  Anti-German Language Law, 82
  Arbitration, 25-26
  Article X of the League of Nations, 113-115
  assessment of first term, 66
  birth, 12
  budget system, 56
  charges of bossism, 45, 63
  coal crisis of 1917, 74-75
  coal strike of 1919, 95
  conflict of interest charges, 65
  criminal syndicalism law, 91-92
  congressional campaigns, 29-32
  death, 138
  defeat in 1914, 66
  divorce, 67
  editor, 20-28
  education of, 12-14
  education program, 56-59, 82, 89, 90, 110, 114
  efficiency, 43, 49, 52, 55-56, 69-71, 103-104, 139
  election of 1912, 39-42
  family, 11-15, 67, 138
  federal aid to education, 110
  film censorship, 51
  Franklin D. Roosevelt and, 106, 122, 133-138
  Georgia politics, 131-132
  good roads, 37, 59-60, 70, 73, 94
  home rule for cities, 47
  Journey Through My Years, 137
  labor relations, 25-26, 47-48, 73-76, 80, 82, 91-92, 95-96, 113, 115
  last will and testament, 138-139
  League of Nations, 102, 109-110, 114-117, 120-124
  League to Enforce Peace, 97
  liquor licensing law, 49-50
  marriage, 16, 67
  newspaper philosophy, 18, 19-27, 127-138
  nomination for president, 101-107
  organized crime, 130
  post-war program, 94-96, 110, 120
  presidential candidate, 88-107, 109-125
  President's Conference on unemployment, 94-95
  prison reforms, 51, 80
  public utilities, 46-47
  race relations, 26, 50
  slush fund charges, 112
  taxes, 47, 55, 103, 104, 109
  teacher, 13-14, 58, 91
  Trailsend, 67, 109, 115
  unemployment, 94-96
  wartime demobilization, 86, 94
  wartime governor, 73-87
Cox, James M. Jr.,, 138, 167, fn17
Cox, John W. C., 138
Creel, George, 81, 101
Crowder, Enoch, 77
Croxton, Fred, 75-77, 82-84, 94
Cummings, Homer, 116, 118, 119
Cunningham, John, 49

Daily Empire, 19
Daniels, Josephus, 82, 116, 122
Darke County, 12
Davis, Harry, 85
  Mayor's War Board, 85-86
Davis, John, W., 106, 122-125
Davis Sewing Machine Company, 33
Dayton
  Dayton View, 21
  Edgmont, 124
  Flood of 1913, 60-61
  growth of, 20-28
    industries, 19-23
    newspapers, 19, 21-23, 129-130
  Riverdale, 21
Dayton Daily News, 18-28, 82, 97, 98

Dayton Gas and Electric Company, 65
Dayton Herald, 23, 30
Dayton Journal, 21
Daytoner Zeitung, 30
Debs, Eugene, 84, 117
Deeds, Edward A., 61
Democratic Party, 70, 119-125, 132-133, 138
   Montgomery County, 22
   Ohio, 68
   National Committee, 119, 133
   national conventions, 70, 101-107
   state conventions, 39, 69-70
Dillon, Edmund, 41
Ditty, Robert, 55
Donnely, Thomas, 74
Dorn, John Gates, 19
Dowling, Joseph, 22-23
Doyle, Michael Francis, 114
Duckworth Democratic Club, 99
Duffy, Thomas, 48

education reforms, 57-59, 73, 82
elections of
   1904, 23
   1908, 29-32, 142
   1910, 35-36
   1912, 39-43
   1914, 63-66
   1916, 68-72
   1918, 88
   1920, 109-117
   1924, 121-125
   1928, 125
electoral reform, 73
Elkins, Stephen B., 16
Faulkner, James W., 74, 81
Federal Fuel Administration, 75
federal highway funds, 94
Feis, Herbert, 134
Felton, Samuel, 16
Fessler, Mayo, 54
Finley, William, 42
Firestone, Harvey, 74, 75
Fisher, Carl, 127
Fitzgerald, John J., 34
flood control, 60-61
flood of 1913, 60-61, 90
Fort Sherman, 76
Franklin, 20

French Lick Springs, 102
Friebolin, Carl, 42
Frizell, William G., 28-32
function of the press, 23
Funk, Antoinette, 106, 113

Galtra, Ed, 122
Garber, Harvey, 63
Garfield, Harry, 75
Garfield, James R., 64
Garford, Arthur, 42
Garner, John Nance, 134
Garrison, Lyndley, 69
Gerard, James, 124
German-Americans, 70, 88, 90-92, 114, 115-116
Gilman, James, 129
Glass Carter, 104, 107
Gompers, Samuel, 37, 98
Graves, Charles S., 53
Grayson, Cary, 102
Great Miami river, 24, 60-61
Greely, Horace, 20
Green, William R., 47
Greenlund Law, 40
Guffey, Joseph, 106

Hague, Frank, 124
Halstead Murat, 13-14
Hamilton, 11, 60
Hamilton County, 15-16
Hammond, Matthew Bray, 48, 69, 76
Hanna, Daniel R., 53, 59
Hanley, Ed, 30, 39
Harding, John E., 29, 142
Harding, Mayme Simpson, 16, 67
Harding, Warren G., 109-117, 120, 125
Harmon, Judson, 30, 35, 38-40, 69
Harris, Roy, 132
Harrison, George, 134
Harrison, Pat, 107, 119
Hearst, William R., 14
Heffernan, William, 57
Henderson, Charles, 37
Hess, William, 49-50
highways, 37, 59, 70, 73, 94
Hitchcock, Gilbert, 98
Hogan, Timothy, 53, 65
Hoover, Herbert, 120
Hoover, J. Edgar, 84

Hough, Emerson, 84
Houston, David, 114
Howe, Henry, 11
Huffman, F. T., 19
Hughes, Charles Evans, 70
Hughes Health Code, 90
Hughes, Oliver, 40
Hull, Cordell, 119, 120, 134-135
Hunt, Henry, 41
Hurley, Ed, 130
Hutchins, Samuel D., 79
Hylan, John, 75
immigration
    Dayton, 24-25
    Third Congressional District, 142
indeterminate sentence law, 51
inheritance tax, 89
innitiative and referendum, 36, 53
intangibles tax, 55
Interstate Commerce Commission, 80
Ireland, 90, 114
Irish-Americans, 114, 116, 122, 124
Italian-Americans, 115, 116

Jacksonburg, 12
Jackson Day Dinner
    1920, 98
Jefferson Day Dinner
    1932, 133
    1934, 135
Jewell, Charles, 95
Johnson, Hiram, 11, 113
Johnson, Thomas L., 11
Jones, Samuel "Golden Rule", 11
judicial reform, 51

Keynes, John M., 134
Knight chain of newspapers, 129
Krock, Arthur, 125, 127
Kroger, Barney, 74
Ku Klu Klan, 122-123

labor relations
    Dayton, 24-25
    Department of Labor, 31
    Federal legislation, 135-136
    Ohio, 47-48, 75
LaFollette, Robert, 11, 30, 35, 124-125
Lamar, Lucius Quintus Cincinnatus, 16

Lane, Franklin K., 82
Langley, Samuel P., 38
law enforcement, 92
League to Enforce Peace, 97
Legislative Reference Bureau, 42-43
Leiserson, William M., 76
Lend-Lease, 136
Liberty League, 135
Liberty Loan drives, 85
Lima, 21, 60-61
Lincoln Highway, 80
liquor licensing law, 48-49
Long, Breckenridge, 123
Love, Tom, 101
Lowerie, S. Gale, 48, 81
Lucking, Alfred, 122
Lusitania, 88

Macon, Robert, 33
Mahoney, Daniel, Jr., 129, 138
Mail Order Journal, 22
Mann-Elkins Act, 35
Mannheim, Karl, 139
Marker, James, 60
martial law, 92
Maxwell, Wilbur, 76
Mayhugh, Charles, 76, 78
McAdoo, William G., 101-107, 116, 119, 121, 122, 124, 133
McCann, Benjamin, 30
McCarthy, John T., 16
McClean, John R., 16, 42
McClure's Saturday Magazine, 22
McCormick, Vance, 102
McGill, Ralph, 132
McGuffey electic readers, 12
McReynold Samuel, 134
Mellet, Don R., 130
Mexico, 68
Miami, 127-129, 145
Miami Canal, 11, 21
Miami Conservancy District, 60-61
Miami Daily News, 128
Miami Herald, 127
Miami University, 12
Michelson, Charles, 124
Middleton, Ohio, 12-15
Middleton Daily Signal, 14-15
Middleton Weekly Signal, 14
minimum wage for women, 48

Montgomery County, 29, 141-142
Moley, Raymond, 74, 82, 134
Moore, Edmond H., 98, 102-107
Moore, John, 95
Morris, Charles, 131
Morrison, Ralph, 134
Mosler Safe Company, 29
Munich Conference, 136
Murdock, Victor, 38
Murphy, Charles, 101-107

National Association for the Advancement of Colored People, 50
National Bankers Association, 45-46
National Board of Fire Underwriters, 82
National Cash Register Company, 20-21, 24, 26, 33
National Defense Act, 91
National Guard, 68
National Home for Disabled Soldiers, 17, 33
National Tax Association, 53
nativism, 83-94, 113-116, 122, 123
Neilen, John F., 16
new South, 128-132
newspaper circulation, 20, 22, 27, 128-130
News Tower, 128
New York Bureau of Municipal Research, 57
New York Central Railroad, 15
New York Times, 112, 102, 122
New York World, 14, 61, 102, 124, 125
Noctor, Thomas R., 98
North Dayton, 21
Norris, George, 34-35

Ohio
　aid to widows with dependent children 49-50
　Agricultural Commission, 48-49
　Constitutional Convention, 38, 40
　home rule for cities, 54
　Industrial Commission, 47-48, 76
　lobbyists, 45
　Public Utilities Commission, 46
　stock regulation, 45, 73
　taxes, 54, 89
　War Council, 75
　Workmen's Compensation Law, 47, 69, 70, 73
　World War I, 73

Ohio Anti-Saloon League, 49, 64, 88, 92, 93
Ohio Building Association, 96
Ohio Branch: Council of National Defense, 73-86
　Committee on Labor and Industrial Relations, 74-77
　County Councils, 84-85
　employment offices, 76-77
　Food Committee, 74, 77, 78
　Patriotic Education, 81-82
　Publicity Committee, 81
　regional councils, 77
　transportation committee, 74, 80, 81
　women's committees, 74
Ohio Civil Service Commission, 57
Ohio Direct Democracy League, 41
Ohio Direct Legislation League, 41
Ohio Equity Association, 53, 55
Ohio Farmer, 49
Ohio Federation of Labor, 48, 74, 88
Ohio Flood Relief Commission, 61
Ohio Good Roads Federation, 59
Ohio Grange, 49
Ohio Industrial Commission, 48, 78, 92
Ohio Manufactures Association, 74, 88, 91
Ohio Mine Workers' Union, 47
Ohio Municipal League, 40, 54
Ohio News League, 26-27
Ohio School Congress, 57-58
Ohio State Board of Commerce, 55
Ohio State University, 47, 74, 76, 78, 79, 81, 90
Olney, Richard, 16

Paddy's Run, 11
Palmer, A. Mitchell, 95, 101-107, 119
Parker, Alton B., 23
parole system, 51
Patriotic Party, 88
Patterson, John, 20, 26
Peabody, George Foster, 95
Peck, Hiram, 40
Peckinpaugh, Alfred, 55
People's Railway Company, 26
Perry, Carl, 81
Pinchot, Gifford, 35
Pittman, Key, 119, 122, 134
Piqua, 20
Pomerene, Atlee, 39, 70, 72, 99

populism, 17, 123
post office, 33, 37
President's Conference on Unemployment, 94-95
prisons, 51-52
prison labor farm, 51
prohibition, 49-50, 63, 89, 93, 113, 115, 123
Prohibition Party, 64
Progressive Party, 40-41, 63, 70
Public Health Council, 73, 90
Pullman, George, 20
Pulitzer, Joseph, 14, 25
Pulitzer Prize, 130
Putcha, George, 84

Quillin, Frank, 25

race relations, 25, 50, 75, 78, 80, 87, 90, 94, 114, 132
Railroads War Board, 79-81
Ralston, Samuel, 123
Ramsover, H. C., 78
recall law, 53-54
Reed, James, 75
Reed, Thomas B., 16
regional planning, 61
reparations question, 120, 124
Resolutions Committee
   1920, 102-103
   1924, 122-123
Red Cross Medal of Merit, 61
Rike, Fred, 60
Robinson, Joseph, 106
Rock, Louis, 130
Rockdale, 13
Rolph, James, 95
Roper, Daniel C., 101, 123
Roosevelt, Theodore, 63, 70
Rural Life Commission, 59
Ryan, Daniel, 74
Ryan, Thomas Fortune, 118

Sadler, Ralph, 138
Sandles, Alfred P., 70
sceintific management, 49
School Relief Act, 89, 90
School Survey Day, 57
Scripps-McCrae League, 42, 69
Seibold, Lewis, 102

self determination, 98
Sharp, William, 38, 40
short ballot, 53
Short Ballot Association, 53
Shaver, Clement, 124
Simms, Charles H., 19
Smith, Alfred E., 102, 106, 132, 138
Smith 1 Percent Law, 56, 61
Smith, Hoke, 17
Snyder, Thornton P., 51
socialism, 26
Sorg, Paul J., 14, 16-18
special service districts, 61
Sprague, Oliver, 134
Springfield Daily News, 25, 131
Springfield, Ohio, 25, 76, 90, 131
Springfield Sun, 25, 131
Stafford, William, 33
Sunday Closing Law, 49-50
Superintendant of Public Instruction, 58
Swain, Charles, 42

Taft, William H., 35, 41
Taggart, Tom, 11, 102-107, 123
Tallmadge, Eugene, 131
Tammany Hall, 101, 102, 127
tariff policy, 32-33
taxes, 55-56
tax assessors, 55
Thatcher, Olvier,
Thompson, William O., 74, 81
Tillman, Benjamin R., 16
tractor program, 78-79
Troy, 60
truck transportation, 79-80
True Democracy League, 64
Tumulty, Joseph, 106, 110, 114, 120, 133

Underwood, Oscar, 119
United Mine Workers Union, 95-96
United States Department of Agriculture, 78-79
United States Employment Service, 77
United States Food Administration, 77, 78, 79
United States Garden Army, 79
University of Cincinnati, 45, 81

Venable, William Henry, 12-13
Villard, Oswald Garrison, 107
Vollmer, Harry, 48
Volstead Act, 102, 104
voter turnout, 144

Wagner Act, 135-136
Walsh, David I., 104, 109
Warburg, James, 134
Warnes, Milton, 55
War Food and Crop Commissioners, 77-78
Washington, D. C., 17-18, 34, 36
water policy, 37, 60-61, 111
Webb-Kenyon Act, 92
welfare capitalism, 26
Weltner, Philip, 132
Western Reserve University, 74
Wheeler, John, 67
Wheeler, Wayne, 49, 104
Whitacre, John J., 63
Whitlock, Brand, 42
White, George, 110, 119, 133
White, William Allen, 122
Willis, Frank B.
   Election in 1914, 64-66
   governoship, 67
   defeat in 1916, 68-72

Wilberforce University, 90
Wilson, William B., 77, 95-96
Wilson, Woodrow
   campaign of 1920, 109-110
   election of 1912, 40
   election of 1916, 68, 70, 71-73, 116
   election of 1924, 121
   1920 Democratic convention, 101-107
   League of Nations, 102
   relationship with McAdoo, 101
   wartime administration, 77, 80, 82-84
Wisconsin idea, 42-43
woman's suffrage, 103
women's wartime committees, 74
World Monetary Conference, 134-135
Woolley, Robert, 101, 119
Wright brothers, 38

xenophobia, 91

Yapple, Wallace, 48
Young, George R., 35

E 748 .C88 C43 1985 c.1

DEC 2 1 1991